Library of
Davidson College

Grimm Library

No. 12

THE LEGEND OF SIR LANCELOT DU LAC

AMS PRESS
NEW YORK

The Legend of Sir Lancelot du Lac

Studies upon its Origin, Development,
and Position in the Arthurian
Romantic Cycle

By

Jessie L. Weston

London
Published by David Nutt
At the Sign of the Phœnix
Long Acre
1901

Library of Congress Cataloging in Publication Data

Weston, Jessie Laidlay, 1850-1928.
 The legend of Sir Lancelot du Lac.

 Original ed. issued as no. 12 of the Grimm library.
 1. Lancelot--Romances--History and criticism.
2. Ulrich von Zatzikhoven, fl. ca. 1200. 3. Chrétien
de Troyes, 12th cent. 4. Arthurian romances--History
and criticism. I. Title.
PN686.L3W4 1972   398.2'2   78-144525
ISBN 0-404-53555-0

398.22
L24w

Reprinted from the edition of 1901, London
First AMS edition published in 1972
Manufactured in the United States of America

Replacement

International Standard Book Number:
Complete Series: 0-404-53550-X
This Volume: 0-404-53555-0

PREFACE

THE Studies contained in the following pages were, in the first instance, undertaken some four or five years ago. From time to time the exigencies of other literary work have compelled me to lay them aside, but the subject has never been lost sight of, and, not infrequently, studies in appearance wholly unconnected with the *Lancelot* legend have thrown an unexpected and welcome light on certain points of the story. Undertaken, in the first instance, with an absolutely open mind (even after I had been working at it for two or three years I should have been sorely at a loss if asked to state a theory of the origin of the story), it was only by slow degrees that the real bearing of the evidence became clear, and I felt that I had at last grasped a guiding thread through the perplexing maze. The results, which perhaps to some readers may appear startlingly subversive of opinions formally expressed by certain distinguished scholars, were wholly unforeseen. They are the outcome of genuine study of original texts; whether, in the long-run they be, or be not generally accepted, I would at least plead that they be judged *on the evidence of those texts*.

In certain cases I have little doubt as to the verdict. So far as the evidence concerning the sources of Malory, and the differing versions of the prose *Lancelot*, is concerned, the facts, now brought forward for the first time, are beyond dispute. They may, I hope they will, be hereafter added to, and confirmed. As they stand they encourage us to hope that further study of the material already available may yield welcome, and perhaps unsuspected results.

We are, so far, only on the threshold of a satisfactory and scientific criticism of the Arthurian cycle, and I doubt whether all who are engaged in this study recognise sufficiently either the extent and complexity of the questions involved, or the absolute futility of, at this early stage, enunciating dogmatic decisions on any of the various points at issue. Is there any one living scholar who is perfectly aware of *all* the evidence at our disposal for any of the great stories of the cycle? If there be, he will know, better than any other, that till critical editions place us in a position to determine the characteristic readings of the MSS. representing not one alone, but *all* those stories, their inter-relation, their points of contact with, and variance from each other, the very best work that can be done will be liable to bear the impress of a temporary character—it will not, it cannot be, final.

Elsewhere, I have urged that this fact be recognised and acted upon, and I cannot but hope that the evidence collected in these studies may help to convince others of the real necessity for a determined effort to edit and render accessible the principal Arthurian texts, and the certain and permanent profit likely to result from such a work.

BOURNEMOUTH, *February* 1901.

CONTENTS

CHAPTER I

	PAGE
INTRODUCTORY REMARKS	1-4
Lancelot not a character of primitive Arthurian tradition	4
First recorded mention by Chrétien de Troyes and sudden growth in popularity	5-7

CHAPTER II

THE 'LANZELET' OF ULRICH VON ZATZIKHOVEN

Lancelot—Theories as to origin of name—M. de la Villemarqué—Professor Rhys—M. Gaston Paris—Professor Zimmer—Professor Foerster—Proposed Celtic derivation unsatisfactory 8-10

Summary of poem 11-17

Discussion of poem—Contradictory character of contents; not necessarily proof of late origin 18-21

Process of evolution sketched 23-25

Connection between *Lanzelet* and *Parzival* of Wolfram von Eschenbach—Not merely a superficial borrowing of names—Necessity for critical edition of the *Lanzelet*, and careful comparison of the two poems 25-29

CHAPTER III

LANCELOT ET LE CERF AU PIED BLANC

Summary of poem 30-32

Lai de Tyolet—Older variant, but real nature of story even then obscured 32-34

viii THE LEGEND OF SIR LANCELOT DU LAC

	PAGE
'False Claimant' *motif* foreign to original *Lai* . . .	34-35
Influence of *Tristan* noticeable in the *Morien* variant—Possible connection with *Lai*	35-38
Reasons for omission of adventure in later versions . .	38-39

CHAPTER IV

LE CHEVALIER DE LA CHARRETTE

Summary of poem	40-42
Structure of poem confused and unsatisfactory — Probable reasons for this	42-46
Versions of Guinevere's imprisonment — Comparison with Siegfried-Brynhild story—Legend primitive and in earliest form unlocalised — Localisation points to an insular redaction	46-49
Relation between Chrétien's poem and other versions—Malory's version cannot be proved to be drawn from prose *Lancelot*—*Iwein* certainly independent of *Charrette*—*Parzival* doubtful—Two latter possibly represent earlier version, imperfectly known by Chrétien	49-53

CHAPTER V

THE POSITION OF CHRÉTIEN DE TROYES IN THE ARTHURIAN CYCLE

Source of Chrétien's poems an important problem . .	54
Professor Foerster's views summarised—The Arthurian legend partly historic, partly romantic—Latter of exclusively continental origin	55-56
Reply to Professor Foerster—Arthurian tradition of greater extent and of wider diffusion than supposed—Evidence for early diffusion of *romantic* tradition . . .	56
Necessity of distinguishing between *mythic* and *romantic* tradition—Former of strongly marked Celtic-Irish character, and mainly preserved in *insular* tradition . .	56-61

CONTENTS

Condition of Arthurian tradition when Chrétien wrote—No longer purely oral—Necessity for understanding what is involved in oral transmission—Mr. Hartland's evidence on this point—The Breton *lais* folk-lore in character—Gradual process of Arthurisation—Evidence of *Yvain*—The process well advanced at the time Chrétien wrote . 61-68

Necessity for determining original character of story before criticising, *i.e.* tales of folk-lore origin demand a different method of criticism from that applicable to tales of purely literary invention—Professor Foerster's theory of origin of *Yvain* examined and rejected as not consonant with archaic character of tale 68-77

Proposed origin of *Perceval* also unsatisfactory, not in harmony with statements made elsewhere by Chrétien—Strong probability that the tale, in its completed form, is older than has hitherto been supposed 78-80

Folk-lore character of *Erec*, *Yvain*, and *Perceval* probably an important element in their popularity . . . 81

The varying geography of Chrétien's poems evidence of varying source 82-83

Probable relation between Chrétien's poems and the Welsh versions—Resemblance does not necessarily postulate dependence 85

General summary of principles resulting from present investigation, and their bearing upon position ultimately to be assigned to Chrétien 86-88

CHAPTER VI

THE PROSE LANCELOT—THE 'ENFANCES' OF THE HERO

Necessity of examining *all* the existing MSS. before a critical study of the legend can be attempted—Present studies concerned only with leading points of story, and certain variants in printed texts 89-90

Arthurian cycle in present form redacted under influence of completed *Lancelot* story 91-93

x THE LEGEND OF SIR LANCELOT DU LAC

PAGE

Enfances of hero in prose *Lancelot* a modified form of story related by Ulrich von Zatzikhoven — Points of contact between prose *Lancelot* and *Parzival* of Wolfram von Eschenbach 93-96
MS. evidence of contact with *Perceval* story . . . 96-97
Parallel with *Bel Inconnu* poems—The *Lancelot* later than either *Perceval* or *Bel Inconnu*—Connection with Lady of the Lake alone of the essence of the story—Necessity for studying character of fairy protectress before deciding original form of *Enfances* 97-99

CHAPTER VII

THE PROSE LANCELOT—THE LOVES OF LANCELOT AND GUINEVERE

Short notice of incidents of frequent repetition in the romance —Impossibility of deciding, with our present knowledge, which belong to original redaction . . . 100-103
Do the mutual relations of Lancelot and Guinevere represent an original feature of the Arthurian story, or are we to consider them a later addition? 103
Early evidence of Guinevere's infidelity—Testimony of the chroniclers—Wace—Layamon . . . 104-107
Mordred not the original lover, but his representative . 107-108
Original lover possibly Gawain 108-111
Lancelot story a later development and independent of earlier tradition—Influence of the *Tristan* legend—Motive determining choice of lover 111-117
Suggested evolution of Lancelot—Guinevere story . 117-118

CHAPTER VIII

THE PROSE LANCELOT—LANCELOT AND THE GRAIL

Intricacy of questions involved—Grail problem, so far, has not been solved — Possibility that mutual relation between *Lancelot* and *Grail* romances may yield us the key to both problems 119-120

CONTENTS

Necessity of distinguishing three distinct *Questes*—Later Grail *Queste* combination of *Grail* (Perceval) and *Château Merveil* (Gawain) adventures 121

Dr. Wechssler's theory of *Grail-Lancelot* cycle examined—Results as deduced by author unsatisfactory . 121-124

Evidence of MS. 751 key to truth—Original Borron *Queste* a Perceval, not a Galahad, *Queste*—Didot *Perceval* represents an early, *Perceval li Gallois* a later, form of Perceval-Lancelot—Grail *Queste* evidence for this discussed 124-132

Origin of the Galahad *Queste*—Dependent upon the *Lancelot*, but by another hand—Contradiction between presentment of characters and essential *motif* of story . 133-140

Motives determining evolution of Galahad *Queste*—Necessity of connecting two main branches of tradition, *Lancelot* and the *Grail*—This only possible under certain conditions which we find fulfilled in the *Queste* . . 140-146

CHAPTER IX

THE DUTCH LANCELOT

Importance of this text as a faithful translation of an excellent original 147-149

Contents summarised 149-151

Close connection with edition 1533, Philippe Lenoire—Importance of these two versions for criticism of Malory's compilation 151

Detailed comparison of texts with Dr. Sommer's summary of prose *Lancelot* and with original text of Malory . 152-164

CHAPTER X

THE QUESTE VERSIONS

Comparison of texts continued—Dutch *Lancelot*—French 1533—Malory—Welsh *Queste*—Dr. Furnivall's *Queste*—Dr. Sommer's summary 166-185

Conclusion—General agreement of the first four against the last two—The former representing a superior family of texts—Malory's source an *Agravain-Queste* MS. belonging to same family as 1533 and Dutch translation—No proof that Malory knew earlier section of *Lancelot* . . 185-188

Variations of *Queste* MSS. apparently due to copyist rather than to compiler—The romance a *Lancelot*, rather than a *Grail*, romance 188-193

CHAPTER XI

THE MORT ARTUR

Comparison of texts continued 195-205
Results confirm previous conclusion, showing continued agreement of 1533 and Dutch translation, and strengthen theory that text used by Malory belonged to same family . . 205

CHAPTER XII

CONCLUSION

Summary of investigation—Results arrived at . . 206-212
The mutual relations of *Perceval* and *Lancelot* stories of primary importance in evolution of Arthurian romantic cycle—Necessity for critical editions of these texts . . 212-214

APPENDIX

The *Lancelot* section of D.L. 215-247

INDEX 248

THE LEGEND OF
SIR LANCELOT DU LAC

CHAPTER I

INTRODUCTORY

To the great majority of English readers, those who are familiar with the Arthurian legend through the pages of Malory and Tennyson, the name which occurs most readily to their minds in connection with the court and Table of King Arthur is that of Lancelot du Lac, at once the most gallant servant of the king, and the secret lover of the queen. To many the story of Lancelot and Guinevere is the most famous of all stories of unlawful love.

True, of late years the popularity of Wagner's music has made their ears, at least, familiar with the names of Tristan and Iseult. Still, that Tristan and Iseult were ever as famous as Lancelot and Guinevere, few outside the ranks of professed students of mediæval literature would believe; still fewer admit that the loves of Arthur's queen and Arthur's knight were suggested by, if not imitated from, the older, more poetic, and infinitely more convincing, Celtic love-tale; that Lancelot, as Arthur's knight and Guinevere's lover, is a comparatively late addition to the Arthurian legend.

Yet so it is. I doubt if any scholar of standing would now argue that Lancelot and his relation to the queen formed an integral portion of the early tradition; if any, conversant with the literature of the cycle, would reckon Lancelot among the original band of heroes who gathered round the British king.

In the introduction to my studies on the Gawain legend, I remarked that, if we desired to arrive at an elucidation of the Arthurian problem as a whole, we must first begin with the elucidation of its component parts—we must severally disentangle the legends connected with the leading knights of the cycle before we can hope to understand the growth and development of that cycle. When we have arrived at some clear idea concerning the stories originally told of the Arthurian heroes, and their relation to each other and to the king, we shall then be in a better position to judge of the nature of the original legend—whether it be mainly the product of literary invention, or in its more important features, the work of mythical tradition. It is not a matter of slight importance to ascertain to which of these two categories the leading heroes of Arthurian romance belong.

In the case of Sir Gawain we were able to detect certain features which, by their persistent recurrence in the great mass of tradition connected with this knight, seemed to indicate a general recognition on the part of the romance writers that they belonged to an early form of his story, and as such were to be preserved even when but incompletely understood. Further I pointed out the parallels existing between certain of his most famous adventures and those recorded in early Irish tradition, parallels which went far to prove, not merely the antiquity

INTRODUCTORY

of the feats ascribed to him, but their source in Celtic myth.

In the following studies I shall endeavour, in the same way, to trace to its origin the legend of Lancelot du Lac, to discover what was the tale originally connected with him, and, if possible, follow the steps which led to the immense development of his popularity. I do not for a moment suggest, any more than in the case of Gawain, the finality of the results arrived at; but I hope at least to present the reader with a sorely needed summary of the Lancelot legend, and to clear the ground for further researches into his story.

In some ways the task before us is less difficult than that involved in the examination of the Gawain legend; the literature connected with Lancelot, if extensive, is not diffuse; by far the greater portion is covered by the prose *Lancelot* and the Grail Romances. On the other hand the story, as compared with that of Gawain, is extraordinarily deficient in characteristic features. The adventures ascribed to Lancelot might just as well be placed to the credit of any other knight: they are the ordinary stock-in-trade of the mediæval romancer. Guinevere's lover he is, but the love-story is of the most conventional character: the more it is studied the more clearly do the records in which it is shrined appear the offspring of conscious literary invention, and that invention of by no means a high order. He is certainly no hero of prehistoric myth, solar or otherwise, as Gawain or Perceval may well be; nor does he by force of sheer humanity lay hold on our imagination, as does Tristan.

How then did Lancelot come into the Arthurian cycle? In the earliest records of Arthurian legend he holds no place. Wace's *Brut*, the French metrical version of the History of Geoffrey of Monmouth, written about the middle of the twelfth century, gives the names of certain of Arthur's knights, Gawain, Kay, Bedivere, Iwein, but never mentions Lancelot. We have an account of Arthur's expedition to France, in the course of which he slew Frollo outside the walls of Paris, an adventure which the compiler of the Prose *Lancelot* places during the war against Claudas to recover Lancelot's patrimony, but in the *Brut* this expedition takes place at an early stage in Arthur's reign, and knows nothing of Lancelot or Claudas.[1]

Dating apparently from the same period, the middle of the twelfth century, is a bas-relief of the cathedral of Modena, representing a female figure standing on the summit of a tower, towards which several armed knights are approaching. Each knight is named, and we find represented Arthur himself, Gawain, Kay, Ider, Carados, and a certain Galuariun, who has not been identified. Lancelot is not among them.[2]

The Welsh Arthurian stories again know nothing of Lancelot, though certain of them contain long lists of heroes of Arthur's court.[3]

So far as we can at present tell, the earliest mention of the knight is that contained in the *Erec* of Chrétien de

---

[1] *Brut*, ed. Leroux de Lincy, vol. ii. ll. 10158-10360. These remarks also apply to Layamon.

[2] Described and illustrated by Zimmerman in *Oberitalische Plastik im frühen und hohen Mittelalter*: Leipzig, 1897. Cf. also *Romania*, xxvii. p. 510.

[3] It is difficult to resist the conclusion that if the Welsh stories were as late in date and as dependent upon French tradition as some scholars maintain, Lancelot would certainly be mentioned in them.

INTRODUCTORY

Troyes, where in a long list of the heroes of the Round Table, ranged according to merit (at least in the case of the earlier names), Lanceloz del Lac is reckoned third, the first two being Gawain and Erec.[1] In the German version by Hartmann von Aue, he occupies the same place, but is called Lanzelot von Arlac. Nothing more is related of him: he plays no rôle in the story, he is a name, and nought else. In a later poem by Chrétien, *Cligés*, the same position, third on the roll of heroes, is ascribed to Lancelot, but here it is Perceval, and not Erec, who ranks second. The hero of the poem, Cligés, appears at a tournament four successive days, in different armour, and overthrows Segramor, Lancelot, and Perceval, finally fighting an undecided combat with Gawain.[2] The *Cligés* reference is particularly noticeable, as the *motif* of the story is the love of the hero for the young wife of his uncle and sovereign. In this connection the loves of Tristan and Iseult are often referred to, but Lancelot and Guinevere never. It seems clear that when Chrétien wrote this poem he did not know Lancelot as the lover of Arthur's queen and the chief of Arthur's knights.

But in the poem which followed the *Cligés*, *Le Chevalier de la Charrette*, Lancelot suddenly appears in both these characters, Gawain's superior and the lover of Guinevere: no explanation of the changed position is offered, but Chrétien takes for granted the familiarity of his audience with the relations between the knight and the queen. To add to the confusion, in the succeeding poem *Le Chevalier au Lion*, Lancelot is only once referred to, in connection with the *Charrette* adventure, and is never mentioned as

[1] Cf. *Erec*, Foerster's ed., l. 1694; Hartmann's *Erec*, l. 1630.
[2] *Cligés*, Foerster's ed., ll. 4765-4798.

one of the knights of Arthur's household; while in Chrétien's last poem, the *Perceval*, he is altogether ignored.[1]

It is very difficult, indeed impossible, to date Chrétien's poems with exactness. The only two which afford clear internal evidence on the point, *Le Chevalier de la Charrette* and *Le Chevalier au Lion*, fall within the years 1164-1173. *Erec* was the first of his Arthurian poems, and between *Erec* and the *Charrette*, certainly one work, *Cligés*, and it may be several, intervened.[2]

Very probably the *Erec* was written early in the decade, 1150-60, and taken in conjunction with the negative evidence afforded by the *Brut* and the Italian bas-relief, it goes to prove that whereas the name of Gawain, as connected with Arthur, was known by the end of the eleventh century,[3] Arthurian tradition knew nothing of Lancelot till the latter half of the twelfth; and that no mention of his relations with Guinevere is found till between 1160-1170, that is, a decade after the first mention

[1] The advocates of Chrétien as an independent and original genius would do well carefully to consider the meaning of such curious inconsistency. If Chrétien were dealing with matter either of his own invention, or of his own free adaptation, he would surely have been more careful of the unities. If, on the other hand, he simply retold tales belonging to different stages of Arthurian tradition, this is exactly what we might expect to find.

[2] In the opening lines of *Cligés*, Chrétien gives a list of his works. This includes a version of the story of *Tristan*, and several translations from Ovid. *Tristan* probably preceded *Erec*, but there is nothing to indicate the relative order of the other works.

[3] Signor Rajna has found the names of Arthur and Gawain in Italian deeds of the first quarter of the twelfth century, and from the nature of some of these deeds it is clear that the persons named therein cannot have been born later than 1080.

INTRODUCTORY

of his name. It is, of course, a well-recognised fact in the study of romance, that the date of a manuscript does not fix the date of the story contained in it; a younger manuscript may contain the same story under an older form. As a rule, the versions contained in Chrétien's poems appear to present a fairly old form of the stories they relate, saving in the case of Lancelot. About this knight, Chrétien either knows nothing or he knows too much. The earlier stages of his story he leaves unrecorded; yet an allusion in the *Charrette* poem[1] shows that he was not unacquainted with the legend concerning his youth and up-bringing. Two versions of this legend have been preserved to us, one in verse and one in prose. In the following chapter we will examine the older of these versions, and inquire into the origin of our hero's name.

[1] *Charrette*, ll. 2347-2362.

CHAPTER II

THE 'LANZELET' OF ULRICH VON ZATZIKHOVEN

THE origin of the name *Lancelot* has been a subject of considerable debate among scholars, and has given rise to the most widely differing explanations. M. de la Villemarqué, who was a warm advocate of the Welsh origin of the Arthurian stories, derived the name from the French *l'ancelot*, a youth or servant, which he held to be a translation of the Welsh Melwas, or Maelwas. This solution was rejected by M. Gaston Paris, in his study on the Lancelot poems,[1] in which he showed that *ancelot* was not a French common name, and that Maelwas did not bear the signification attributed to it. Professor Rhys,[2] adopting the theory of the Welsh origin of the name, which in its present form he admitted only exists in Welsh literature as borrowed from French or English sources, decided that it represented a Welsh variant of Peredur, the root of this latter name being *Pâr=a spear or lance*. 'The characters,' says Professor Rhys, 'were originally the same, though their respective developments eventually differed very widely.' I doubt if this solution ever found any adherents except its author: it is sufficient

---

[1] *Romania*, vol. x. p. 492.
[2] *Studies in the Arthurian Legend*, chap. vi.

'LANZELET' OF ULRICH V. ZATZIKHOVEN

to remark that the derivation of Peredur, on which it rests, is by no means universally accepted, and that Lancelot is in no special way connected with a spear or lance.[1] It is certainly true that the Lancelot story shows signs of having been affected by the Perceval legend, but as we shall see the borrowings are restricted to one special and purely continental form of the story.

M. Gaston Paris, in the study referred to above, suggested that Lancelot might be either a Celtic name altered, or, more probably, the substitution, by French poets, of a name of Germanic origin for one of Breton form strange to the ears of their French audiences, *e.g.* it might be a diminutive form of *Lanzo*. This is also the conclusion of Professor Zimmer.[2] The prefix *Lant* is often found in names of Frankish origin transferred to Breton ground: such names are Lando, Landolin; Lanzo, Lanzolin, etc.

In the introduction to his edition of the *Charrette*, recently published,[3] Professor Foerster announces his complete adhesion to this view.

It certainly seems that the evidence points strongly to this conclusion. The fact that Lancelot's name does not appear in the earliest obtainable Arthurian documents shows that he did not belong to the original 'stoff' of the cycle; the entire silence of Welsh literature, and the

---

[1] The only adventure of the kind I can recall is that of the fiery lance of the *Charrette* and prose *Lancelot*, an adventure which is the common property of several knights, and by no means confined to Lancelot.

[2] *Zeitschrift für französische Sprache und Litteratur*, vol. xii. Heft I.

[3] *Der Karrenritter*, herausgegeben von Wendelin Foerster: Halle, 1899.

practical silence of English vernacular romances,[1] seem to show that he formed no part of the *insular* Arthurian tradition. For my own part I unhesitatingly accept Professor Foerster's dictum, '*Lancelot ist den Kymren gänzlich unbekannt, und ist unter allen Umständen Kontinentaler*[2] *Herkunft.*'[3]

A weak point in the proposed Celtic solutions appears to me to be that both entirely ignore the qualifying title *du Lac*, by which Lancelot is invariably known. Neither M. de la Villemarqué nor Professor Rhys appear to consider it of any special importance, yet if I mistake not this is just the significant point of the Lancelot story, and that which from the very outset differentiates it from the legends connected with Peredur or Maelwas. From the moment of his appearance in Chrétien's list of Arthur's knights to that in which the prose *Lancelot* records his death in the odour of sanctity, Lancelot is Lancelot *du Lac*, and the earliest version of his story which we possess amply justifies his claim to the title.

---

[1] Cf. *Anturs of Arthur*, where the ghost foretells to Gawain the treason of Mordred, the destruction of the Round Table, and his own death. Lancelot is not mentioned. Nor does he appear in *Syr Gawayne and the Grene Knyghte* or in *The Avowynge of Arthur*. In some of the other poems, *Galogres and Gawayne*, *The Carle of Carlile*, *The Marriage of Sir Gawain*, and *Sir Libeaus Desconus* he is mentioned, but plays no important part. The ballad of *Sir Lancelot du Lake* in the Percy Collection is a version of an adventure related in the Prose *Lancelot*.

[2] Cf. *Karrenritter*, Introduction, p. xxxix.

[3] The materials for this study had been collected, and my conclusion as to the origin of the Lancelot story arrived at, before the publication of Professor Foerster's book. I am glad to find myself supported in any point by such an authority, but think it well to avoid misconception by stating that my results have been arrived at through independent study.

The poem of Ulrich von Zatzikhoven[1] is certainly later than either the *Erec* or the *Charrette* of Chrétien, but the tradition it embodies is anterior to the poem itself. Written in the opening years of the thirteenth century, it is, as explicitly stated in the text, the translation of '*daz welsche buoch von Lanzelete*,' brought to Germany by Hugo de Morville, one of the hostages who in 1194 replaced Richard of England in the prison of Leopold of Austria.[2] The date of the original French version cannot, of course, be fixed. In any case it must have preceded its introduction into Germany; judging from internal evidence it represented an early and immature version of the Lancelot legend. The story as related in the *Lanzelet* is as follows: Lanzelet was son to King Pant of Genewîs and his wife Clarine. By a revolt of his people Pant was driven from his kingdom with his wife and child. In his flight he came to a stream, and there, overcome by his wounds, sank down and died. The queen had laid her child under a tree while she tended her husband, and before she could reach it again a water-fairy (*mer-feine*) came in a cloud of mist and carried off the infant. The fairy was a queen, ruling over ten thousand maidens, who knew no man. Her kingdom was called *Meide-lant*; there it was ever May-tide, and her palace had such virtue that whoso abode one day within it might never know sorrow till the day of his death. There the little Lanzelet was brought up, in ignorance of his name and rank, till he reached the age of fifteen,

[1] *Lanzelet* von Ulrich von Zatzikhoven, ed. Hahn: Frankfurt, 1845. Out of print and difficult to procure.

[2] This account, and the mention of England, l. 7054, seem to render it possible that the original poem may have been written in this island.

knowing nothing of knighthood, nor even how to bestride a horse. Then eager to try his lot in the world outside he demanded leave to ride forth. This the fairy granted, but refused to tell him his name and parentage; he must first conquer the strongest knight in the world, Iweret, of the fair wood Beforet.

She gave him rich armour, white as a swan, the best that might be, a surcoat (*wafen-roc*) decked with golden bells; sword and shield, and a goodly horse. But the lad did not know how to ride, so let the bridle hang loose and held on by the saddle-bow. In this fashion he rode till he met a knight, Johfrit de Liez, who rebuked him for his childish bearing, and took him to his castle, where he was kindly welcomed by the host's mother and her maidens, and instructed in riding and the use of knightly weapons.

His next adventure is to ride with two knights to the castle of one Galagandreiz. In the night the daughter of the host, condemned by her father to perpetual virginity, offers her love to the three knights in turn; is accepted by Lanzelet, who fights a duel with her father, slays him, and weds the maiden. One day he rode forth seeking adventures, and found a road which led him to the castle of Limors. The folk attacked, and would have slain him, but for the intervention of Ade, niece to the lord of the castle. Lanzelet is thrown into prison, and only escapes by fighting single-handed, first with a giant, then with two lions, and finally with the lord of the castle himself. Having slain this last, he becomes the '*ami*' of the maiden Ade. (Whether he marries her or not is not clearly stated. In any case we hear no more of his first wife, the daughter of Galagandreiz.)

Meanwhile the fame of Lanzelet's exploits has penetrated

to Arthur's ears, and Gawain is sent to find the unnamed hero, and bring him to Arthur's Court. They meet, and fight an undecided combat, terminated by the arrival of a messenger with tidings of a tournament between King Lot of Johenîs and Gurnemanz, *den fürsten wîs*. Lanzelet betakes himself hither, wearing each day a different suit of armour, green, red and white, overthrows many knights, including King Lot, whom he set free out of friendship for Gawain, and without revealing himself, rides away with Ade and her brother.

They come to a castle, Schâtel le Mort, the master of which, Mâbûz, is a magician, and son to the fairy who had brought Lanzelet up. Lanzelet rides to the castle, which has this property, that whoever crosses its drawbridge at once loses all courage and hardihood. Lanzelet falls under the spell, and is taken prisoner in the most ignominious manner, much to the dismay of Ade, who rides off with her brother and disappears from the story. The land of Mâbûz adjoins that of Iweret of Beforet, who is in the habit of raiding his neighbour's territory. Mâbûz, who is by nature a coward, determines that Lanzelet, whose fame is well known to him, shall be his champion. He has him carried by his men without the walls of the castle, when his natural courage at once returns. He rides to a fountain, beside which hangs a brazen cymbal on which he must strike three times with a hammer to summon his foe. In the meantime Iblîs, the fair daughter of Iweret, has had a dream of an unknown knight whom she meets beside the fountain; she rises early to seek the scene of her dream, and finds the original of her vision in Lanzelet. She beseeches him to carry her off without waiting for the conflict, but Lanzelet refuses. Iweret arrives and a fierce fight ensues, in which he is slain. Lanzelet weds Iblis and becomes master of Beforet.

A messenger now arrives from the Fairy of the Lake, revealing Lanzelet's name and parentage (his mother, Clarine, was sister to Arthur). The object of her theft of the child is now accomplished: she desired to secure a champion who would free her son Mâbûz from his too powerful enemy. Lanzelet decides to seek Gawain, whom he now knows to be his kinsman. On their way they meet a squire who informs them that the King Valerîn (or Falerîn, the spelling varies), has appeared at Arthur's court and laid claim to Guinevere, on the ground that she had been betrothed to him previous to her marriage with Arthur. If Valerîn cannot find a champion to oppose him he will carry off the queen. Lanzelet undertakes the combat, and defeats Valerîn.

(We must note here that Lanzelet's service to the queen is of a *preventive* character, *i.e.* he saves her from the possibility of abduction, he does not rescue her after the abduction has taken place.)

Lanzelet then leaves his wife at court, and goes forth to seek the castle of Plurîs, which he had passed on his journey from *Meide-land* and the adventure of which he desires to test. There he is challenged by one hundred knights, whom he successively overthrows, and weds the queen (Ulrich says quaintly, '*ich enweiz ob erz ungerne tet, wan diu künigîn was ein schœne maget*, 5530-1). Iblîs remains at Arthur's court, grieving for the disappearance of her husband, during whose absence she successfully withstands the *Mantle* test, an incident of not infrequent occurrence in Arthurian romance.

Hearing that Lanzelet is a prisoner at Plurîs, Gawain,

Karjet (Gaheriet?), Erec, and Tristan go in search of him, and, by means of a ruse, succeed in freeing him. The queen of Pluris disappears from the story.

On their way to court they learn that, while engaged in hunting the white stag, Guinevere has been carried off by Valerin, and imprisoned in a magic castle, surrounded by a dense thicket peopled with all kinds of serpents. Tristan, ' der listige Tristan'[1] *suggests that they should seek the aid of Malduz*[2] *or Malduc, the magician, the Lord of the Misty Lake (Genibeleten Se), who will enable them to penetrate Valerin's stronghold. Erec announces that neither he nor Gawain should take part in the expedition as they have respectively slain Malduc's father and brother. Arthur therefore sets forth accompanied by Karjet (Gaheriet), Tristan and Lanzelet (this is the order), and are later joined by Dodine le Sauvage. By the good offices of the enchanter's daughter, to whom Arthur appeals, Malduc consents to aid them on condition that Erec and Gawain are delivered up to him, to which these heroes willingly consent. Malduc then, by means of spells, disperses the serpents guarding Valerin's castle, slays him and his men, and wakens Guinevere from the magic slumber into which Valerin has cast her.*

I have italicised this passage as extremely important for the criticism of the story. It will be seen that so far from Lanzelet being the means of Guinevere's escape, he plays

[1] This is entirely in accordance with Tristan's character as represented in the poems. He is in the highest degree *rusé* and resourceful.

[2] Is it not possible that this *Malduz* the magician may be the original of *Mauduiz li Sages* whom Chrétien ranks as eighth of Arthur's knights? Cf. *Erec*, 1699. Hartmann's version gives Malduiz; *Diu Krône*, 1379, Malduz der Weise. The identification seems clear.

practically no part in the story, all he does is to accompany the king. The rescuer is Malduc; recourse to him is suggested by Tristan and made possible by the self-sacrifice of Gawain and Erec; but saving in the discussion as to whether Malduc's terms shall or shall not be accepted, Lanzelet's name is not even mentioned.[1]

Erec and Gawain are cast into prison by Malduc and nearly starved to death, but are rescued by one hundred of Arthur's knights, headed by Lanzelet and aided by a giant, Esealt der lange. They all return to Arthur's court, where great feasts are held.

Iblîs tells her husband of a curious adventure which had befallen one of the knights: how he had met in a forest a terrible dragon which, speaking with a human voice, besought a kiss from the knight; he refused and the dragon flew away lamenting. Lanzelet resolves to test the adventure, rides to the forest, finds the dragon, and gives the desired kiss. The monster bathes in a stream at hand, and becomes a fair maiden, Elidiâ, daughter to the king of Thile; she has been transformed into a dragon for trans-

[1] I am quite at a loss to account for the mistake into which such authorities as M. Gaston Paris and Professor Foerster have apparently fallen. In M. Paris's study the idea that Lanzelet is the rescuer is perhaps rather implied than stated, but when I wrote the *Charrette* chapter (viii.) in my *Studies on the Legend of Sir Gawain*, in which I followed the article in *Romania*, I was certainly under the impression that the latter was the case. In the introduction to the *Karrenritter*, p. xliv., Professor Foerster distinctly says that Lanzelet frees the queen. I have read and re-read the text carefully and made my final summary direct from it, and there is no doubt that Lanzelet has nothing to do with the matter. The passage in question is contained in ll. 6975-7445. How too did Professor Foerster come to ignore the real character of Guinevere's imprisonment? Cf. *Charrette*, lxxi.

'LANZELET' OF ULRICH V. ZATZIKHOVEN

gressing the rules of *Minne*, and condemned to remain in that form till kissed by the best knight on earth. She remains at Arthur's court, where she is made judge of all disputed questions relating to *Minne*.

Here the story of Lanzelet practically ends. He wins back his lands of Genewîs without difficulty, promising to treat his subjects better than his father did. He and Iblîs betake themselves to the heritage of the latter, Beforet, where they receive Arthur and Guinevere with great pomp. The poem concludes by telling us that they have four children, three sons and one daughter, that they live to see their children's children, and die both on the same day.

The poem of Ulrich von Zatzikhoven has scarcely received the attention which, as a factor in the criticism of the legend, it undoubtedly demands. The questions arising out of it are not only interesting, but, as I shall presently show, in one instance at least, of the very highest importance. The questions may be grouped as (*a*) those relating to the structure and sources of the poem itself; (*b*) those which affect its relation to the other Lancelot romances. For the first it is obvious that we are dealing with a poem of very loose construction; the various parts do not harmonise with each other, and no attempt has been made to make them do so. Thus we have no fewer than four love affairs attributed to Lanzelet, and in three out of the four he weds the lady; yet these amours, one of which is subsequent to his marriage with Iblîs, are dropped as of no account. Professor Foerster[1] considers that this looseness of construction points to a late date, and that the source of the *Lanzelet* was a biographical

---

[1] *Karrenritter*, Introduction, p. xliv.

romance of the weakest order. According to Professor Foerster the clearer the composition, the better knit the incidents, the older the romance.

Now it seems to me that there are two orders of ill-constructed romances, and that we shall do well to differentiate between them. In one case we have a number of incidents of secondary character, obviously borrowed or imitated from those occurring elsewhere, strung together more or less cleverly on the thread of a hero's individuality. The incidents are all to be found in other romances, and as a rule none of them have any suggestion of Celtic or mythic origin. The literary style is superior to the matter. Such romances are *e.g. Rigomer, Torec, Le Chevalier à la Manche*. A very favourable example is *Méraugis de Portlesguez*. These are all certainly late romances.

In the other case we have a romance even more ill-constructed, but consisting not of incidents but of whole short tales, manifestly independent of each other, and some of them of distinctly antique and mythic character: the literary style is poor and the whole is less a romance, properly speaking, than the material out of which a romance can be evolved. This, I believe, marks an early stage of development, and of this we have naturally but few specimens. The *Lanzelet* is, I believe, one.

If I mistake not, the groundwork is a series of *lais*, each complete in itself, and having no connection with what precedes or what follows it. It is in no real sense a biographical romance, though perhaps it might be called a tentative effort in that direction. The *Mantle* episode certainly formed a single *lai*; the *Fier Baiser*, now found with other adventures, probably originally did so.[1] Certain

---

[1] I think it is worthy of note that though Lanzelet is the hero of the

of the episodes, too, possess a distinctly archaic character, *e.g.* the description of the fairy's kingdom as a isle of women where no man penetrates, a conception much older than the *Fata Morgana* of the prose *Lancelot*; and the description of Guinevere's prison, the magic slumber in a fair dwelling, *ein wünneclichez haus*, surrounded by a dense thicket infested with serpents, is the sleeping beauty story in its oldest 'other world' form.[1] The position of Gawain in the story is that held by him in the earlier, pre-Lancelot romances.

I cannot accept the suggestion of a biographical *Lancelot* from which both the *Lanzelet* and the *Charrette* were drawn. If we remember that the first mention of Lancelot in Arthurian romance can only be traced to the second half of the twelfth century, it does not seem probable that by 1164 (when, or about when, Chrétien wrote his poem) he could have become the hero of a fixed biographical romance. Nor, the *motif* of his *liaison* with Guinevere once introduced into the story, is the compilation of such a version as the *Lanzelet* subsequently probable. Professor Foerster feels this difficulty, and suggests a solution, which a little more consideration would have shown him to be untenable. On page xlvi. of his introduction to the *Karrenritter*, he says, '*wenn wirklich Kristian zuerst den Ehebruch eingeführt hat, so ist doch die Annahme zulässig dass Verehrer Arturs und seiner Frau diese neue ehrenrührische Erfindung zwar gekannt, aber mit Entrüstung abgewiesen*

tale here and not Guinglain, Gawain's son, as elsewhere, yet in this poem Lanzelet is Arthur's nephew, and of Gawain's kin, which he is not in any other version. The *Fier Baiser* is thus still restricted to the family of Gawain.

[1] Cf. my *Legends of the Wagner Drama, Siegfried*.

haben, um ja nicht des idealen Königs Ehrenschild zu beschmutzen.' But a few pages further on the writer himself refers to the story of Guinevere and Mordred as told by Geoffrey[1] and Wace. He must therefore be well aware that there can be no possible question of Chrétien's having *introduced* the *motif* of Guinevere's faithlessness; that is one of the oldest and most original features of the Arthurian story. The question is *not*, 'Did the queen have a lover?'—that was answered in the affirmative long before Chrétien's day—but, 'When did Lancelot become her lover? Was it through the version of the *Charrette*?' a very different matter.[2]

Taking into consideration the construction of the poem, and the character of the contents, I think we are justified in considering the composition of Ulrich von Zatzikhoven as a collection of *lais* which have not yet been worked over or taken final literary shape. When the scattered Lancelot stories did this, it was under the influence of a *motif* foreign to the original legend, his love for Guinevere. How that came to be introduced into the legend is a matter for separate consideration, but I do not think there is room for doubt that it was this introduction which determined the final and literary form of the Lancelot story. All conflicting elements, such as the various

---

[1] I say especially 'as told by Geoffrey and Wace,' for these writers give us clearly to understand that the queen was a consenting party, and no victim to Mordred's treachery. It is quite a different version from that of the prose *Lancelot*.

[2] I shall have occasion to refer very frequently to Professor Foerster's introduction. It is a full and powerful statement of views which so far as they affect the origin and evolution of the Arthurian legend I believe to be radically unsound. It is most useful to have at hand a summary so clear and concise.

love affairs, were rejected and only the original germ retained.

And what was this germ? Authorities will no doubt differ. Some perhaps will say it was the story of Guinevere's imprisonment and rescue, but they must remember that in the *Lanzelet* this is *not* the work of the hero. I think myself that the root of the Lancelot tale was simply a Breton *lai*, relating the theft of a king's son by a water fairy: this seems to be the one abiding and persistent element in the tale, all else is uncertain and shifting. Here the hero is Arthur's nephew; elsewhere he is but the son of an old ally; at one time his father is a tyrant, '*chassé*' by his own people; again he is a noble king, the victim of treachery and a foreign foe. Sometimes Lancelot's mother lives to see him restored to his kingdom; sometimes she dies while he is yet in the care of the fairy, and never sees her son again. He has two cousins on the father's side, Bohort and Lionel, and a bastard half-brother Hector; he has no relations on his father's side, but is cousin to Gawain through his mother. He is Guinevere's lover; he is not Guinevere's lover. He is unmarried; he is very much married—three times at least! He has four children born in wedlock; he has but one son, the offspring of a *liaison*. He is the most valiant knight of Arthur's court; he is scarce worthy of mention. Among all this shifting tangle and contradiction, there is but one thing, and one only, fixed and certain, he is Lancelot *du Lac*. I do not see how we can avoid the conclusion that in this record of his youth we have the one fixed point of departure for all the subsequent unfoldings of romance.

Not that this story was always unvarying in its details,

on the contrary we find in it marked divergences. Thus in the *Lanzelet* the motive of the theft is clear, the fairy desires a champion and protector for her cowardly son; the motive in the prose *Lancelot* is not apparent; probably it was a mere capricious fancy for a beautiful child.

And if the motive was not always clearly understood, still less so was the character of the fairy. In fact she seems to have considerably puzzled the mediæval romancers. In the first instance the story would be excessively simple, she would probably be such a water-fairy as we find in *Tidorel*, and Ulrich seems to have retained this idea when he calls her a *Merfeine* or *Merminne*, but as the *lai* gained popularity, and it became necessary to supply details as to her kingdom, etc., it would be supplemented from other legendary sources. Ulrich's own description, the land of ten thousand maidens where no man penetrates, is manifestly the *Meide-land* which in *Diu Krône* Gawain visits, and which is universally admitted to be a remembrance of the 'Isle of Women' of old Celtic tradition. It may have touched the Lancelot *lai* through the medium of the Gawain's story, but as a 'property' of old Celtic belief it may well have been known independently. I think it probable that this identification may explain a very curious passage in *Diu Krône*, where Kei reproaches Lancelot who has failed in the glove test in the following terms:

> '*er hât daz vil rehte erspeht,
> daz iz di gotinne
> verkurt an ir minne,
> diu iu zôch in dem sê.*'—ll. 24517-20.

Certain it is that while the queen of the 'Isle of Women' does not appear to be addicted to child-stealing, she does entice, or abduct, earthly knights to be her lovers. It is not impossible that a version of the *Lancelot* story, redacted by some one familiar with the real character of the kingdom, may have represented him as the queen's lover. It is also not impossible, were this the case, that the story of the imprisonment of Guinevere in the other world, a story which, as we shall presently see, must have existed at a very early date, may have led to her being confused with the queen of that kingdom, and to the transfer of Lancelot's affections from the one to the other.

The prose *Lancelot* version is entirely different, and far less archaic: there is no real lake, the appearance is but a *mirage*; men are admitted; Lancelot has not only his cousins for companions, but other knights as well. The lady herself is conceived of more as a mortal versed in enchantment than as a fairy proper. In the *Suite de Merlin* she is identified with the Demoiselle Chaceresse, daughter of the King of Northumberland;[1] and in both these romances, the *Lancelot* and the *Merlin Suite*, she is the lover and the betrayer of Merlin. It may not be out of place to remark here that the tendency of later romances, as exhibited in the *Suite* and notably in Malory, is to connect the Lady of the Lake rather with Arthur than with Lancelot.

It may be asked, how did so simple a *lai* as we here postulate attain so great a popularity? The incidents would be few, and the characters at first probably anonymous.[2] Here, I think, we may take into account a factor

---

[1] *Merlin*, G. Paris and Ulrich's ed., vol. ii. pp. 136-137.

[2] In the prose *Lancelot* the hero is always addressed as 'king's son.' Cf. in this connection Professor Ker's review of my *Legend of Sir Gawain*, Folk-lore, vol. ix. p. 266. I incline to think that the question of a hero's possessing from the first a name and a well-

hitherto practically ignored, the music of the *lais*. As we know they were intended to be sung, and each was connected with its own melody. It would be a truism nowadays to say that the success of a song depends less upon the words than upon the music to which the words are set, and though less true of an age in which the songs of the people were also its folk-tales, yet the influence of music upon the development of popular legends is a point we do ill to ignore. It may help us to solve certain puzzles. Certain heroes of course represent what we may call the general stock-in-trade of Aryan tradition : their names vary with the lands in which their tales are told, but whether Cuchullain or Gawain, Siegfried or Perceval, the hero represents a traditional tale which antedates any special form of recital; such a tale would be assured of welcome, and practically independent of musical aid. But in the case of Lancelot we have no such pre-historic tradition, no striking parallels in early legends. Previously unknown, he leaps into popularity, as it were, at a bound. Even the most ardent adherent of Chrétien de Troyes cannot appeal to the popularity of that writer to help us

marked story depends upon whether he has or has not an existence in *myth*. If of mythical origin he probably would have both, if an actor in folk-tale very likely neither; thus while I should reject Professor Ker's correction as regards *Gawain*, I would certainly hold it true of *Lancelot*. In the case of this latter hero, I think his name may well have been determined by his title du Lac. The tendency of early verse is towards alliteration, probably mere chance determined the *Lancelot*, the one essential was that it should begin with an *L*. It should, I think, also be noted that while in the *Lanzelet* the hero's ignorance of his name and birth are genuine, in the prose *Lancelot* he knows who he is, and the wrong done to his father and uncle by Claudas. The pseudonyms '*Filz du Roi*,' '*Beau Varlet*' are here unnecessary ; a meaningless survival from the original tale.

with a solution, for his Lancelot poem, the *Charrette*, is but seldom referred to in contemporary literature. Much of Lancelot's later popularity is doubtless due to his rôle as the queen's lover; but how account for the initial popularity which caused him to be chosen for that rôle? I can only explain the phenomenon of a knight, whose very name is unknown before the middle of the twelfth century, becoming before the end of that century the leading hero of a cycle to which he was originally a stranger, by supposing that there was some special charm in the *lai* originally connected with him, by means of which his story took hold of the public fancy. Had that charm been in the *lai* itself, in word or form, then I think it would have been preserved to us. We possess more than one beautiful *lai*, the hero of which, originally independent of the Arthurian cycle, became by virtue of his story admitted within the magic precincts. Failing that, I think the charm must have lain in the air to which it was wedded, and which so pleased the ears of the hearers that they demanded its repetition, and lengthening, by the addition of episodes foreign to the original tale. Thus other *lais*, whose fate had been less happy, might for a time at least win a spurious popularity, till the 'survival of the fittest,' which operates in literature as elsewhere, discarded the weaker portions, and fixed the outline of the story in the form we know. This theory may or may not be correct, but I can suggest none other that will meet the problems of the case; and at least it has the advantage of offering an hypothesis which may be of use in other stories besides the one under discussion.

But there is another point in the discussion of Ulrich's poem which urgently demands attention. What is the connection between the *Lanzelet* and the *Parzival* of Wolfram von Eschenbach? A connection of some sort there is, and that a fairly close one. Take for instance the passage describing the hero's departure from his magic home for the world of men, a passage extending over two hundred lines (ll. 400-666). He does not know how to sit his horse, how to hold the bridle,[1] or use his weapons; is ignorant of his name and birth; is called *der kindische man* (l. 598), *der namenlôse tumbe* (l. 2045), all features which irresistibly recall Perceval to our mind, but are in no way characteristic of Lancelot.[2]

The tourney at which Lancelot makes his first appearance at Arthur's court has been undertaken between King Lot von Johenis and *Gurnemanz den fürsten wîs* (l. 2630). It commences with a vesper play:

> '*engegen der vespereide*
> *riten über jene heide,*
> *dort zwêne, dâ her drî.*'—ll. 2855-7.

In the *Parzival*, Book II., we read of the tourney before Kanvoleis that it began with a vesper play:

> '*von Póytóuwe Schyolarz*
> *und Gurnemanz de Grâhárz,*
> *die tjostierten ûf dem plân.*
> *Sich huop diu vesperîe sân,*
> *hie riten sehse, dort wol drî.*'—ll. 295-9.

In connection with which we may note that both

[1] This feature is, I think, peculiar to Wolfram; Chrétien does not mention it.

[2] Professor Hertz, in his edition of the *Parzival*, p. 440, records these points of contact, but does not discuss the question of the relation of the two poems. Professor Foerster in his introduction simply notes that the instruction by Johfrit de Liez recalls the *Perceval* story.

Chrétien and Hartmann von Aue spell the name of Gurnemanz with *o*, not with *u*, as does Wolfram. Other names, some of them peculiar to Wolfram's version, occur in the *Lanzelet*, such as Galagandreiss (Galogandres), also found in Hartmann's *Erec* though not in Chrétien; Iwân de Nonel, l. 2935 (*Parzival*, v. 312); Iblîs, l. 4060 (*Parzival*, xiii. 895). Ulrich's Iblîs is connected with the cloister *jaemerlichen urbor*, Wolfram's with *Terra de Lâbur*; Kailet, l. 6032 (*Parzival*, ii. 737); Maurîn, whose name in each case is similarly qualified, *mit den lichten schenkeln her Maurîn*, l. 3052, *Mit den schœnen schenkeln Maurîn* (*Parzival*, xiii. 1069).[1] In the description of Iweret we read, *einen wâfen roc fuort er und guldîn schellen dran er schein ein engel niht ein man*, ll. 4428-30, which should be compared with the description of Karnachkarnanz.

> '*den dûhte er als ein got getân:
> er'n het ê 'so lichtes niht erkant.
> ûfem tôwe, der wâpenroc erwant.
> mit guldîn schellen kleine.*'—*Parzival*, iii. 175 *et seq.*

Now how are all these points of contact to be explained? Scholars are agreed in placing the date of Ulrich's poem in the opening years of the thirteenth century, therefore anterior to the *Parzival*. Did Wolfram borrow from Ulrich? If it were a mere question of a name here and there we might think so, but the points of contact amount to more than this. We have the characteristics of Perceval postulated of Lancelot; we have correspondence in details, even verbal identity; further, the prose *Lancelot*, as we shall see, presents other points of contact with Wolfram's poem

---

[1] Layamon '*Brut*' knows Maurin of Winchester as a kinsman of Arthur's, ll. 20238 and 24336. I have not found the name elsewhere.

in details where he differs notably from Chrétien. It is not probable that Wolfram, who never alludes to any adventures related in the *Lanzelet*, and to all appearance knows nothing of the hero save the *Charrette* adventure, should have borrowed from two such widely different versions of his story. The fact that where Lancelot appears to have borrowed from the *Perceval* legend, the borrowed matter is marked by characteristics special to one version of the story is, to say the least, curious. If the *Lanzelet really* preceded the *Parzival*—a philological question upon which I am not qualified to pronounce an opinion—and Ulrich, as is generally supposed, closely followed his source, only one conclusion seems possible, *i.e.* that that source knew, and quoted, the poem of Kiot. It is significant that in the mention of Gurnemanz he is spoken of as *den fürsten wîs*, which shows that to the writer he was not a mere name, but a well-known character, distinguished by the qualities which mark him in the *Parzival*.

My own impression is, however, that Ulrich knew Wolfram's poem, or at least part of it (between the *Lanzelet* and the last three books of the *Parzival* there do not appear to be any points of contact). There are numberless small coincidences in language and phrase, trifling in themselves, but which as a whole seem to argue a familiarity with the words of the *Parzival*. Such a correspondence is more likely on the part of Ulrich than on that of Wolfram, who by his own confession could not read or write, and must have become orally familiar with his source. But it is quite clear that a critical comparison of the two works is urgently needed, both in the interests of Arthurian tradition and of German literature. The popular impression, *i.e.* that Wolfram merely borrowed a few names from the *Lanzelet*, will not stand the test of investigation. Two conclusions alone are open, from which we must make our choice: either to admit the existence, beyond any doubt, of the French poem, other than Chrétien's, which Wolfram declared to be his source;[1] or to place the date of Ulrich von Zatzikhoven some few years later than that usually assigned to him. We await the aid of some one of the many competent scholars Germany possesses to solve this puzzle for us.

[1] It appears to me that, in view of Herr P. Hagen's excellent demonstration of the correctness of the many curious Oriental references with which the *Parzival* abounds, and his remarkable identification of Wolfram's Grail with a sacred *Bætylus* stone, it is impossible any longer to deny the possession, by Wolfram, of a source other than Chrétien's poem. But whether the *Lanzelet* offers another proof or not I should hesitate to say. If it does, the evidence, extending as it does over so much of the *Parzival*, is of the greatest value as an indication of the extent of Kiot's work.

CHAPTER III

LANCELOT ET LE CERF AU PIED BLANC

BEFORE examining Chrétien's poem of the *Charrette*, which, whatever the date of composition, belongs by the nature of its contents to the later stages of Arthurian tradition, it will be well to direct our attention to a short episodic poem, undoubtedly French in origin, but, so far as we at present know, only to be found in a translation incorporated in the vast compilation known as the Dutch *Lancelot*.[1] The contents of the poem are as follows: A maiden arrives at Arthur's court, attended by a brachet. She is the messenger of a queen who demands a champion to accomplish the following feat: in her land is a stag with one white foot, guarded by seven lions; she promises her hand to whoever will slay the lions, and present her with the white foot of the stag. The brachet will be guide to any knight who may undertake the adventure. Kay announces his intention of being the first to try his fortune, and sets out, guided by the dog. After riding some distance he comes to a deep and swiftly

---

[1] *Lancelot*, ed. Jonckbloet, vol. ii. ll. 22271-23126. The summaries in this chapter, and all subsequent references to the Dutch *Lancelot*, are taken direct from the text. A summary of the romance here discussed is given by M. Gaston Paris, *Histoire Littéraire de la France*, vol. xxx. p. 113.

flowing river, which the dog promptly swims. Kay's courage, however, fails him at the sight of the water, and he turns back, feigning a sudden illness, which had prevented him from pursuing the quest. Lancelot then determines to try his fortune: he sets out, passes the river in safety, and is attacked by the seven lions. After a fierce conflict, in which he is desperately wounded, he succeeds in slaying them, and secures the white foot. At this moment a stranger knight appears, and Lancelot, exhausted by the fight, gives him the foot, bidding him carry it to the queen, and say that the knight who has achieved the adventure lies sorely wounded, and prays her aid. The knight promises this, but having received the foot, deals Lancelot a treacherous blow with his sword, and leaving him for dead rides off to the castle, and claims the reward due to the slayer of the lions.

The queen is much distressed, as the knight is both ugly and cowardly, and summons her lords and vassals to ask their advice. They recommend that the marriage be postponed for fifteen days, greatly to the disappointment of the knight.

Meanwhile Gawain has become anxious at the non-return of Lancelot, and sets forth to seek him. He finds him apparently dead, revives him, and conveys him to the dwelling of a physician, whom he instructs as to the proper treatment,[1] and then rides himself to the court to punish the treacherous knight.

He arrives on the eve of the marriage, accuses the knight of his treachery, challenges him to single combat and slays

[1] Throughout the Dutch *Lancelot* we have constant references to Gawain's skill in healing. Cf. *Parzival*, x. 104. Chrétien does not appear to know this trait in Gawain's character.

him. The queen is much rejoiced at the news. Gawain brings Lancelot to the queen, who regards him as her future husband; but, on the excuse of calling together his kinsmen for the marriage, Lancelot contrives to leave the country, 'not for anything in the world would he have been faithless to Guinevere.' He and Gawain return to Arthur's court, and the queen is left vainly awaiting her bridegroom.

This conclusion is of course obviously lame and ineffective. The hero should wed the maiden, whose hand was the previously announced reward of successful accomplishment of the feat. That Lancelot undertakes the adventure at all can only be explained by supposing that the tale was connected with him previous to his being generally recognised as the queen's lover.

That he was not the original hero of the tale is proved by the fact that we possess a Breton *lai* which relates the story in a better and more coherent form, ascribing it to a certain *Tyolet*, whom we do not meet in any of the later Arthurian romances.[1]

The main points in which the versions differ are: (*a*) the maiden who comes to Arthur's court is herself the prize of the victor. This is a better version, as it simplifies the action, and accounts for the anxiety felt at the absence of the knight, who should have returned to court at once on achieving the venture. (*b*) Gawain's action (which is the same in both poems, with the exception that instead of his slaying the traitor, Tyolet arrives in time to prevent a combat) is clearly explained; the brachet, which has

[1] The *lai* of *Tyolet* was published by M. Gaston Paris in vol. viii. of *Romania*, '*Lais Inédits*.' I have given a prose translation in vol. iii. of *Arthurian Romances unrepresented in Malory*.

acted as guide, returns alone to court, and leads Gawain to the scene of the combat. In the *Lancelot* version it is difficult to understand how Gawain, who had no guide, finds his friend so quickly. (*c*) Tyolet weds the maiden, and returns with her to her own land, where he becomes king.

Here we have an unmistakable instance of a *lai* originally told of another hero being transferred to Lancelot.

The story itself, however, seems to be older than its connection with either hero; even in the *Tyolet* version, superior as it is to the *Lancelot*, the real meaning of the tale appears to have been overlooked or misunderstood. In its original form I think it was clearly a transformation tale. The stag was the enchanted relative of the princess who sought the hero's aid, and the spell which detained him in animal form could only be broken by the cutting off of the foot. We know that the smiting off of a member of the body (generally the head) is a well-recognised form of terminating an enchantment, and in this case the proposed solution would explain what, in the tale as it stands, appears a piece of unredeemed brutality.

A peculiarity of the *Tyolet* version is that it falls into two well-marked divisions, the first recounting the upbringing of the hero, and his arrival at Arthur's court, a tale bearing a marked affinity to the Perceval *Enfances*; the second being the 'white-foot' adventure. Now in this first part the hero, going into the woods in search of game, sees and follows a stag, which is transformed into a man before his astonished eyes. I suspect that this episode formed the connecting link between the two sections of the *lai*, the real meaning of the latter stag not having been lost when the two were united. A confirmation of this theory is found in the fact that one of the numerous 'shape-shifting' changes of Merlin was into the form of a stag with a white fore-foot.[1] I also think this may well be the origin of the mysterious white stag guarded by lions which meets us so often in later Arthurian story. In the *Queste* stag and lions change into Our Lord and the Four Evangelists, thus preserving the transformation character.

But whatever the original character of the story, it has, in the form in which we now possess it, become affected by *a motif* extremely popular in mediæval times, that of the *False Claimant*. The leading characteristics of this widely spread tale may be summed up as follows. The hero at great risk to himself performs a feat, and possesses himself of a proof (previously agreed upon) that he has done so. The traitor comes on the scene, possesses himself of the proof (either attempting to slay the hero himself or believing him to be already dead), and claims the reward; not knowing that the hero has possessed himself of a further proof of his deed. The hero, left for dead, recovers, and appearing at the critical moment, confutes the traitor by the production of the second and decisive proof.

Of this story practically countless variants exist; Mr. E. S. Hartland, in his *Legend of Perseus*, vol. iii., has tabulated a large number gathered from all parts of the world. The most general version appears to be that in which the feat consists in the slaying of a dragon, to be testified by the production of the head. The hero, not content with cutting off the head, also cuts out the tongue, and is thus enabled to confute the traitor, who has omitted to look within the monster's jaws. It will be noted that

[1] Cf. *Merlin*, Sommer's ed. chap. xxiv. p. 302.

neither in the *Tyolet* or *Lancelot* versions does the hero possess such a proof: in the first instance the impostor is put to shame by Tyolet's inquiry as to who slew the lions; in the second Gawain settles the matter by slaying the traitor. This lack of an important feature of the original tale seems to indicate that the *lai* in its primitive form did not belong to this group of stories, though from the character of the feat related the borrowing of features from so widely known a folk-tale was amost natural development.

A very good example of the *False Claimant* is found in some versions of the *Tristan* legend, notably the poems of Gottfried von Strassburg, and his source, Thomas of Brittany: very few of the prose versions have retained it.[1]

M. Gaston Paris seems inclined to connect the 'whitefoot' adventure with this. Ultimately, of course, the stories must go back to a common source; but the *Cerf au pied blanc* presents the adventure in so general a form, that one can hardly connect it with any special variant of this very widespread folk-tale. The *Tristan* variant is, as I have said above, an especially good example, with many well-marked features, none of the more characteristic of which are reproduced in the *lai*. But we have in the same vast compilation the account of another adventure of the same character, also ascribed to Lancelot, which does appear to be directly drawn from the Tristan story.

In *Morien*[2] we learn that Morien, Gawain, and Lancelot,

---

[1] *Tristan*, vol. i. Book XIII., ed. Bechstein, *Deutsche classiker des Mittelalters*; also my translation of same, *Arthurian Romances*, No. ii. vol. i.

[2] Dutch *Lancelot*, vol. i. l. 42,540 to end. The portion dealing with the adventure begins l. 43,593; the adventure itself, l. 46,514; also summarised in *Hist. Litt.* vol. xxx.

seeking for Perceval and Agloval, come to a hermit's cell at four cross-roads. They ask whither the roads lead, and learn that that on the right hand leads to a waste land devastated by the ravages of a devil in the form of a beast. Lancelot determines to brave the adventure and, in spite of the remonstrances of the hermit, chooses this road. The writer of the tale informs us (but it should be kept in mind that the hermit *does not* tell Lancelot) that the lady of the country has promised her hand to whoever will slay the monster. A knight who has long loved her, but is too cowardly to dare the venture, keeps a watch upon all those who may attack the beast, with the secret intention of, if possible, slaying the victor and taking the credit of the deed to himself. Lancelot arrives at the monster's lair, which is surrounded by the bones of men and animals slain by the fiend. No description of the creature is given, but it is quite clear from the incidental details that the writer conceived of it as a dragon; Lancelot's sword and spear can make no impression on its skin; its claws pierce through shield and hauberk and score deep wounds on the knight's body; it breathes forth venom, which would have slain Lancelot but for the ring he wore (no doubt the ring given him by the Lady of the Lake); finally, as it opens its jaws to devour him, the knight thrusts his spear down its throat and pierces the heart. The monster utters a loud cry, which is heard over two miles off, and expires. The traitor knight, hearing the cry, knows that the monster is slain and rides to the spot. Lancelot is binding up his wounds; the traitor approaches, making feint to aid him, deals him a treacherous blow and leaves him for dead; then he cuts off the foot and is riding away when Gawain appears upon the scene and challenges him. Lancelot recovers from his swoon in time to bid Gawain slay the traitor, which he does. Before Lancelot can recover from his wounds news comes that the King of Ireland has invaded Arthur's kingdom, and is besieging the queen in one of her castles. Lancelot and Gawain go at once to her aid, and nothing is heard of the lady whose hand was to have been the reward of the venture. But, as I have noted above, there is no sign that Lancelot knew anything of the promised guerdon; his conduct is therefore more intelligible and less unchivalrous than in the *lai*.

The special points of contact with the *Tristan* story are these: (*a*) The nature of the animal, which is undoubtedly in both cases a dragon. (*b*) The hero undertakes the adventure unsolicited. Tristan lands in Ireland, hears of the dragon's ravages and goes off secretly to slay it. He has no thought of winning Iseult for himself. In both versions of the *lai* the lady herself invites the adventure. (*c*) The character of the traitor: in both *Tristan* and *Morien* he is represented as being too cowardly to dare the feat himself but as watching his opportunity to rob a brave man of the fruit of his valour. In the *lai* variants 'opportunity makes the traitor'; in these two versions the traitor is on the watch for his opportunity. (*d*) In both cases he is attracted to the spot by the death-cry of the monster. The appearance of Gawain, on the other hand, the death of the traitor, and the fact that it is the *foot* and not, as it should be, the *head*, which is cut off, clearly show the influence of the *lai*.

The ending is, of course, unsatisfactory, and it is curious that the writer, who in the details noted above clearly shows a knowledge of the excellent and complete version of the *Tristan* legend, should not have finished his story more in accordance with that tale. It is not impossible that the original adventure as contained in the *Morien* poem *was* the stag adventure, and that the compiler of the Dutch *Lancelot*, who evidently possessed an extensive collection of Arthurian documents, knowing that he was going to relate the story later on, purposely altered the earlier portion more in accordance with the dragon adventure of the Tristan tale, retaining the later portion for the sake of the rôle played by Gawain, who is one of his heroes, and who, it is scarcely necessary to say, does not appear in the *Tristan* legend. Unfortunately we have no other version of the *Morien* save that of the Dutch *Lancelot*, so the question must remain undetermined; all we can say with certainty is that the adventure as there related is combined from two distinct variants of the same original *motif*

An interesting feature of the *Morien* story is that it shows the *Lancelot* legend influenced by the *Tristan* at a point practically unconnected with the central *motif* of that story, the loves of Tristan and Iseult.

The story of the *cerf au pied blanc* as attributed to Lancelot does not appear to have obtained any popularity. In no variant of the prose *Lancelot* is it related, or even alluded to; the version preserved by the Dutch compiler is, so far, the only one that has been discovered. But existing as it does, it clearly points to a date at which the Lancelot story was still told in isolated *lais*, and before the introduction into the legend of his love for Guinevere. Once fixed as Guinevere's lover, we can understand how the tale dropped out of the completed legend: alter the ending as they might the obstinate fact would remain that Lancelot voluntarily undertook an adventure the successful achievement of which would necessitate him becoming the husband of a stranger maiden; it was an *impasse* from which he could only escape at the cost of an insult to one or the other queen, and very wisely the compilers of his legend ignored the story.

It also seems probable that the original character of the tale itself was not properly understood by its compilers: an evidence, if evidence were really needed, of the extreme antiquity and, if I may use the word, 'unlocalised' character of the elements which went to compose the Arthurian cycle.

CHAPTER IV

LE CHEVALIER DE LA CHARRETTE

With the poem, the title of which heads this chapter, we reach a fresh stage in the Lancelot tradition, and one which, though it has already been the subject of acute and scholarly discussion, still presents many points of difficulty.[1]

The story related in the poem is so well known, and the poem itself so accessible, that it is unnecessary to do more than summarise the leading features. It is, as we all know, the story of Guinevere's abduction by Meleagant, and her rescue by Sir Lancelot.

A knight (Meleagant) appears at Arthur's court, and boasts of the Breton subjects he holds in captivity. Arthur can free them if he will commit Guinevere to the care of a knight who will fight a single combat with him; if he (Meleagant) be defeated, all the prisoners shall be freed; if he be victor, Guinevere, too, is his captive. Kay, by

---

[1] The poem itself has been discussed by M. Gaston Paris in *Romania*, vol. xii., and by Professor Foerster in the introduction to his edition. The question of Guinevere's rescuer has been treated by Professor Rhys in his *Studies in the Arthurian Legend*, and in M. Gaston Paris's article just referred to, and that on Ulrich von Zatzikhoven's *Lanzelet* in *Romania*, vol. x. I have also devoted a chapter in my *Legend of Sir Gawain* to the subject.

demanding from Arthur a boon, the nature of which is unspecified, and which the king grants before hearing, obtains permission to escort the queen. Gawain follows, meets Kay's horse, riderless and covered with blood, and is then confronted by an unnamed knight (Lancelot), who begs the loan of a steed. Gawain gives him his, and follows on a spare steed as quickly as possible, only to find traces of a sanguinary conflict, and his own horse slain. He overtakes Lancelot, who, meeting a dwarf driving a cart, mounts after a momentary hesitation, and the two continue the pursuit together. Meleagant's land (or rather that of his father Baudemagus) is surrounded by deep water, crossed by two bridges, one of a sword-blade, the other under the water. Lancelot chooses the first, crosses in safety, fights with Meleagant, and frees Guinevere, who, however, receives him coldly, being offended at his momentary hesitation before mounting the cart. Lancelot, in despair, tries to commit suicide; Guinevere, hearing a rumour of his death, is overwhelmed with grief, and on his next appearance receives him with the greatest favour. They pass the night together, Lancelot gaining access to the queen's chamber by means of a heavily barred window, and severely wounding his hands in wrenching asunder the bars. The traces of blood on the bed-clothes cause the queen to be accused of a *liaison* with Kay, who, severely wounded, is sleeping in the ante-chamber. Lancelot undertakes to prove Guinevere's innocence by a combat with Meleagant, which shall take place at Arthur's court; but, having set out to seek Gawain, is treacherously decoyed into prison by his foe. Meleagant, by means of forged letters, persuades the queen that Lancelot has returned to court, whither Guinevere repairs, escorted by Gawain, who has meanwhile arrived on the scene. Lancelot, who has been released on parole by his jailor's wife, to attend a tourney, is subsequently walled up in a tower by Meleagant, from which prison he is released by his rival's sister, and reaching court at the last moment, overcomes and slays Meleagant.[1]

The capital importance of this poem lies in the fact that here, for the first time, so far as our present knowledge goes, we meet with those relations between Lancelot and the queen which form so important a part of the completed Arthurian legend. Are these relations, then, an invention of Chrétien, or were they already familiar to the public for whom he wrote? Here I shall only treat this question incidentally, deferring a full study of the point to a subsequent chapter; the questions which mainly concern us relate rather to the nature (*a*) of the story itself, (*b*) of Chrétien's share in its development.

In the introductory lines we learn that the poem was written at the instance of the Countess Marie de Champagne, who supplied '*Matiere et san.*' I take this to mean that she only supplied a verbal outline of the story, and left it to Chrétien to fill in details. Thus, as regards source, Chrétien stands in a different position in this poem than in his other romances. In every other instance he had either in *livre* or *conte*[2] (which latter I take to be the recital of a professional story-teller) a fixed source from which he drew his tale.

---

[1] The concluding portion of the poem is by Godefroy de Leigni, who, however, worked with Chrétien's knowledge and approval, so that practically the work may be held to be Chrétien's throughout.

[2] Livre, *Cligés* and *Perceval*; conte, *Erec* and *Chevalier au Lion*. The concluding lines of the latter, 'qu'onques plus conter n'an oï,' clearly indicate this. I shall return to this subject in the next chapter.

LE CHEVALIER DE LA CHARRETTE 43

The internal evidence agrees with these indications: the *Charrette* is far inferior to Chrétien's other work; the construction is feeble in the extreme, and bristles with contradictions and obscurities. Why, for instance, does Meleagant suggest that Guinevere shall be put in charge of a knight and follow him? Why not challenge a single combat at the court, where there would be a public to see that the rules of such combat were observed? It may be that the original scene of abduction was a wood, and this is an awkward attempt to combine a later version, *i.e.* Arthur's court, with a primitive feature; but in any case it starts the story on wrong lines. Gawain (who is also mounted) follows *directly* on Lancelot's track, but before he comes up with him there has been time for a fierce conflict to take place. These conflicts with a valiant knight do not as a rule terminate so quickly, even though the odds be unequal! Gawain, who of course knows Lancelot well, apparently fails to recognise him, even when he unhelms for supper. The maiden of the castle warns them against sleeping in a certain bed; whoever does so will scarce escape with his life. Lancelot braves the adventure, but the next morning when he is found safe and well, the lady expresses no surprise. We are told that the maiden whom Lancelot frees from the knight at the ford knows him and *is afraid he will know her*, but no explanation of this is vouchsafed, and her identity is not revealed. We are expressly told that the kingdom of Gorres is surrounded by a water which none may pass, but before Lancelot even arrives at the water and bridge he is in the kingdom of Gorres, peopled by captive Bretons. No explanation is given of how Guinevere knew of Lancelot's hesitation to mount the cart; there was no witness but the dwarf, and if he noted so momentary an indecision he must have had a curiously keen appreciation of the rules of *Minne*; and how did he come to see Guinevere? But perhaps it was a case of telepathy. In the same manner Kay becomes mysteriously aware of what has passed between Lancelot and the queen. And these instances might be indefinitely multiplied. Chrétien's *Lancelot* is scarcely less incoherent than Ulrich von Zatzikhoven's; and we begin to wonder if there were not some inherent weakness in the legend itself, which rendered it impossible for any one to give an intelligible account of the hero's proceedings.[1]

I think it is clear that the decided inferiority of the *Charrette* as compared with Chrétien's other poems is due to the deficiencies of his source. He was left in the lurch, and his genius was not of a nature to extricate him from his difficulties. When he had before him a story the form of which was already practically fixed, and which required polishing rather than re-arrangement, Chrétien could put it into charming language, and make a finished and artistic piece of work out of a simple original. I should express the charm of his work as being that he clad the folk-tale in the garments of the court, and taught it to move easily in its foreign trappings. But when his materials were scanty, and he was called upon to supplement them from his own imagination, he was unequal to the task; and

[1] The manifold discrepancies of Chrétien's version were long ago remarked upon by M. Gaston Paris, and even Professor Foerster, with all his enthusiasm for the poet, is constrained to admit their existence, but he considers some of the puzzles were of Chrétien's own making, and he intended later to clear them up. Why then did he not explain them to Godefroy de Leigni, who finished the poem with Chrétien's approval?

LE CHEVALIER DE LA CHARRETTE 45

he was artist enough to know it, and to leave unfinished a work which did him little credit, while he turned to one the nature of which precisely suited his special talent. It is not, I think, without significance that the best of Chrétien's poems follows immediately on his worst. He had a reputation to retrieve, and he did it gallantly in the *Yvain*.

Nor is Chrétien really successful in depicting lovers as lovers: they are little more than lay figures; they talk at great length, and indulge in analysis of their feelings, expressed in the most graceful and ingenious language; but one

> '*Iseut ma drue, Iseut m'amie,*
> *En vous ma mort, en vous ma vie!*'

is worth all Chrétien ever wrote on the subject; the breath of the god is not in it. Yet, so far as the *Charrette* goes, this is scarcely to be laid to his blame. Nowhere, save perhaps in one chapter of Malory, is there the least ring of reality in the loves of Lancelot and Guinevere. They go through all the prescribed gestures of their rôle with admirable precision. Guinevere is by turns gracious, disdainful, frantically jealous, and repentant of her jealousy; Lancelot is courteous, humble, despairing, hopeful: their relation to each other is all that *Minne dienst* can require between a knight and his lady, but nowhere in the whole wearily drawn-out story does the real, pent-up human feeling break through. We can never imagine these two taking one another by the hand and wandering off into the wilderness, content, and more than content, with each other's presence. The story of Lancelot and Guinevere is artificial, not natural; it demands the setting of the court, not of the woodlands. Only in the passage where

Malory describes their parting do they, for a moment, become real; and the effect produced is probably due to the simplicity of the old knight's language, and the virile force of the English tongue.

Nor do I think that these relations are due to Chrétien. He treats them as an already established fact, well known to his readers, and needing no explanation. Certain episodes of the poem, the finding of the comb, the testing of the knight's fidelity to the queen by the lady in whose castle he passes the night, presuppose a state of things generally familiar. Every one knows who Lancelot is; every one will know why he, and no other knight, shall rescue the queen.

That there was a previous story of Guinevere's rescue from imprisonment under analogous circumstances is quite clear: the references found in the Arthurian romance are too numerous, and too archaic in form to be derived from a poem so late in date, so artificial in character, and so restricted in popularity as the *Charrette*. Of this story we have at least three distinct accounts: (*a*) that given by Ulrich von Zatzikhoven, where the 'other-world' character of the imprisonment is strongly marked, but the rescue is the work of an enchanter, and not of Arthur or any of his knights; (*b*) that given in the *Vita Gildæ*, when the abductor is Melwas, king of *Æstiva Regis* (Somerset), the place of imprisonment Glastonbury, and there is again no special rescuer, Arthur marches at the head of his armies to her relief, but it is the intervention of St. Gildas and the Abbot of Glastonbury which brings about the desired result; (*c*) the account given in the poem under discussion.[1]

---

[1] I do not here include either the mediæval Welsh fragments or Malory's account. The meaning of the former cannot be accurately

Of these three variants the version of the *Lanzelet* stands by itself; it represents the 'other-world' under an entirely different, and probably more primitive, aspect, and makes no effort at localisation.¹ The other two variants fall together, Melwas, the king of *Æstiva Regis*, which is admittedly Somerset=Meleagant of Gorres, whose chief city is *Bade*=Bath, also in Somerset. These later versions have been localised, and I think it is clear that the localisation took place on English soil, *i.e.* it is an insular and not a continental variant.

Now, from the very nature of the story it is clear that in its *earliest* forms it would not be attributed to any special locality, and therein the *Lanzelet* version again appears to be the elder; further, the variants must have arisen at a time when it was clearly understood that, however they might apparently differ, Valerîn's thorn-girt dwelling and Meleagant's water-circled castle meant one and the same thing, *i.e.* that both were recognised methods of describing the 'other-world.' In this connection it is instructive to recall the versions of Brynhild's wooing by Siegfried; her residence is universally admitted to be an 'other-world' dwelling, and we find it depicted under forms closely corresponding with the variants of the Guinevere story;

ascertained, and the latter practically represents the same version as that of the *Charrette* poem, though the question of *source* cannot, as I shall prove later on, be held to be definitely settled.

¹ Cf. Simrock, *Handbuch der deutschen Mythologie, Dornröschen.* Some of the details of Arthur's journey to Valerîn's stronghold are worth the attention of folk-lore experts, *e.g.* the curious account of the *Schrîenden Mose,* that at certain times utters loud cries, *drî tage vor sunegihten sô schrît daz mos und selten mêr,* and the curious fish in its stream, which are '*ebenlanc und ebenkurz,*' and of which '*die Engellende*' have many. Cf. *Lanzelet,* ll. 7040 *et seq.*

e.g. Waberlohe (*Volsunga saga*)=Valerîn's hedged magic slumber; Castle surrounded by water (*Thidrek saga*)=Meleagant's stronghold; Glasberg (*Folk-songs*)=Glastonbury. The parallelism is significant.[1]

It is quite clear, I think, that such a story can be in no way ascribed to the invention of a poet living towards the end of the twelfth century, but must be of very much earlier date. Chrétien was dealing with a late variant of a primitive and very widely known theme. But could this variant, which, as seems probable, only reached him through the medium of a tale related by the Countess Marie of Champagne, have come from England, to which country the localisation of Glastonbury, Somersetshire, and Bath point? It is quite possible. We must remember who Marie de Champagne was: she was a princess of France, the daughter of King Louis VII. and Eleanor of Aquitaine, who, on her divorce from the French king, married Henry of Normandy, afterwards Henry II. of England. That is, at the time Chrétien wrote, the mother of his protectress was Queen of England and wedded to a sovereign who took a keen and personal interest in all that concerned King Arthur. The *possibility* of transmission is as clear as daylight; the question of course is, Would Marie be inclined to take advantage of it? The relations between her father and his divorced wife were certainly curious, as Louis made no objection to the marriage of the eldest son of Henry and Eleanor with his daughter by his second marriage, but whether there was intercourse between mother and daughter I have not been able to discover. But the question ought to be easily solved by some historical

[1] On these varying forms of the '*other-world*' dwelling, cf *Rassmann Heldensage*, vol. i. p. 152.

LE CHEVALIER DE LA CHARRETTE

specialist who has made a study of that period. The point is interesting and important, and it is to be hoped some one will clear it up for us.

A question of secondary interest is whether Chrétien's poem is the source of contemporary and later allusions to the story. Of such allusions, or rather versions, we have two of special importance, that contained in Malory's compilation, and that given by Hartmann von Aue, in his *Iwein*. With regard to the former, I can only say that though I am in a position to offer new and important evidence with regard to the manuscript Malory used, and his method of composition, yet that evidence leaves the *Charrette* question unsolved. Of *direct* evidence there is none; the *indirect* and *inferential* evidence tends to show that Malory's source was *not* the poem of Chrétien de Troyes. The two points on which we can be certain are, (*a*) that Malory did not know the earlier part of the prose *Lancelot* at all, that his manuscript began at a point subsequent to the *Charrette* adventure; and (*b*) that he does not invent adventures, and but rarely details. Dr. Sommer's conclusions, as set forth in his *Study on the Sources of Malory*, are founded on very insufficient premises, and will need to be thoroughly revised to bring them into accordance with our present knowledge. This question I shall discuss fully in a later section. The *Iwein* version is of great importance, and though I have previously referred to it,[1] yet in the light of Professor Foerster's strongly repeated assertion that Hartmann knew no other version of the story than that given by Chrétien, I think it is worth while going over the evidence again.

---

[1] *Legend of Sir Gawain*, chap. viii.

It must be remembered that Hartmann's *Iwein* is a translation of Chrétien's *Chevalier au Lion*, and though rather more diffuse, follows its source closely. In the French poem which, as we have noted above, immediately succeeded the *Charrette*, Chrétien deftly introduces more than one allusion to Guinevere's abduction. He says that Guinevere has been carried off by a knight *d'estrange terre*, who went to the court to demand her; but he would not have succeeded in carrying her off had it not been for Kay, who deceived or deluded (*anbricona*) the king into putting the queen in his charge (ll. 3916-39). In another place, he says that the king, '*Fist que fors del san Quant aprés lui l'an anvoia. Je cuit que keus la convoia Jusqu'au chevalier qui l'an mainne*' (ll. 3706-11). Now, let us suppose that, as Professor Foerster insists, Hartmann had not read the *Charrette* and knew no other version of the story, what would he, who knew French well, and translates without blunders and confusion, understand by this? We must note particularly what Chrétien tells and what he omits. He distinctly says that the knight came to the court and demanded the queen (the real version of the poem is less blunt, as we have seen); that Arthur, deluded, put the queen in Kay's charge to lead her to the knight, and that they followed him. He does *not* say that the whole catastrophe came about through Arthur's granting a boon before he knew in what it consisted; he implies that the folly lay in Arthur's sending the queen after the knight, not in the circumstances which forced him to do so.

Now what does Hartmann say? In his version a knight appeared before Arthur and demanded a boon, the nature of which he refused to specify beforehand.

Arthur granted it. It was that he should carry off the queen. This he did. The knights armed and followed. Kay was the first to overtake him, and was struck from his horse with such violence that his helmet caught in a tree and he hung suspended. He was not carried off captive. One after another all the knights are vanquished, and the queen carried off. Gawain is not at court; he returns the next day, and goes in search of the queen. Lancelot is not mentioned throughout; and the inference is that Gawain frees her.

What is specially noticeable in this account is that Hartmann agrees with Chrétien in the very feature which the French poet does *not* specify, *i.e.* the cause of the queen's abduction—a boon rashly granted, though he transfers the asking from Kay to the knight; while he differs from Chrétien in the feature which he *does* specify, *i.e.* that Kay takes Guinevere *after* the knight. Further, he adds details which would clear up some of the inconsistencies in Chrétien's own account: *i.e.* if Gawain were not present at the time, and all the knights followed one after the other and were defeated by Meleagant, we can quite understand that when Gawain returned the next day and followed on the trail, he *would* find traces of the severe and bloody conflict for which Chrétien's version leaves no room. On the face of it, Hartmann's version is much the more logical and coherent of the two. I have remarked above on the extreme awkwardness of the action at the outset of the story; that Meleagant should carry off Guinevere by a ruse similar to that employed by Gandîn in the *Tristan* poems is far more in accordance with mediæval tradition. If Hartmann's divergence is a mere 'invention,' he not only deserves praise for his sagacious skill in constructing a story,[1] but excites admiration for the acuteness which enabled him to detect the leading *motif* of the adventure to which his source afforded absolutely no clue.

Wolfram von Eschenbach's references to the *Charrette* adventure are curious; at first sight it seems certain that he is referring to Chrétien's poem, but on closer examination the matter is not so clear. Thus he says that Lancelot crossed the sword-bridge, fought with Meljakanz (Meleagant), and freed Guinevere—all of which agree with Chrétien.[2] But, on the other hand, he mentions Kay's suspension on the tree (Hartmann's version), and does not know that Meleagant was slain by Lancelot, or that the captive Bretons were freed by his coming—both Meleagant and the Breton knights are fighting at the tournament of Beaurösch.[3] Indeed, Wolfram appears to know far more of these latter than can be gathered from Chrétien's poem. Of course, we cannot here say whether these references are due to Wolfram or to his source, which, as recent research has clearly shown, was certainly the work of a man of varied and extensive learning.[4] Nor is it at all clear that Wolfram knew Lancelot as Guinevere's lover;

---

[1] As a rule, whenever in the *Iwein* Hartmann does depart from his source, it is with the effect of making the story more coherent and probable. I have noted several instances of this in my study on the *Yvain* poems, *Modern Quarterly for Language and Literature*, July and November, 1898.

[2] Cf. *Parzival*, Book VII. 1472.

[3] Cf. *Parzival*, Book VII., as above; also 590 *et seq.* and 1355 *et seq.*

[4] Cf. *Der Gral*, P. Hagen : Strassburg, 1900. I am unable to accept the author's contention that the *Bætylus*-Grail represents the original form of the talisman; but he certainly proves the correctness of the many curious references to Oriental literature which are peculiar to Wolfram's version of the story, and cannot possibly have been within that writer's own knowledge.

he simply says that her imprisonment grieved him '*im was gevancnisse leit, die frou Ginòvêr dolte,*' which might be postulated of any loyal servant of Arthur's. Again when, at the beginning of Book xii., the poet recites Gawain's love-sorrows, he compares his pains first to those suffered by various heroes in the achievement of knightly deeds in general, and then rehearses the parallel cases of sundry lovers. In the first list Lancelot and the sword-bridge appear in company with Iwein and the fountain, and Erec and the '*Schoie de la kurt*' adventure, neither of which were undertaken for the sake of love (why Garel slew the lion and fetched the knife, we do not know), but among the lovers he and Guinevere are not mentioned.

Taking into consideration the fact that the story is, by its very nature, far older than any literary form we possess; that there was certainly in existence one version at least other than Chrétien's (proved by the *Lanzelet*); and that Chrétien's source was avowedly an *informal* one, I do not think it impossible that in the poems of Hartmann and Wolfram we have references to the original form of the story of which Chrétien had only an incomplete knowledge. Hartmann's version is certainly not drawn from the *Charrette*; in Wolfram's case we can only give the verdict '*not proven.*'

In the whole investigation I think we can only consider two points as satisfactorily settled: the original character of the story, and the fact that Lancelot was not at first the hero of the adventure.

CHAPTER V

THE POSITION OF CHRÉTIEN DE TROYES IN THE ARTHURIAN CYCLE

AT the stage which we have now reached in our examination of the *Lancelot* legend, it is, I think, imperative to form a clear idea of the position which, in the great body of Arthurian literature, shall be assigned to the author of the romance we have last studied. On the question of the literary excellence of Chrétien's handling of his material all are more or less agreed, but the problem of his relation to his sources, the question whence he drew the stories he told with such inimitable grace and felicity, is one which has long provoked a lively interchange of argument. The romances of Chrétien de Troyes form one of the chosen battlegrounds of widely differing schools of Arthurian criticism.

Inasmuch as during the varying fortunes of a long-continued conflict the elementary principles underlying the views respectively advocated have a tendency to become obscured, and gradually misunderstood, it is well that from time to time they should be clearly and formally re-stated, in the light of such knowledge as recent investigation may have cast upon them. We are then in a better position to judge whether they retain, unimpaired, the

CHRÉTIEN AND THE ARTHURIAN CYCLE

force and cogency their adherents have ascribed to them. Professor Foerster has apparently felt this necessity, and, impelled by it, has, in the introduction to his edition of the *Charrette*, given to the world what he evidently intends us to regard as his matured and final conclusion on the question of the source of Arthurian dramatic tradition.

Doubtless a similar statement from some leading scholar among the many who hold views differing from Professor Foerster will be forthcoming; in the meantime the present study appears to me to offer an excellent opportunity for the re-statement of certain principles, and the reiteration of certain facts, which cannot safely be left out of consideration in such a study, and which Professor Foerster's argument practically ignores.

To understand the position of Chrétien de Troyes to his sources, whatever they may have been, we must, in the first place, have possessed ourselves of the answer to two leading questions. (*a*) What is the nature of the Arthurian tradition itself? (*b*) What was the popular form assumed by that tradition at the time Chrétien wrote? These are the main points, but they, of course, involve subsidiary issues.

Generally speaking, the tendency of the school represented by Professor Foerster is to regard the Arthurian tradition as divided into two branches, historic and romantic. The former branch being *primarily* represented by the *Historia* of Geoffrey of Monmouth, the popularity of which practically introduced Arthur to the literary world, and *secondarily* by certain passages in the earlier prose romances. This branch contains features of *insular* origin, reminiscences of the historic Arthur and his fights with the Saxons; but the second and far more important branch, the romantic, is of purely *continental* origin. Arthur, as a romantic hero, is the product of Breton tradition and folk-lore; Armorica, and not Wales, is the cradle of Arthurian (romantic) legend; and it was Geoffrey's *Historia* which gave the requisite impulse to the formation of this tradition.

So much for theory, what now are the facts?

Without in any way minimising the popularity and influence of Geoffrey's work, either in its original form or in the translation of Wace, it is quite clear (*a*) that it did not represent *all* the historic tradition current concerning Arthur; (*b*) that his popularity was of considerably earlier date. A comparison with the *Brut* of Layamon[1] will prove the first point; for the second, we have already noted Professor Rajna's discovery of Arthurian names in Italian documents as proving that such names must have been popular in Italy at the end of the eleventh century. Further, from the testimony of the bas-relief at Modena we see that the traditions associated with the British king were not purely historic, but that he and his knights were already the heroes of tales which have not descended to us. We cannot, therefore, fix with any approach to certainty the date at which Arthur became a romantic hero, but evidence points to a period anterior to that generally admitted.

Then ought we not to distinguish between *romantic* and *mythic*? Professor Foerster's arguments appear to me to

---

In this connection, cf. Dr. Brown's study on *The Round Table before Wace*, vol. vii. of *Harvard Studies*: Boston, 1900; and the incidental demonstration that Layamon had access to Welsh traditions unknown to Wace.

ignore Arthur as a *mythic* hero. Romance and myth are not the same thing; though their final developments are apt to overlap, their root origins are distinctly different.

The mythic element in Arthurian legend cannot be ignored—in fact, it is practically admitted; but some scholars appear to lose sight of its character. Yet if that character be rightly apprehended it will, I think, be recognised that the distinguishing features are not due to any demonstrable Armorican element; that the connection of Arthur with Celtic myth must have taken place on *insular* rather than on *continental* ground. Thus while Arthur may, or may not, represent the *Mercurius Artusius* of the Gauls, it is not possible to deny that he, and at least one of his knights, Gawain, stand in very close relation to early Irish mythic tradition. The persistence of Irish elements in the Arthurian story is not a theory but an established *fact*. Where would these stories, Arthurian and Irish, be most likely to meet and mingle, in Great Britain, or in Armorica? The first is *a priori* the more probable; not only is the distance less, but we know that during the centuries between the life of the historic Arthur and the appearance of Arthurian story a constant interchange of population went on between Ireland and the northern parts of the British Isles. The conclusion at which we should naturally arrive would be that stories in which the Celtic element was presented under a form identical with early Irish tradition would reach Brittany *viâ* Great Britain, and would not be of Armorican origin.

And this conclusion is strongly supported by the facts. We have two remarkable stories told of Gawain, both of which find striking parallels in early Irish legend, both are excellently preserved in insular versions, neither is adequately represented by any known continental text. I allude of course to *Sir Gawain and the Green Knight* and *The Marriage of Sir Gawain*.[1]

Of the first the existing French versions are, one and all, poor; immensely inferior to the English poem, and showing in certain cases, notably in *Perceval li Gallois*, a manifest lack of comprehension of the story. The German version, *Diu Krône*, is perferable to any of the French, but in no case is the story so well and fully told as in the English poem, which cannot possibly be derived from any known continental source. Of the main point of the second story, the wedding of a young knight to a 'Loathly Lady,' the French poems have no trace, though some seem to have retained a confused remembrance of the transformation of a hideous hag into a maiden of surpassing beauty. Mr. Maynadier, in his study of all the known variants, pronounces unhesitatingly for the direct dependence of the English upon the Irish tradition.[2]

In the first story, the Green Knight, the original hero of the beheading challenge, is Cuchulinn, who, if he does not himself represent a god, is certainly the son of a god. In the second the lady is 'the sovereignty,' and through granting her request the hero obtains the sovereignty of Ireland.

---

[1] For the first, cf. *Legend of Sir Gawain*, chap. ix., where I have discussed the variants of the poem. For *The Marriage of Sir Gawain*, cf. Mr. Maynadier's exhaustive study of *The Wife of Bath's Tale*, vol. xiii. of the present series. In the case of the *Green Knight* there are certain peculiarities of names which point to an intermediate French stage, which, in this instance at least, cannot well have been other than an Anglo-Norman poem.

[2] The French variant which seems to have most affinity with the tale referred to is that of the Didot *Perceval*, printed by M. Hucher in vol. i. of his *Saint Graal*, p. 453.

Both are thus distinctly mythical in character; and though the English versions, as we now possess them, are of comparatively late date, in neither case can the Irish version be later than the eleventh century, while the internal evidence points a period anterior to the introduction of Christianity.

Let us take another instance, the story of Guinevere's abduction and rescue. Of purely mythical origin, the story was at first unlocalised, but when localised it is on insular and not on continental ground. To say, as Professor Foerster does,[1] that the mention of Bath is no proof of an insular source simply shows that the writer has not grasped the real facts of the case. The mention of Bath does not cover the whole ground, it must be taken in connection with *Æstiva Regis* (Somerset) and Glastonbury. The latter is, if I mistake not, the real point of identification. A confusion between Glastonbury, Avalon, and the abode of the departed had taken place previous to William of Malmesbury: the exact date cannot be ascertained, but M. Ferd. Lot considers the author of the identification to have been an Irish monk writing in the tenth century. In a subsequent note M. Lot further identified Melwas= Meleagant, whom all scholars admit to be a king of the other-world, with the Irish 'king of the dead,' *Tigern-Mas*, of which name he considers Mael-was to be the Welsh translation.[2]

Now it seems to me quite obvious that the connection of the king of the other-world with the place looked upon as the special dwelling of the departed must have *preceded*

[1] Introduction, *Charrette*, p. cxxvii.
[2] Cf. 'Nouvelles Etudes sur la provenance du cycle Arthurien,' *Romania*, vols. xxvii. and xxviii.

his being considered as lord also of the surrounding lands, *i.e.* Tigern-Mas=Maelwas must have been connected with Glastonbury=Avalon *before* he was thought of in connection with Bath and *Æstiva Regis*. It is most probable that such a connection would take place on *insular* not on *continental* ground, and as a matter of fact the only text which connects Melwas with Glastonbury, the *Vita Gildæ*, is an insular text, as is that which connects Glastonbury with Avalon. Here, too, again, if M. Lot be right, we find Irish influence at work.

It is probable that we may be able to add to this list the story of Arthur's fight with the demon cat. The story is certainly told in a continental text (*Merlin*), and located on continental ground, but the identification of the monster with the *Cath Palug* of Welsh tradition and that again with the mysterious *Chapalu* of French romance depends on insular evidence.[1]

In his notice of Herr Freymond's monograph [2] M. Gaston Paris suggests that the source will be found to be 'un trait sans doute fort ancien, de mythologie celtique, que Gaufrei de Monmouth n'a pas accueilli'; while M. Loth, in a note appended to this critique, remarks that the original vanquisher of the cat was certainly not Arthur but Kay. The localisation of the story in Savoy, Herr Freymond considers to have been due to the narration of pilgrims, and discusses the relations of the houses of Savoy and Flanders with our Anglo-Norman kings.

Here then we have a group of stories, possessing a distinctive (Celto-mythic) character, all of which are either

---

[1] Cf. *Artus Kampf mit dem Katzenungetum*, E. Freymond, Halle: 1899.

[2] *Romania*, vol. xxix. p. 121 *et seq.*

CHRÉTIEN AND THE ARTHURIAN CYCLE

better preserved, solely retained, or originally localised in these islands; *i.e.* the evidence of facts is here in favour of an insular rather than a continental origin. Nor do I think we shall be wrong if we ascribe a decided importance to the fact that the tales told in these islands appear to have been of a mythic rather than of a romantic character.

Granting then, that at Chrétien's time, and long previous, there was current a body of tradition, historic, mythic, romantic, dealing with the British king, how was it handed down, and in what shape did he find it? Of course it will generally be admitted that for a long time the transmission of such stories would be entirely—in Chrétien's days it would still be partially—oral.[1] But in saying this we must have a clear idea of what, in the case of traditional stories, oral transmission implies. It does *not* mean a game of 'Russian scandal,' where the point is to see how much a story told from mouth to mouth can be made to vary from its original form in the process; professional story-*tellers* were, and are, more conservative than story-*writers*. The tales crystallise into certain formulæ of incident and expression which survive often after the real signification has been forgotten.[2]

In the words of a recognised authority on folk-lore: 'Among many peoples the *ipsissima verba* of traditional tales are insisted upon; the form, and even the details of the form, are often as much a part of the tradition as the

---

[1] The evidence of the *lais*, and the fact that Marie de France was Chrétien's contemporary, forbids us to postulate an entirely oral transmission.

[2] Of this the '*runs*' of Celtic and Gaelic story-tellers form a good example. Cf. Hyde's *Beside the Fire*, p. xxv.

substance of the tale.'[1] Therefore when we find two stories of marked traditional and folk-lore character agreeing with each other in sequence of incident, detail, and even words, we do not necessarily conclude that the versions are connected by borrowing: they may be, but it is at least equally possible that they represent independent versions of the same oral original.

This is, of course, well understood by the folk-lore student; but unfortunately it is too often ignored by the literary critic, who is too prone to devote attention to the literary form, while he ignores the essential character of the story. Yet in solving the problem of sources it is this latter which is the determining factor.

In examining into the sources of Chrétien de Troyes it is well to remember that it is easy to exaggerate the necessity for a literary source; it is difficult to exaggerate the conservative tendencies of a professional story-teller of that date.

But besides the Arthurian legend proper, there was also current in Chrétien's time a great mass of popular folk-lore, which, certainly on the Continent, probably also on our island,[2] was told, or rather sung, in the form of mythical tales or *lais*. These *lais*, in the first instance in the Breton tongue, and independent of the Arthurian cycle, were later translated into French eight-syllabic verse, and largely Arthurised—if I may use the word.

The process in vogue appears to have consisted of two stages: in the first, the king at whose court the events took place (himself generally anonymous) was identified with Arthur; in the second stage, the original hero was replaced by one of Arthur's knights. Among the speci-

[1] Mr. E. S. Hartland, to whom I submitted the question.
[2] Cf. M. Ferd. Lot 'La patrie des lais Bretons,' *Romania*, vol. xxviii.

mens which have been preserved we have examples of all the stages: *lais* entirely independent of Arthur; *lais*, the scene of which is laid at Arthur's court; *lais* in which the hero is one of Arthur's knights; but one and all are in the same metre, that of Chrétien's poems. Of an intermediate French form we have no trace.

The *lai* of *Tyolet*, to which we have previously referred, is an excellent example of this gradual 'Arthurisation.' As we have it, the court at which the events take place is that of Arthur, the loyal friend of the hero is Gawain, but nowhere else do we meet with Tyolet as one of Arthur's knights: the inference is that we have here a *lai* in the first stage of assimilation. The *lai* consists of two parts; the latter half, the stag adventure, is found in a separate form, but here the hero is one of Arthur's most famous knights, Lancelot—the process of assimilation is complete.

The first part of the *lai* has many features which recall the more famous 'Perceval' *Enfances*. That *Tyolet* is anterior to the evolution of the Lancelot story we have shown above[1]; the probability is that it is also anterior to the great popularity of the *Perceval* story. When Perceval was once universally recognised as the son of the widowed lady of the forest, there would be little probability of the tale being told of a hero practically unknown to Arthurian story. His adventures taken over by more famous knights, Tyolet disappeared from the roll of heroes.

Again, among the *lais* we have an important group dealing with the main idea of a knight beloved by the wife of his lord, rejecting her advances, incurring her displeasure, and finally departing to fairyland with a fairy bride. Of this story we have three important

[1] Chap. iii.

variants, agreeing in their main features but differing in detail: the *lais* of *Graalent*, *Guingamor*, and *Lanval*. Of these three, the scene of the two first is laid at the court of an anonymous king; the action of the third, translated by a contemporary of Chrétien, passes at the court of Arthur. But, though the *lai* of *Guingamor* has only reached us in its earlier and independent form, Chrétien himself refers to it in an Arthurised version. He brings Guingamor to Arthur's court, and says of him,

> '*de l'Isle d'Avalon fu sire.*
> *De cestui avons oï dire*
> *Qu'il fu amis Morgain la fee,*
> *Et ce fu veritez provee.*—*Erec*, ll. 1955-8.

M. Ferd. Lot[1] suggests that the identification is probably due to Chrétien himself, but if we examine the passage closely I do not think we shall find it to be so. It occurs in a list of knights who visit Arthur's court for the marriage of Erec. The passage immediately preceding deals with a certain Maheloas of l'Ile de Voirre.[2] He then names

---

[1] 'Morgue la Fée et Morgan Tud,' *Romania*, vol. xxviii. p. 327.

[2] Professor Foerster's references to this character (*Charrette*, lxxiii.) are perplexing. He prints Chrétien's description of the 'Ile' side by side with a parallel passage from Giraldus Cambrensis, *Topographia Hiberniæ*, informing us that both are 'ganz einfach eine naturgetreue Beschreibung von Irland.' He cannot mean us to understand that the one description is borrowed from the other; the work of Giraldus is at least thirty years later than the *Erec* (*circa* 1186), and that chronicler would hardly go to a romancer like Chrétien for the description of a country he knew personally. But *is* it a '*Naturgetreue*' description of Ireland at all? Professor Foerster is compelled himself to admit naïvely, '*Gewitter und Stürme fehlen nicht ganz!*' Is this not rather a description of the fabled Irish Paradise which Chrétien and Giraldus alike have borrowed from a source common to both?

two brothers, Graislemier de Fine Posterne and Guingamor. The first named is generally identified as Graalent-Mor, the hero of the *lai* to which I have referred above.

The fact that Chrétien makes the two knights brothers clearly indicates that he knew the close kinship existing between their stories; but why, if dealing with a free hand, he should have made Guingamor, and not Graalent, the lord of Avalon it is difficult to say. If free to choose we should have expected the latter; the *lai* of *Graalent* stands in far closer connection with that of *Lanval* (being a variant of the same story) than with that of Guingamor; and Lanval weds the mistress of Avalon. Or, since both were brothers, both might have been represented as dwelling in that mystic island which had not one queen alone as its denizen but nine. The real explanation alike of the connection and the separation of the two knights appears to me to be that Chrétien knew the one *lai*, and not the other, in an Arthurised form.

Certainly it seems more probable that the gradual assimilation by the *lais* of an Arthurian character would, so far as the Continent is concerned, take place on Breton rather than on French grounds. They are originally Breton *lais*; Arthur is a Breton,[1] not a French, hero; where would Breton folk-lore and Breton traditionary romance be more likely to coalesce than in the home of both? I do not myself believe that such coalition was the work either of Marie de France or Chrétien de Troyes.

In any case it is beyond the shadow of a doubt that when Chrétien wrote his first Arthurian poem there was

[1] Of course I here use the word *Breton* in a general sense as opposed to *French*. I do not intend to imply that Arthur is of *Continental* origin.

already afloat a vast body of popular folk-lore connected with the Arthurian legend, and existing under the form of short poems in rhymed, eight-syllabic verse, the same metre, in fact, as that adopted by Chrétien himself. It is also certain that he knew these *lais*; highly probable that he knew some of them, as his contemporary Marie de France did, in their Arthurised form. As we shall see presently, there is strong ground for the presumption that for the main incident of his most famous poem, *Yvain*, he was indebted to such a *lai*.

Now, without accepting the mechanical theory of Herr Brugger,[1] which would make the first Arthurian romances consist of *continental lais* automatically strung together, I certainly think that the *lais* played a more important part in the evolution of these romances than we generally realise. In a previous chapter[2] I have indicated what would probably be the method of procedure. The original *lai* would be expanded by the introduction of isolated adventures; other *lais*, which through demerit of style or music had failed to win popularity, would be drawn upon for incident, or incorporated bodily; one or more popular *lais* would be added, and the whole worked over and polished up into a complete and finished romance. At first the parts would hang but loosely together, and there would be a good deal of re-selection and discarding of incident before the work crystallised into shape, though the form of the *original* tale, which was the kernel of the subsequent romance, would not be likely to vary much.

The *Lanzelet* of Ulrich von Zatzikhoven is, as I suggested

[1] *Ueber die Bedeutung von Bretagne, Breton*, Zeitschrift für französische Sprache, xx. 79-162.
[2] Cf. chap. ii.

CHRÉTIEN AND THE ARTHURIAN CYCLE 67

above, an example of a romance arrested in development: the kernel of the whole can be detected, but the parts fit badly, and it has never been really worked up into shape. But, unless I am much mistaken, we have in the Welsh tale of *The Lady of the Fountain* a specimen of the same process at work, of capital importance for critical purposes, since we also possess the completed work, *i.e.* the Mabinogi has preserved Chrétien's *Yvain in process of making.* The adventures are practically identical, sequence and incident agree in the main, but in the Welsh version they are much more loosely connected, and there are significant breaks which seem to show where the successive redactions ended. If we follow the indications of the version we shall conclude that *as first told* the story ended with Yvain's achievement of the 'spring' adventure and his marriage with the lady. This would, I think, represent the original *lai*, which in its primitive form might well be unconnected with Arthur's court: the king was probably anonymous. The next step would be to Arthurise the story; Yvain must start from Arthur's court, and naturally the court must learn of his success: this was arranged by bringing Arthur and his knights to the spring where they are themselves witnesses, and victims, of Yvain's prowess. It is significant that in *all* the versions extant Yvain is influenced in his secret departure from court by the conviction that *Gawain* will demand the adventure of the spring, and thus forestall him; but in the Welsh variant alone is this forecast literally fulfilled and the undecided conflict between Yvain and Gawain fought at the spring. And here the Welsh version breaks again. This was evidently the end of the Arthurised *lai*, and the point where the conflict between the friends was *originally* placed. All the variants bear the trace of this second redaction; the Welsh tale alone indicates clearly what was the primitive form. Yvain's transgression of his lady's command (probably first introduced for this purpose), a transgression much more serious in the Welsh, where he stays away for three years, than in the other versions, offered an elastic framework for the introduction of isolated adventures; finally, when the whole was worked over in romance form, his combat with King Arthur's invincible nephew was transferred to the end of the poem, where it formed an appropriate and fitting climax to his feats.

The theory suggested above is based upon certain recognised peculiarities in the evolution of the Breton *lais*; but the question whether we are justified in making such use of ascertained facts naturally depends upon whether the story related in the romance in question was in its origin one that we might expect to find related in a *lai*; if it were *not*, then, however rational the hypothesis may otherwise appear, we should regard it with suspicion as lacking solid foundation.

Granting then that a considerable share in the completion of Arthurian romantic tradition was due to the influence of *lais* originally independent of that tradition, that the process of fusion had already commenced when Chrétien wrote his poems, and that he was himself familiar with such *lais*, each of the above points having been already proved, our next step must be to examine the *character* of the stories related by Chrétien.

Two of the five works we possess (I do not count the *Guillaume*, which whether it be by Chrétien or not lies outside the scope of our inquiry) must at once be put on one side. Neither *Cligés* nor the *Charrette* story (in

CHRÉTIEN AND THE ARTHURIAN CYCLE 69

the form Chrétien tells it) can be based upon *lais*. But the character of the three more famous poems, *Erec*, *Yvain*, and *Perceval*, is precisely that of a romance composed of traditional and folk-lore themes. In the case of *Erec* and *Perceval* this is partially admitted even by the most thoroughgoing advocate of Chrétien's originality, though Professor Foerster would limit the element to the *Sparrow-hawk* and *Joie de la Court* adventures in the first, and to Perceval's *Enfances* as representing a *Dümmling* folk-tale in the second.[1]

On this subject I shall have more to say later on; for the present I will confine my remarks to *Yvain*, on the construction of which Professor Foerster holds a theory, highly complicated in itself, and excluding, as a necessary consequence, any genuine folk-lore element.[2]

According to this view the main idea of the poem is borrowed from the story of *The Widow of Ephesus*, a tale of world-wide popularity, the oldest version of which appears to be Oriental (Grisebach considered it to be Chinese), and which in Latin form, as told first by Phædrus and then at greater length in the compilation of *The Seven Sages of Rome*, was well known in mediæval times.[3] With this is combined other elements: a Breton local tradition, classical stories (the Ring of Gyges and the Lion of Androcles), and other stories of unspecified origin.

On the face of it, this theory postulates a highly artificial source, and one calling for great powers of invention and combination; and when we examine it, we find the main

---

[1] Cf. *Charrette*, lxxxi. and cxli.

[2] Cf. on this point Professor Foerster's Introductions to his editions of the *Yvain*, 1887 (large ed.), 1891 (small ed.).

[3] Cf. Grisebach, *Die Treulose Witwe*: Wien, 1873.

idea wholly inadequate to sustain the elaborate fabric reared upon it. I have carefully studied *The Widow of Ephesus*, both in earlier and later variants, and can only see the slightest possible resemblance to the *Yvain* story; true, in both a widow, overcome with grief for the loss of her husband, speedily forms a fresh attachment, but situation, details, *motif*, all are radically different. In every variant of the first story the lady's action is prompted by mere sensual caprice; in the second, it is the outcome of a sound instinct of self-preservation. True, Laudine does eventually fall in love with *Yvain*, but she contemplates marriage with him before she has ever beheld him, influenced by the advice of her servant, who paints in strong colours the defenceless condition of the land, and who is aware of Yvain's passion for her lady. In *no* variant of the earlier tale does the lady marry the slayer of her husband (a point, I believe, essential to the *Yvain* story). Indeed, in many her advances are rejected by the object of her passion; in *all* she is represented as refusing to leave the grave, and none are free from the repulsive details accompanying her new-fledged passion, though these are amplified in the later versions. In insisting on the fact that the lady's re-marriage (often entirely lacking in the earlier story), '*unter hässlichen unser Gefühl schwer verletzenden Bedingungen*,' is the central point of both stories,[1] Professor Foerster overshoots his mark. The conduct of the Lady of Ephesus is certainly offensive in the highest degree, not so that of Laudine. For a woman, especially if she were an heiress, in mediæval times marriage was an absolute necessity. The true parallel to

[1] Cf. review of *The Legend of Sir Gawain*. Zeitschrift für französische Sprache, No. 20, p. 95.

Laudine is here *not* the widow of many wanderings, but the Duchess of Burgundy, in *Girard de Viane*, who, on the death of her husband, promptly appeals to Charlemagne. '*A quoi sert le deuil?—donnez-moi un autre mari. Donnez moi donc un mari qui soit bien puissant.*'[1] *Un mari bien puissant* was a necessity of those days. The real truth is, that the situation was already in the story, and mediæval compilers explained it in accordance with the social conditions of the time, and the parallel situations in contemporary stories.

A minor objection to the theory is, that it would make, not the hero, but the lady, the real centre of the story, which is certainly not the case. But, as we shall see, the tale in its original form is far older than Chrétien, *and could by no possibility have been invented at so late a date as Professor Foerster suggests.*

Yvain, as one of Arthur's knights, is of a date considerably anterior to Chrétien. We find him in Wace's *Brut*, as a valiant hero, on whom Arthur, after the death of Aguisel, bestows the crown of Scotland.[2] Now, Professor Foerster himself states, and I think the great majority of scholars will fully agree with him, that neither *Erec, Yvain*, nor *Perceval* were *originally* Arthurian heroes, and undoubtedly their connection with Arthur's court was of the slightest. If their connection with Arthur marks a secondary stage in the story, and *Yvain* in the *Brut* is already an Arthurian knight, it is pretty obvious that the original tale connected with him, by virtue of which he was admitted into the magic circle of Arthurian romance, must be older

---

[1] Cf. Gautier, *Epopées Françaises*, vol. ii. p. 89 ff.; also Helisant, in *Garin le Loherain*.

[2] Cf. *Brut*, ed. Leroux de Lincy, vol. ii. ll. 13597-99.

even than Wace; in other words, he must have been the hero of a popular adventure upwards of thirty years, at least, before Chrétien wrote his poem. And if that original story was not the fountain-story, what was it?

But if we look at the tale aright, I think we shall discover that its essential character is so archaic that it may well be as old as the most exacting criticism can require. What is it but the variant of a *motif* coeval with the earliest stages of human thought and religious practice—the tale of him '*who slew the slayer, and shall himself be slain*'? The champion who must needs defend his charge single-handed against all comers, and whose victor must perforce take his place; and how old this tale may be, Mr. Frazer has taught us.[1]

This surmise is strengthened by the nature of the challenge; Yvain's pouring the water, which is followed by a storm, is a simple piece of sympathetic magic—of rain-making, and, as such, is practised even to-day by savages in different parts of the world. Such a story must, by its very nature, have been originally *un*localised, even as it cannot be dated; it could be postulated of *any* place, it might be practised everywhere—it belongs just as much, and just as little, to South Africa in the present day as to the wood of Broceliande in the twelfth century.

To treat such a story as a local tradition is a grave error. It may have recalled in its details certain stories told of the Fountain of Barenton, and, therefore, when transported to the Continent from Wales (to which country the earlier redaction certainly belongs), the continental story-tellers, finding the Fountain unlocalised, as it naturally was in the original tale, connected it with the Breton forest.

[1] Cf. *The Golden Bough*, J. G. Frazer.

But it is obvious that such connection is purely arbitrary, and has no critical value. It is at variance with all the geography of the story, which is located in Wales or on the Welsh border; and neither the compiler of the Welsh version nor the English translator of Chrétien's poem admit it, but adhere to the earlier and unlocalised form.

I may here quote a remark of the distinguished folk-lore authority to whom I have previously referred. Mr. E. S. Hartland says: 'The rain-making incident has always seemed to me a very good evidence of the traditional origin of the (*Yvain*) story. At all events it is an incident very closely connected with savage magic.'

I do not suppose it would very much astonish any competent student of these questions if some missionary in Africa, or traveller in the South Sea Islands, was to publish a savage variant of our romance: the substitution of the slayer for the slain, and the practice of rain-making by the pouring out of water, are customs alive in certain parts of the world to this day. But what would Professor Foerster say? Would he still maintain that his '*Meister*' invented the story, and credit the savage folk, whoever they might be, with the remains of a vanished civilisation and literary culture?

I think it also highly probable that in the *Balaan*, and *Balaain* story, and in *Meraugis de Portlesguez*, we have variants of the same theme. In each of these cases the hero must take the place of the champion he defeats, and hold the post till in his turn he be defeated and slain; while at the same time he succeeds to his predecessor's relations with the lady of the castle, whose *ami* he becomes.[1]

---

[1] Cf. *Merlin*, ed. Paris and Ulrich, vol. ii. pp. 44-56; *Meraugis de Portlesguez*, ll. 2915 *et seq.*

It will be observed that Herr Ahlström's suggestion that the lady may originally have been a fairy—a suggestion contemptuously scouted by Professor Foerster[1]—might be accepted without any detriment to the original signification of the story, whereas Professor Foerster's theory excludes any possible archaic origin, and is demonstrably out of harmony with the very primitive rain-making incident.

It is obvious that such a tale as I have indicated above, belonging as it does to the family of folk-lore and traditional tales, is precisely the kind of story that might be related in a *lai*; and this was, I believe, its original form. It is significant that Chrétien records the fact that there was a *lai* more or less closely connected with the lady who became Yvain's wife; and, according to the reading of one MS., that connection was very close indeed, being nothing less than the relation of how Yvain won her to wife.

I print here the reading to which I refer, together with that of Professor Foerster's edition:—

MS. 12560, *Bib. Nat.* (Anç. fr. 210), fol. 14, recto 2nd col.	Professor Foerster's critical edition.
Veanz touz les barons se done	*Veant toz ses barons se done*
La dame a mon seignor ' Y.'	*La dame a mon seignor Yvain.*
Par la main de son chapelain	*Par la main d'un suen chapelain*
Einsint la dame de lenduc	*Prise a Laudine de Landuc*
La dame qui fu fille au duc	*La dame qui fu fille au duc*
Lan ( ) donez dont len note ·|· lai.[2]	*Laudunet don an note un lai.*

—*Yvain*, ed. 1891, ll. 2148-53.

[1] *Vide supra, Legend of Sir Gawain*, Zeitschrift für franz. Spr.

[2] M. Ferd. Lot, to whom I am indebted for the verification of this passage, writes: 'Le ( ) répresente un léger blanc occasionné par un défaut du parchemin, en sorte qu'on pourrait lire en deux mots *Lan donez* (d'où *l'ont donez*); on peut lire La*n*-donez aussi bien que La*u*donez.'

CHRÉTIEN AND THE ARTHURIAN CYCLE

(Translation.)

All the barons beholding, gives herself	*All her barons beholding, gives herself*
The lady to my lord Yvain.	*The lady to my lord Yvain.*
By the hand of her chaplain	*By the hand of one her chaplain*
Thus the lady of Ienduc,	*He has taken Laudine de Landuc,*
The lady who was daughter to the duke,	*The lady who was daughter to the duke,*
They have given to him of which (whom) one notes a lay.	*Laudunet of whom (which) one notes a lay.*

It will be observed that, grammatically, the phrase 'don an note un lai' may refer to the wedding quite as well as to the supposed Laudunet, while *in no other passage in the entire poem* is the lady's name or that of her father mentioned.

The MS. which offers the interesting variant quoted above is, Professor Foerster tells us, in the dialect of Champagne (Chrétien was a Champenois) of the thirteenth century, and stands in close relation to the source of Hartmann von Aue's translation.[1]

For many reasons it appears to me that this reading deserves more attention than it has yet received. It is, to say the least, curious that Chrétien should go out of his way to remark upon a *lai* dealing with an absolutely unknown personage and one to whom he never refers again. Chrétien's poems stand, *not* at the commencement of the Arthurian tradition, but at a very advanced stage of its evolution: had there been current at that date, the end of the twelfth century, a *lai* important enough to be chronicled in this unusual manner (I can recall no other instance in Chrétien's poems), some trace of the hero of

[1] Cf. Introduction to *Yvain*, large edition, where it is referred to as G.

the *lai*, if not the poem itself, would surely have been preserved to us. On the other hand, the version given in the Welsh tale has a break precisely at this point, showing where the primary redaction ended, and the character of the tale is, as we have seen, such as might well be preserved in a *lai*. I believe that Chrétien is here indicating the original source of this section of his poem.

The passage, moreover, has a curious affinity with one to which I shall have occasion to refer later on, where the carelessness of a copyist in running together two or three words has created what the editor of the text read as a proper name, a reading adopted by his critics. But here the text had not been worked over, and the result was a confused reading which has baffled more than one commentator. The mere chance that the right reading (here undoubted) has been preserved in a text hitherto unaccountably neglected has enabled me to detect the error; but had the copyists of the *Queste* been as careful to preserve the grammatical sense as those of the *Yvain*, we should have been much puzzled to decide whether *D'Estrois de Gariles* was or was not originally *des trois de Gaule*![1]

It is a question for experts in palæography which is the more likely error to be made, the running of two or three words into one, eventually read as a proper name, or the separation of the letters composing a proper name into two or three words.

It appears to me that the arguments advanced for the above view are, as compared with Professor Foerster's arguments, *objective* versus *subjective*. Professor Foerster sees in the story of Yvain and his lady a resemblance to the tale of the *Widow of Ephesus*, *therefore* he concludes

[1] Cf. chap. x. p. 182, where the passage referred to is given in full.

CHRÉTIEN AND THE ARTHURIAN CYCLE 77

that Chrétien based his romance on that story; but in support of his theory he offers no *proof* whatever: there is no evidence that Chrétien knew the tale, no reference to a book in which it might be contained, no correspondence of name or phrase, and the most characteristic incidents, the dwelling by the grave, and the insult to the corpse, have no parallel in the romance.[1] The evidence is purely subjective; satisfactory to the framer of the theory, but not satisfactory to others.

The evidence for the theory advanced above is, on the contrary, purely objective. The story must be of such a character that it might be told as a *lai*—it is of such a character, *i.e.* folk-lore and traditional; *proof*—the rain-making incident, and correspondence with the *motif* of 'slayer and slain.' We must have proof that Chrétien knew the *lais* current in his day—he refers to one of the most famous, *Guingamor*, and couples the hero with that of another, *Graalent*. We should like a reference to a *lai* connected with the story—we have the reference, at the very point where, according to our theory, we might expect to find it. Further, the reading of one MS., and that neither a late nor a poor one, gives a remarkable indication of the contents of the *lai*. If on these grounds we decline to accept the *Widow of Ephesus* theory we are surely neither prejudiced nor oblivious of facts.[2]

---

[1] To say, as Professor Foerster does, that the spring=grave is to misrepresent the incidents; the castle in which the lady dwells is some distance from the spring, as we see in Yvain's chase of his flying foe.

[2] I do not know that it is has any real bearing on the question, but the passage from *Flamenca* quoted by Wolff (*Lais*), p. 51, is curious: '*L'uns viola lais del cabrefoil, E' l'autre cel de Tintagoil; l'uns cantet cels des fis amanz, E l'autre cel que fes Ivans.*'

Nor is Professor Foerster more fortunate in his theory of the origin of *Perceval*. He states it at great length in the introduction to the *Charrette*,[1] but the main points may be summarised thus. The book given to Chrétien by Count Philip of Flanders was a *Grail* as distinct from a *Perceval* romance. The two were independent stories and their combination was the work of Chrétien de Troyes. 'Dieser original Gralroman enthielt natürlich keinen Perceval und auch nicht dessen Sagen-motiv, sondern wird den uns sonst bekannten Gral-texten ähnlich gewesen sein.'[2] 'Sollte das *livre* aber, aller Unwahrscheinlichkeit zu trotz, dennoch ein Perceval (d. h. Dümmlings-) Roman gewesen sein, so erklärt sich ebenfalls warum das *livre* nicht gefunden worden ist: *der Name Perceval stand natürlich nicht in demselben sondern ist durch Kristian von einem schon in Erec genannten Ritter auf den Helden übertragen worden.*'[3]

Into such pitfalls can the obstinate adherence to a preconceived idea lead the most distinguished scholar! What are the facts? In *Erec*, Chrétien mentions Perceval by his full title, Perceval li Galois, as at Arthur's court, but does not include him in the list of knights of the Round

---

[1] P. cxli. *et seq*.

[2] It should be noted that Professor Foerster offers no arguments; he only makes assertions. There may, or there may not, have been a Grail romance which knew nothing of Perceval, certainly we have no traces of such, but how *can* we tell what would be the character of such a story? There are any amount of theories on the subject. Wechssler has his, Hagen his, diametrically opposed to each other. Theories unsupported by proof are useless as argument. Professor Foerster is very fond of telling us this; but the moment we get on to the question of Chrétien de Troyes and his sources, *adieu* proof. We are wrapped in the mists of subjectivity.

[3] The italics are mine.

Table;[1] but in *Cligés*, written some years later than *Erec*, and according to Professor Foerster himself *between twenty and thirty years before the Perceval*, the whole position is changed: Perceval is not merely one of Arthur's knights, but second in rank, inferior only to Gawain, thus displacing *Erec*, whose praises Chrétien had sung at length, and superior to Lancelot, whom the poet also celebrated before he wrote of Perceval.

This is the position. Cligés has come to a tournament at Ossenefort, and has on the first two days overthrown successively Segramore and Lancelot; on the third day:

> '*Del ranc devers Ossenefort*
> *Part uns vassaus de grant renon,*
> *Percevaus li Galois ot non.*
> *Lués que Cligés le vit movoir*
> *Et de son non oï le voir,*
> *Que Perceval l'oï nomer,*
> *Mout desirre a lui asanbler.*'—*Cligés*, 4826-32.

This is the Perceval who was only a name to Chrétien! But Chrétien's hero knows him! Can we avoid the conclusion that, at the time *Cligés* was written, Perceval was already the hero of a well-known and highly popular tale; so popular that the author felt justified in displacing in his favour the hero (Erec) whose deeds he had already sung with such marked success? If the story of Perceval li Galois be due to Chrétien, then we must believe that, having conceived the tale in his mind, and paved the way for its reception by the above reference, he yet abstained from presenting it to the public for nearly thirty years! Or could Perceval have been the hero of some other tale, the popularity of which has waned before

[1] Cf. *Erec*, l. 1526; list of knights, l. 1691 *et seq.*

that of Chrétien's poem? Of any story connected with him save the *Enfances-Grail* adventure there is no trace, and of these we have variants of the former *minus* the Grail tradition (*Peredur* and the English *Sir Percyvelle*); but all the Grail stories know the *Enfances*.

It is also significant that Chrétien in the *Erec* mentions both Gurnemanz (Gornemant) and L'Orguelleus de la Lande, both of them noted characters of the *Perceval* story; in fact, but for that story the former would be nothing more than a name to us.

I have remarked in a note to chap. ii. that Chrétien apparently also knew the enchanter of the *Lanzelet*. I had not noted this till I had completed my study of the poem, and, as a footnote is apt to be overlooked, I draw attention to it here. In the list of the knights of the Round Table given in *Erec*, Chrétien ranks as eighth Mauduiz li Sages; in Hartmann's translation the name is given as Malduiz li Sages; *Diu Krône* has Malduz der Weise; the *Lanzelet* spells the enchanter's name Malduz or Malduc, and qualifies him as der Wîse.[1]

I do not think there can be the least doubt that it is one and the same individual who is referred to in these quotations, and the only adventure known of him, and one which would fully account for his sobriquet *li Sages*, is one which is preserved in a poem bristling with *Perceval* allusions,[2] the *Lanzelet* of Ulrich von Zatzikhoven.

[1] Cf. *Erec*, l. 1699; Hartmann, *Erec*, l. 1635; *Diu Krône*, l. 1379 (Adventure of the Cup); *Lanzelet*, ll. 7353-64.

[2] If Malduz, or Malduc, were a well-known enchanter, and connected with the Arthurian story, as he appears to have been, how did he vanish from it? Was it the greater popularity of *Merlin* which displaced him? What is the origin of his name? It sounds as if it might be Celtic, or can he be in any way connected with Maugis, the resourceful cousin of '*Les quatre fils Aginon*'?

I have said above that a critical edition of the *Lanzelet* is urgently needed, and I should not be surprised if the result of a close examination of that poem were to show good reasons for fixing the date of the *Perceval* story (as a *Perceval* and not a mere *Dümmling* story) at a much earlier period than we have hitherto been inclined to admit.[1]

Is it not the fact that story-tellers in mediæval times depended for their popularity less upon the *manner* in which they told their stories than on the stories themselves? *i.e.*, if they wished to write a really popular poem they took a subject already popular, and which they knew would be secure of a favourable hearing. Are we really so unreasonable when we contend that it was the traditional, folk-lore, popular character of the stories told in *Erec*, *Yvain*, and *Perceval*, which made them so much more popular than *Cligés*? The *Charrette* is so manifestly inferior to Chrétien's other works that we will not call it as evidence; it was, and deserved to be, little known. But *Cligés* stands on a different footing. The story is interesting, it is well written, and the love-tale of Alexander and Soredamors contains some of the poet's most characteristic writing; yet, compared with the other poems, it took little hold on the popular fancy. Was it not because the story was unknown to the general public with whom the tale itself counted for more than the skill with which it was told?

---

[1] So far as the *Perceval* story is concerned, there is certainly evidence of varying forms, *e.g.*, Whence did the continuators of Chrétien, notably Gerbert, draw their versions? And what of the *Perceval* embodied in the Dutch *Lancelot*, which appears to be independent, so far as the working out of the adventures suggested by the Grail messenger are concerned, of any known version?

I cannot but think that to treat such stories as the three named above, solely as *Arthurian* stories, is to base our criticism of them on an entirely false foundation: they are only Arthurian in a secondary sense, and criticism of them, to be accurate and scientific, must be founded as much on folk-lore as on literary data. Nor, I submit, are arguments, which may be sound enough as applied to the rise of the Arthurian romantic legend, of necessity equally sound when applied to stories of independent origin incorporated in that legend. I do not say for a moment that Arthur as a *romantic* hero is a continental creation, personally I very much doubt it; but of this I am quite certain, were that continental origin proved up to the hilt, it would still leave unsolved the problem of the origin of these stories.

Before closing this chapter I would touch for a moment on the geographical questions involved; for it seems to me that not sufficient account has been taken of the marked difference between the geography of these three and that of Chrétien's remaining two poems. The first three have a common character. Yvain's adventures pass in and on the borders of Wales. He starts from Carduel en Galles (Kardyf in the English version), and after one night's rest reaches the fountain. It is at Chester, not otherwise an Arthurian town, but one well within the bounds of the story, that his wife's messenger finds him. Erec is '*d'Estregalles*'; the towns are Caradigan, Carduel, Cærnant, Nantes. So with Perceval, who is *li Galois*, we have Carduel, Dinasdron, the Forest of Broceliande— exactly the geography we might expect in stories of Welsh origin redacted on Armorican ground. Many of the names here, as in certain of the *lais*, may be either insular or continental, inasmuch as they are common to the Celtic race on both sides of the Channel.

But in *Cligés*, and in a minor degree in the *Charrette*, we are on different ground: the geography is that neither of Wales nor of Brittany. Here we have Dover, Wallingford, Winchester, Windsor, Southampton, Oxford, Shoreham, Bath, London; while we note a marked omission of the distinctively *Arthurian* localities. The *Charrette* opens at *Carlion*, which it, however, apparently confuses with *Camelot*.

Now this is surely significant. If Chrétien had a free hand in the arrangement of his stories, if they were really compounded of elements drawn from all sources and thus combined for the first time, why did he shift his *mise-en-scène* backwards and forwards in this curious manner? Why turn from the geography of *Erec* to that of *Cligés* and the *Charrette*, only to revert to his first love in *Yvain* and *Perceval*? Is it not most probable that in those three stories, at least, he was dealing with traditional matter, the localising of which had already been effected?

In the case of *Cligés* and the *Charrette* it seems not improbable that closer investigation may find grounds to support the theory of a possible Anglo-Norman transmission, which would account for the southern England geography.[1]

A point on which we may well lay stress is, that the

---

[1] Professor Foerster's attempt to base an argument on the source of *Cligés* cannot for a moment be accepted, cf. Introduction, *Charrette*, cxxxviii. We only know that the source was a book; but what that book contained, no one can say. We can never argue from the *un*known to the known. We do not know much of Chrétien's sources for the other poems, but the grounds for an investigation *do* exist in the above instances, they do *not* in *Cligés*. We must find out how Chrétien dealt with *Erec*, *Yvain*, and *Perceval* before we are in a

independence of Chrétien as a story-teller does not stand or fall with the existence or non-existence of Anglo-Norman Arthurian poems. Their importance, in relation to Chrétien, may easily be exaggerated by those unfamiliar with the character of oral tales. If we once accept as a principle the well-ascertained fact that such stories have a tendency to fall into a set form, a fixed sequence of incident and detail, would always be related in practically the same words, and, moreover, could well contain more than one *sagen motif*, we shall realise that the necessity of postulating a written source as explanation for the agreement in sequence, incident, and phrase, becomes infinitely less pressing.[1]

To my mind, the correspondences between the Welsh Arthurian tales and Chrétien's three poems in question offer no proof that the former repose directly on these poems as basis; but I consider it extremely probable that many of the perplexing features of the question—*e.g.* the occurrence in the Welsh stories, and in translations of Chrétien's poems, of details not to be found in the best MSS. of those

position to offer the slightest hypothesis as to his treatment of *Cligés*. The fact that Mark of Rome gives a short summary of the story is interesting, but so brief a *résumé* is of little critical value. It is certainly not a *book*, therefore cannot possibly be identical with Chrétien's source.

[1] On this subject, cf. any scientific collection of folk-tales, *e.g.*, *The Science of Fairy Tales*, by Mr. E. S. Hartland, or in the same author's *Legend of Perseus*, the tabulated variants of the Dragon story in vol. iii. These would help the reader to realise the number of *motifs* often combined in a single story. The *lais* of *Lanval*, *Graalent*, and *Guingamor*, comparatively short though they be, yet combine at least three distinct story-*motifs*, *i.e.* what we may call the Joseph and Potiphar's wife, Tannhäuser, and Lohengrin themes. Any one of these *lais* would be capable of considerable expansion.

CHRÉTIEN AND THE ARTHURIAN CYCLE

poems—may be accounted for by copyists and translators familiar with an oral version of the tale, filling in details which Chrétien had either never heard, or had purposely omitted. If we postulate, as from the character of the stories we are justified in doing, a very widespread knowledge of those tales, apart from any written source, we shall not be surprised at the existence of a large number of minor variants; the impossibility of explaining which on purely literary grounds drives Professor Foerster and those who share his views to the unsatisfactory expedient of multiplying MS. 'families.'[1]

To sum up the considerations advanced in the preceding pages, I think we are justified in saying that the real *crux* of Arthurian romance is the period *before* and not *after*

---

[1] I have studied the *Yvain* versions carefully, and have read those of *Erec*, but not compared them critically; but I should not be surprised if it were ultimately found that in *The Lady of the Fountain* we have the story at a stage anterior to Chrétien, and probably that at which it came into his hands, *redacted by the Welsh scribe under the influence of Chrétien's poem*; while in *Geraint* we have the process reversed, *i.e.* a rendering of *Chrétien's poem modified by the earlier version.* In the statement, '*Gwiffert Petit he is called by the Franks, but the Cymry call him the Little King*,' we have, I think, a hint of this. The writer must have been too good a French scholar to think the one term a translation of the other; it rather implies that the Welsh knew the character only by a sobriquet borrowed from his diminutive size, which is exactly what we should expect, the earlier stages of story-telling being anonymous. So far as the correspondence in word and dialogue is concerned, the conclusion to be drawn depends entirely on the nature of the parallel passages; if they be merely such ordinary dialogue (question and response) as would naturally spring from the incidents of the story, both may well be reminiscences of the oral version. Analytic, self-communing passages would, of course, point to a later stage in evolution; but the Welsh version dialogue is of the simplest description.

Chrétien de Troyes. Not that the latter period does not offer us puzzles: it does, many and great, but when we arrive at some definite and *proven* conclusion as to the materials with which the earliest compilers of metrical romance were dealing, we shall have made a great step towards unravelling the problem of their successors. So far, I do not think we have arrived at such a conclusion; many theories are in the field, but none seem entirely to meet the conditions of the question. My own conviction is that, whether oral or written, Arthurian romantic tradition is of much older date than we have hitherto been inclined to believe.

To arrive at any solid result in our investigations there are certain principles which we must always keep in view, *e.g.*, if the Arthurian tradition consists (as it admittedly does) largely of folk-lore and mythic elements, it must, so far as these elements are concerned, be examined and criticised on methods recognised and adopted by experts in those branches of knowledge—and not treated on literary lines and literary evidence alone. Thus it is essential to determine the original *character* of a story before proceeding to criticise its literary *form*. To treat stories of folk-lore origin from an exclusively literary point of view is to render a false conclusion not merely probable but *certain*.

In every case where an oral source appears probable, or even possible, we must ascertain, from the evidence of experts in story-transmission, what are the characteristics of tales so told, and what is the nature of the correspondence existing between tales of common origin but of independent development.

The evidence of proper names is valuable only in a secondary degree, as testifying to the place or places of redaction. But the older the story the less valuable they are as indications of original *source*, the oldest tales having a strong tendency to anonymity. So we find that in the *lais* the older versions only speak of 'a king,' the later identify that king with Arthur.[1]

If we take these elementary tests, and apply them to those of the poems of Chrétien de Troyes for which a traditional origin may safely be postulated, we shall I think arrive at the conclusion that there is little ground for ascribing *inventive* genius to the poet, whose superiority over his contemporaries was *quantitative* rather than *qualitative*. He differed from them in degree, not in kind; he had a keener sense of artistic composition, a more excellent literary style. Given the same material as his contemporaries he produced a superior result; when the material was deficient, as in the *Charrette*, the result was proportionately inferior.

There is no necessity to belittle him as '*ein sklavischer Übersetzer*'; there is no ground that I can see for crediting him with an inventive genius foreign to his age. The truth lies, as it so often does, midway between the two extremes.

In this connection I may well quote Dr. Schofield's sober and carefully reasoned conclusion to his *Study of the Lays of Graalent and Lanval*: 'The process of combining separate episodes to make an extended poem, we may well believe, had begun before the time of Marie's contemporary, Chrétien de Troyes. He simply carried it one step farther, and devoted his great literary talent to presenting in more attractive form, with more modern courtly flourishes, the stories already existing. Doubtless

[1] Professor Foerster recognises this argument in a measure, but does not appear to realise its full bearing.

he himself made new combinations, and in so doing was guided by a poet's sense of appropriateness, choosing such general and subordinate episodes as would contribute best to the development of his hero's character.[1] To him we must certainly ascribe the interesting psychological discussions so numerous in his works. But still his power of invention is not great. His art is shown above all in the way in which he combines and arranges separate stories, or embellishes those already told at considerable length.'[2]

These words, I believe, state in generous terms the position which scientific criticism will ultimately assign to Chrétien de Troyes: they represent the very utmost that can reasonably be claimed for him.

[1] I should myself be inclined to limit Chrétien's share in the work to the re-arrangement of existing combinations. I do not think he ever made any new combination, unless it were in the case of *Cligés*, and that is only a 'perhaps.'

[2] Cf. *Lays of Graalent and Lanval*, p. 175.

Herr Brugger's article, referred to on p. 66, did not come into my hands until these studies were in proof. Inasmuch as the theory regarding the Arthurisation of the *lais* stated in this chapter and in chapter ii. might lead some readers to the conclusion that my views are identical with those set forth in the article in question, I think it well to state (*a*) that I only postulate of certain early metrical romances an origin which Herr Brugger apparently attributes to *all* Arthurian romances, prose or verse; (*b*) that when Herr Brugger speaks of *origin* he uses the word loosely, and in a *secondary* sense, whereas I use it in a *primary*; *e.g.* to say that a story which reached French writers through a Breton source may therefore be accurately described as of Breton origin is, in my opinion, both inaccurate and misleading, especially in the face of Professor Foerster's strongly reiterated denials of an insular Arthurian *romantic* tradition. The immediate source of the French writers does not solve for us the problem of the origins of Arthurian tradition; it is a mistake to employ an argument, or use terminology, confounding two distinct questions.

CHAPTER VI

THE PROSE LANCELOT—THE 'ENFANCES' OF THE HERO

In the preceding chapters we have examined certain romances of the *Lancelot* cycle lying outside the great prose compilation which represents its final form. The *popular* 'Lancelot' legend was the legend as told in the prose *Lancelot*, and the *Grail* romances therewith incorporated. It is with these romances we must now deal.

The elements composing this vast compilation (which in its completed form appears to have aimed at embracing the entire Arthurian cycle in all its ramifications) are so diverse that it would, under any circumstances, be a matter of great difficulty to decide how best to analyse and examine the composite structure; and this initial difficulty is much increased by the fact that so far the material at our disposal, abundant though it be, is in an inchoate and unorganised condition. There is no critical edition of the prose *Lancelot*; and as we shall see in the following studies, not merely the MSS., but the numerous printed editions derived from the MSS., differ so widely from each other that until a critical text based on a comparison of *all* the available versions is in our hands, it will be quite impossible to do more than form a tentative hypothesis, or advance a guarded suggestion as to the gradual growth and formation of the completed legend.

I would therefore entreat any readers of this and the subsequent chapters to bear in mind that I am not attempting any critical study of the prose *Lancelot*, as a whole—the time for such a study has not yet come—but rather I am examining (*a*) certain points of the prose legend which are of capital importance in themselves, or must have existed in some form even in a shorter version of the story, *e.g.*, such as Lancelot's youth, and first appearance at court, his relations with Guinevere, and connection with the Grail story; (*b*) certain interesting variants in the texts we possess, variants which are of the greatest importance to English scholars as clearing up many of the difficulties connected with the character of the source used by Malory in his compilation.[1] My aim is to prepare the way for a critical examination of the prose *Lancelot* rather than to myself offer such a critical examination.

In a previous chapter I hazarded the suggestion that the original germ of the whole story might prove to be a *lai* recounting the theft of a child by a water-fairy, and in spite of the unwieldy dimensions to which the tale has grown, I think this suggestion will be found to hold good.

As I hinted above, the *Lancelot* legend is not confined to the prose *Lancelot*, but it has affected romances originally

---

[1] The printed editions of the prose *Lancelot* chronicled by Dr. Sommer, *Sources of Malory*, p. 8, note, are 1494, Ant. Verard; 1513, Philippe Lenoire; 1533, Jehan Petit. There was also an edition 1533, *Philippe Lenoire*, which represents a very important text, and one which Dr. Sommer does not appear to know. A copy is in the Bodleian (Douce collection).

entirely unconnected with our hero, such as the *Merlin* and the *Tristan*. In the earliest forms of the story neither of these tales have anything whatever to do with Lancelot; in the latest versions *Tristan* has been practically incorporated into the *Lancelot*, while *Merlin* forms an elaborate introduction to it.

Though it has undergone a certain amount of modification, the tradition at the base of the *Merlin* and prose *Lancelot* appears to be identical with that related by the *Lanzelet*. The names Ban of Benoic and Pant of Genewîs are quite near enough to represent the same original, probably modified in the *Lanzelet* by translation into another tongue. The story of the king driven from his kingdom and dying of a broken heart is the same, *au fond*, though the *motif* has been varied, and in the prose *Lancelot* the king's misfortunes are caused by treachery, and not by his own misgovernment. This is a very natural modification, and one likely to be caused by the growing popularity of the son, which would have a tendency to react favourably on the character of the father.[1]

It is clear that both versions of the *Merlin* story know the *Lancelot* legend in its completed form. Thus the

[1] It is difficult to know exactly what value to place on the traditional relationship of uncle and nephew as postulated of Arthur and Lancelot in the poem of Ulrich von Zatzikhoven. This is so completely a *lieu commun* of heroic romance. Except in the case of a hero of distinctly mythical origin such as Gawain, I am inclined to consider it as marking a secondary stage in the evolution of a hero, he would have attained to a certain degree of popularity before it was postulated of him—thus Perceval and Caradoc are each, in turn, Arthur's nephews. In the case of Lancelot it probably represented an intermediate stage between entire independence of Arthur (the original) and son of a faithful ally (the final) form.

Vulgate *Merlin* knows of his two cousins, Lionel and Bohort, whose introduction into the legend marks that secondary stage, when not merely the hero, but the hero's race in its entirety, is selected for special honour.[1]

In the Ordinary, or Vulgate, *Merlin*, the enchanter is never brought into direct contact with Lancelot, but is betrayed to his doom before the birth of that hero takes place. In the *Suite de Merlin*, however, he and his treacherous love visit the castle of King Ban, and see the child, whose future fame Merlin prophesies; while the lady is identified with the fairy who brings up Lancelot.[2]

The *Suite* also refers in a prophetic manner to certain subsequent feats of Lancelot, and introduces the personages of the *Tristan* story, such as Morholt (Le Morhout),[3] a clear proof that it is posterior to the incorporation of this legend with the Arthurian cycle.

Of the two *Merlin* versions, the *Suite* therefore appears to be the later, but the Vulgate *Merlin* also refers to the

---

[1] *Merlin*, Sommer's ed., chap. xxxiii. The *Lancelot* legend appears to me to offer a very interesting parallel to the methods employed by the compilers of the *Chansons de Geste*, which are so ably pointed out by M. Leon Gautier in his *Epopées Françaises*. The original story of the hero forms a nucleus from which other romances depart in a downward direction—dealing with sons and, perhaps, grandsons;—in an upward, dealing with father and grandfather—till a complete cycle is thus formed. We have exactly this process in *Lancelot*—the *Queste* extols the deeds of his son, the *Merlin* those of his father; and we have indications that the story was well on the way to the evolution of a secondary branch, that of Bohort and his son. None of the other Arthurian heroes has undergone a parallel development.

[2] Cf. *Merlin*, ed. Paris and Ulrich, vol. ii. pp. 137, 143.

[3] *Ibid.* pp. 231 *et seq.*

THE PROSE LANCELOT

Grail romances,[1] so that it seems clear that both have been redacted subsequent to the completion of the *Lancelot* story.

To return to the prose *Lancelot*. The story of the hero's youth, while agreeing in the main with that told by Ulrich von Zatzikhoven, is yet marked by important modifications and additions. The brothers Lionel and Bohort appear on the scene, and become Lancelot's companions, while the whole conception of the kingdom of

---

[1] Cf. *Merlin*, ed. Sommer, chap. xxvii. It may be as well here to remark that Professor Foerster apparently attributes considerable importance to the pseudo-historical account of Arthur's wars with the Saxons contained in the prose romances, notably the Vulgate *Merlin* (cf. *Charrette*, p. xcvi., and review of *Legend of Sir Gawain*, Zeitschrift für Franz. Sp., Band 20, p. 102), asserting that the prose romances contain, side by side with the later, the remains of the oldest stages of Arthurian tradition. To me it seems patent that these romances have simply borrowed from the *Chronicles*. There is nothing in them which cannot be found in Geoffrey or his translators, and the fact that they represent the *romantic* legend in a demonstrably late form, and not in one consonant with the pseudo-historic indications, while there is no trace of any fundamental revision of the story, such as might be expected, seems to make it quite clear that they are of comparatively late invention. They by no means stand on the same footing as do Wace and Layamon, which are of distinct value in determining earlier forms of the legend. To take one instance alone, the *Merlin* gives a long account of the sons of King Lot, who play a most important part in the action of the story, but the genuine early tradition gives Gawain no brother save Mordred, and Layamon distinctly says, 'he wes Walwainnes broðer, næs þer nan oðer' (ll. 25467-8). The existence of these sons marks a secondary stage in the story; but they are in all the *prose* romances. An exception should perhaps be made in favour of the Didot *Perceval*, which gives the *Mort Artur* section in a form differing from the other prose romances and much more closely in accord with the *Chronicles*. I shall return to this point later on.

the Lady of the Lake is radically modified. It is no longer a *Meide-lant*; Lancelot has knight-attendants as well as cousin-playfellows, indeed, save for the *Mirage*, which counterfeits a lake and thus keeps off unwelcome intruders, the country is to all intents and purposes an ordinary earthly kingdom.[1]

When the lad (who is always called by his protectress *Fils du roi*, and has a more than adequate idea of his own importance) leaves the kingdom, which he does in order to seek knighthood at Arthur's hands, he goes gorgeously equipped, with armour, steed, and retinue of servants.

But his arrival at Arthur's court is most interesting and suggestive. Arthur meets him without the town, and consigns him to the care of *Ywain*, who, the next day, leads him to the palace through a crowd of spectators eager to look upon his beauty.

In a previous chapter I have commented upon the strong resemblance between the account of Lanzelet's entry into the world, as described by Ulrich von Zatzikhoven, and that of Parzival, as related by Wolfram von Eschenbach. Both alike are ignorant of knightly skill and customs; both are unable to control their steeds, they cannot even hold the bridle; both are alike fair to look upon, but apparently foolish (*tumbe*); both are ignorant of their name and parentage. Different as the account of the prose *Lancelot* is from this, and no difference could well be wider, yet here again the *Lancelot* falls into line with the *Perceval* story, and again in the form peculiar to Wolfram von Eschenbach; for there, too, Parzival makes

---

[1] The two accounts should be carefully compared.

THE PROSE LANCELOT

his entry on foot, through a crowd eager to behold his beauty, and his guide is the squire *Iwanet*.[1]

It will be remembered that in Chrétien's version of the story Perceval's entry is made under quite different circumstances. He rides into the hall, and advances so close to the king that his horse's head touches him, and subsequently he refuses to dismount.

The correspondence of the name Ywain=Iwanet is also significant. In the case of Wolfram's poem it has been generally concluded that the name was a diminutive of *Iwein* or *Iwan*, and therefore distinct from the name Chrétien gives to Gawain's squire who aids Perceval to disarm his fallen foe— *Yonet*. Hertz, in his recent translation of the *Parzival*,[2] takes this view, though he would differentiate the Ywain referred to from King Urien's famous son, and in my translation of the poem I adopted the same view. But further study has led me to doubt this solution. I now think it more probable that the name is in both cases the same, *i.e.* a form of the Breton *Yonec*, which we find with the varying spelling, *Iwenec* and *Yonet*.[3] Thus both Chrétien and Wolfram refer to the same character; and the compiler of the prose *Lancelot* probably knew the *Perceval* story under a form analogous rather to Wolfram than to Chrétien. Whether the form *Ywain* was adopted through a mistake, or from a desire to substitute a well-known hero for an obscure squire, it is impossible to say, in any case the correspondence, though less striking

---

[1] Cf. *Parzival*, Book III. l. 937 *et seq.* I unfortunately omitted to note the reference in the prose *Lancelot*. The passage is on p. 127, vol. iii. of M. Paulin Paris's abridged edition.

[2] Cf. *Parzival*, Hertz, n. 66, p. 495.

[3] Cf. *Lais inédits*, M. Gaston Paris, *Romania*, vol. viii.

than the similar passages of the *Lanzelet*, is worth noting.[1]

Again we find that Guinevere, failing to obtain an answer from the youth, who is struck dumb by her beauty, makes some contemptuous remarks as to his lack of sense, and leaves the hall. This may be compared with *Parzival*, Book III. ll. 988-9.[2]

A further indication of contact with the *Perceval* romances is afforded by the love-trances which overtake the hero at the most inconvenient moment, and are repeated *ad nauseam* in the most clumsy and inartistic manner. It is noticeable that on the occasion of the first attack (in the case of Lancelot one can only regard these trances as an intermittent malady) the knight is clad in red armour and leans on his spear—as does Perceval when he sees the blood-drops on the snow. In the prose *Lancelot* it is invariably the sight, and not the memory, of Guinevere which causes the trance, a far less poetical conception than that of the *Perceval*.

But in face of the passage quoted by M. Paulin Paris, in his translation of the prose *Lancelot*, probably few will

[1] Lancelot's eagerness to receive knighthood should be compared with that of Parzival. Thus Lancelot says to Yvain, 'Dictes a monseigneur le roy qu'il me face chevalier comme il a promis—car ie le veuil estres sans attendre plus,'—and again, 'ie ne seray plus escuyer.' prose *Lancelot*, ed. 1533, vol. i. Cf. this with *Parzival*, Book III. ll. 1001-2, 'nune sûmet mich nicht mêre phleg mîn nâch riters êre,' and 1158-9, 'i'ne wil niht langer sîn ein kneht, ich sol schildes ambet hân.' The correspondence is striking.

[2] 'En verité ce varlet n'est mye bien sage, ou il a este mal enseigné.' Yvain suggests that a woman has forbidden him to tell his name (which might be compared with *Parzival*, Book III. l. 1464). By his speech he must be *de Gaulle*. Ed. 1533, vol. i. (The 1533 edition has in each volume a summary of chapter contents, thus reference is easy.)

contend that the story of *Perceval* was not anterior to, and well-known by the compiler of, the first mentioned romance. *Et le grant conte de Lancelot convient repairier en la fin à Perceval qui est chiés et la fin de tos les contes ès autres chevaliers. Et tout sont branches de lui, qu'il acheva la grant queste. Et li contes Perceval meismes est une branche del haut conte del Graal qui est chiés de tos les contes.*[1]

We should note here that when this particular passage was written the writer evidently knew nothing of Galahad as the Grail Winner, though he knew the *Lancelot* story in an advanced stage. We shall have occasion to refer to this later on.

In the account of Lancelot's first appearance at court we find an incident which appears to connect the story with a cycle of poems bearing a curious resemblance to the *Perceval* cycle—the *Bel Inconnu* poems. Immediately after the hero has received knighthood, as they sit at meat in the hall, a messenger arrives, sent by the 'Dame de Nohan,'[2] asking for a champion to aid her against the King of Northumberland. Lancelot (whose name we must remember is not yet revealed, and who is referred to by the compiler as *Le Beau Varlet*) at once requests that the adventure be given to him, and, though Arthur demurs on account of his youth and inexperience, insists that he has a right to it, as the first boon he has claimed since he was knighted.

It is under precisely similar circumstances that the hero of the *Bel Inconnu* stories undertakes his first adventure.

Others have been struck by this resemblance, and M.

---

[1] MS. 751, fol. 144 vo., quoted by M. Paulin Paris in vol. iv. of *Romans de la Table Ronde*, p. 87.

[2] This *Dame de Nohan* is probably the same as the *Dame de Noauz* mentioned in the *Charrette*, i. 5389.

Philipot, in his review of Dr. Schofield's *Studies on the Libeaus Desconus*,[1] maintains that the *Lancelot* story (more particularly in the version known to Ulrich von Zatzikhoven) is the elder of the two, and the source of the parallel adventure of the *Bel Inconnu* group.

With this view I cannot agree. I have elsewhere[2] given reasons for holding the true order of the *Enfances* to be as follows, *Perceval, Le Bel Inconnu, Lancelot*, and to this view I adhere. We must remember that the French original of the *Lanzelet* must in any case be prior to 1194; how much earlier we have no means of deciding, but the *Lanzelet* has points of contact with both the *Perceval* (Enfances) and the *Bel Inconnu* (Fier Baiser) story. Further, the prose *Lancelot*, though differing very widely from Ulrich von Zatzikhoven's poem, yet, as we see, also offers parallels both to *Perceval* and *Le Bel Inconnu*; such parallels being entirely different from those of the *Lanzelet*. To assert that these stories borrowed from the *Lancelot* would involve the existence, at an early date, of a fully developed and widely diffused *Lancelot* legend, a conclusion which the absence of all reference to the hero in the earlier Arthurian romances forbids.

To my mind, when we have three separate cycles of romance closely connected with each other, if we desire to discover which is the oldest of the stories we should ask in the first instance, in which of the stories are the incidents common to all the essence, in which are they the accidents, of the tale. It is quite clear that they are not essential to the *Lancelot* story. The characteristics of ignorance, simplicity, and headlong impulsiveness attributed to him by Ulrich von Zatzikhoven, are entirely foreign to his character as elsewhere represented; even in the *Lanzelet* they are

[1] Cf. *Romania*, vol. xxvi. p. 290.   [2] *Legend of Sir Gawain*, p. 65.

promptly discarded: but they *are* the very essence of Perceval's character, he, and no other, is the *schöne tumbe* of romance. Again, the adventure of the *Fier Baiser* has absolutely nothing to do with Lancelot; it is manifestly dragged into the *Lanzelet* version 'by the head and shoulders,' and has no connection with the context, but it is the crown and completion of the adventures of Gawain's nameless son.[1]

Whatever be the connection between the *Perceval* and *Bel Inconnu* stories, I think it is clear that both were well known before the development of the *Lancelot* legend took place, and that in the process of development this latter borrowed from both. A close examination of the variants of the *Lancelot* 'Enfances' will, I think, strengthen the hypothesis advanced in a previous chapter, *i.e.* that the connection of the hero with a water-fairy *alone* is of the essence of the tale, all the rest is comparatively late in development, and markedly *non*-original and secondary in character.[2]

[1] M. Marillier in a review of the *Voyage of Bran* and *Legend of Sir Gawain*, contained in *Revue des Religions* (July-August 1899), is inclined to connect the adventure of the *Fier Baiser* ascribed to the son with the adventure of the *Marriage of Sir Gawain* ascribed to the father. Both are disenchantment stories, and both appear to belong to the class of disenchantment by personal contact. The point is an interesting and a suggestive one.

[2] The character of the fairy and the nature of Lancelot's upbringing demand a special study, for which, so far, the materials are not available. The Lady of the Lake touches on the one hand the Queen of the Other-World, on the other, Morgain la Fee. I understand that a study on the characters of Lady of the Lake, Vivienne, and Morgain, is being prepared under the direction of Dr. Schofield. For the details of Lancelot's childhood, we must wait till a critical edition of the prose *Lancelot* shows us whether we have any variants or traces of early redactions, to bridge the gulf between the poem of Ulrich van Zatzikhoven and the final prose romance.

CHAPTER VII

THE PROSE LANCELOT—THE LOVES OF
LANCELOT AND GUINEVERE

IN the previous chapter I remarked that the time, and the material, for a really critical study of the prose *Lancelot* were not yet ripe, and that I should, therefore, confine myself to the discussion of the more striking features of the story, *i.e.* the *Enfances*, the *liaison* with Guinevere, and the connection with the Grail Quest. These form what we may call the persistent element in the completed *Lancelot* legend; the great mass of adventures filling in the framework, varying (as we shall presently see) so considerably, that till we have some idea of the growth and various redactions of the story it is hopeless to attempt to criticise them.

Certain remarks, however, we can safely make. The story as we have it at present is marked by a constant repetition of similar incidents. I have already alluded to one, the love-trance. What we may perhaps consider an exaggeration of this *motif*, the love-madness, also occurs more than once and has affected the *Tristan* story. This is certainly not an original feature, but I think it is a question whether the source be the *Chevalier au Lion* or the *Prophecies of Merlin*; personally I incline to the latter solution, and think the name of Merlin's wife, Guendolen,

THE PROSE LANCELOT

may have suggested its introduction into the *Lancelot* story.[1]

Another incident of frequent repetition is the release of the hero from prison in order that he may attend a tournament. Of this we have at least three instances: the version of the *Charrette*, where it is the wife of the seneschal, his jailor, who assists him; and two belonging specially to the prose *Lancelot*. In one instance it is from the prison of the Dame de Malehault that he attends the tournament and returns, as in the *Charrette*; in the other he is freed from the prison of the three queens by the daughter of the Duc de Rochedon, and does not return. This latter also corresponds with his being freed from the prison of Meleagant by the daughter of King Baudemagus, whom Malory, doubtless under the influence of the *Charrette* story, substitutes in his translation for the heiress of Rochedon.

Again we find that certain adventures, some of considerable importance, are related in some versions of the story while they are omitted in others, but in the absence of a critical and comparative edition it is impossible to say which of the great mass of adventures now composing the prose *Lancelot* belonged to the original redaction. Nor can this again be satisfactorily settled till we have determined the mutual relation between the *Grand S. Graal*, the *Queste*, and the *Lancelot*. In short, the *Lancelot* problem involves a number of minor problems of extreme intricacy, and till these be solved we only stand on the threshold of Arthurian criticism.[2]

[1] Cf. Introduction to M. Paulin Paris's *Romans de la Table Ronde*, p. 81 *et seq.*, also M. de Villemarqué's *Merlin*, p. 121.

[2] Dr. Wechssler's interesting study on '*die verschiedenen Redak-*

A point in which it appears to me that we have a suggestion of the original tale, expanded from a source foreign to that tale, is in the account of the expedition undertaken to recover Lancelot's ancestral kingdom from the hands of King Claudas. There is no doubt that the hero should, as a matter of poetical justice, regain his inheritance, and in the *Lanzelet* we find it summarily recorded that he does so,[1] but under entirely different circumstances from those recorded in the prose *Lancelot*. The latter account is of extreme length, and apparently a free imitation of the Arthurian expeditions of the *Chronicles*; the incident of Frollo's defeat before Paris is certainly borrowed from Geoffrey or his translators. As it now stands the incident is lacking in point and practically unnecessary to the story, since Lancelot prefers to continue Arthur's knight rather than become a sovereign in his own right, and therefore bestows the lands on his cousins and bastard half-brother. The retention of a feature which evolution has thus robbed of its significance appears to afford evidence both of the original independence of the tale and also of the priority of Ulrich von Zatzikhoven's version.

Leaving on one side then the minor adventures into which the successive redactions have introduced considerable variation, we will turn to that feature of the story which, practically unvarying in form, appears to offer us a fairer prospect of arriving at some real and definite

tionen des Graal-Lancelot Cyklus' will be referred to later on. It is an excellent statement of certain aspects of the problem, but further research shows some of his conclusions to be very doubtful. His judgment with regard to the *Queste* variants is certainly at fault.

[1] l. 8050 *et seq.*

conclusion—the love of Lancelot for the wife of his liege lord. Setting aside the many minor questions to which the subject gives rise, it seems to me that the main problem of the amours of Lancelot and Guinevere is, Do they represent the latest form of an original feature of the story, or are we to consider them as an addition to the tale, an element imported into it under the influence of the popular *Tristan* legend?

This much is certain, there is no literary evidence of growth in the story; either it is non-existent, as in the *Lanzelet*, or complete, fully developed, and decked out in all the artificialities and refinements of *Minne-dienst*, as in the *Charrette*. As we noted in our discussion of the latter poem, Chrétien evidently credits his audience with a previous knowledge of the relations between the queen and his hero; he nowhere hints that he is about to tell them something new, nor does he offer any explanation why Lancelot rather than Gawain, who, as the *Merlin* informs us, was 'the queen's knight,' should achieve the rescue of his liege lady. There can be no doubt that he was dealing with a situation thoroughly familiar to, and understood by, his hearers.

A point which we are much tempted to overlook in the criticism of Arthurian romance is the length of time intervening between the period at which the events recorded are supposed to have happened, and the earliest known literary record of those events. If we estimate this intervening period as five centuries, we are speaking well within the mark. It is obvious that we have here ample time for forgetfulness, dislocation, or rearrangement of the original legend. Yet that that legend survived I hold for certain. Had Arthur been completely forgotten, the immense popularity achieved by the romances of his cycle would constitute a literary phenomenon practically unique; the seed that in the twelfth century burst into such glorious flower had been germinating for ages. The question is, what was the nature of that seed—what the relation of the original Arthurian legend to the completed Arthurian romance?

On this point it behoves us to tread warily, and to avoid dogmatising. I have suggested elsewhere that probably the historic germ of the Arthurian legend is to be found in his fights with the Saxons, his betrayal by his wife and nephew, and his death in battle with the latter. Certainly there is a genuine historic element in the account of his wars; and it is significant that the older Arthurian chroniclers—Geoffrey of Monmouth and his translators—all agree in relating at considerable length the story of Guinevere's betrayal of her husband; while the Welsh tradition, which does not know Lancelot, is even more emphatic on the subject of her infidelity.[1]

We must remember that, alike in Geoffrey, Wace, and Layamon, the account of Guinevere's relations with Mordred is totally different to that familiar to us through Malory, and borrowed by him from the *Mort Artur*. In the latter, the queen is no accomplice in Mordred's treason, but resists his advances *vi et armis*, barricading herself in the Tower of London, where the traitor vainly besieges her.

In the chronicles the whole position is different: they shall speak for themselves. This is Wace's account:

[1] Cf. Rhys, *Studies in the Arthurian Legend*, chap. iii. The author remarks that to this day in some parts of Wales it is held an insult, as implying a reflection on her moral character, to call a girl Guinevere.

THE PROSE LANCELOT

> '*Que Mordret fist en Engleterre*
> *La roine sot et oï,*
>
> . . . .
>
> *A Evroïc ert à sejor,*
> *En pensé fu et en tristor.*
> *Membra lui de la vilenie*
> *Que por Mordret se fu honie;*
> *Le roi avoit deshonoré*
> *Et son neveu Mordret amé,*
> *Contre loi l'avoit esposée,*
> *S'in estoit honie et dampnée;*
> *Mius vausist morte estre que vive,*
> *Mult en estoit morne et pensive.*
> *A Karlion s'en est fuie,*
> *S'in entra en une abaïe,*
> *Iloc devint none velée;*
> *Tote sa vie i fu celée.*
> *Ne fu oïe, ne véue,*
> *Ne fu trovée, ne séue.*
> *Por la vergogne del mesfait*
> *Et del pécié qu'ele avoit fait.*'—*Brut*, ii. ll. 13607-30.

In the corresponding passage, Geoffrey of Monmouth gives as his authorities 'Breton' tradition and the clerk Walter of Oxford (cf. note to above passage). Layamon in his account is even more severe towards the guilty pair:

> '*Arður bi-tahte*
> *al þat he ahte.*
> *Moddrade and þere quene*
> *þat heom was iquene.*
> *þat was ufele idon*
> *þat heo iboren weoren.*
> *þis lond heo for-radden*
> *mid ræuðen uniuoȝen.*
> *and a þan ænden heom seolven*
> *þe wurse gon iscenden.*

> *þat heo þer for-leoseden*
> *lif and heore saulen.*
> *and œdder seoðða laðen*
> *nauer œlche londe.*
> *þat nauer na mā nalde.*
> *sel bede beoden for heore saule.*'
>
> *Brut*, Layamon, Madden's ed., ll. 25500-14.[1]

In the passage corresponding to that quoted above from Wace, Layamon adds the detail, that none knew the manner of the queen's death, *whether she had drowned herself*:

> '*nuste hit mon to soðe.*
> *whaðer heo weore on deðe*
> (*and ou ȝeo hinne ende*)[2]
> *þa heo seolf weore*
> *isunken in þe watere.*'—ll. 28481-85.

From these passages it is abundantly clear that Guinevere was no victim of treachery, but a willing sinner; and that the tradition of her infidelity to her husband existed prior to the formation of the Arthurian romantic cycle.

Granting, then, that the feature formed part of the early Arthurian legend, are we to consider that the version given by the chronicles faithfully represents the original tradition, and that it was Mordred who was Guinevere's original

---

[1] 'Arthur gave in charge all that he had to Mordred and the queen. That was evil done that they were born, for the land they destroyed with sorrows enow. And at the end themselves the Worse (devil) began to destroy that they there forfeited (lost) their lives and their souls, and ever since are loathed in every land, that never a man will offer prayer for their souls.'

[2] This line is lacking in the oldest MS., but can be supplied from the later recension: 'Man knew not, in sooth, whether she were dead (and how she hence departed), whether she herself were sunk in the water.'

lover? I think not. It is an extremely curious feature of the problem, that though in each of the pseudo-historic versions Guinevere, as we have seen, is genuinely in love with Mordred, and is roundly condemned by the chroniclers for her conduct, in no single one of the Arthurian *romances* is there any trace of the slightest affection existing between them. Mordred, save as traitor in the final scenes, plays no rôle in the story; he is never represented as a *persona grata* at court; in one important version, as we shall see, the queen dislikes him because she suspects his true relation to Arthur. Guinevere's moral character is held to be untarnished, even by her *liaison* with Lancelot.

I suspect that we have here to deal with a lapse of tradition. Mordred is not the original lover, but he represents him; and between that original lover and Lancelot there intervenes a period in which Guinevere's lapse from virtue was smoothed over, and partially forgotten. It is certainly remarkable that in each of the three great prose branches, the *Merlin*,[1] the *Tristan*, and the *Lancelot*, Guinevere's moral character is apparently unaffected by her conduct with Lancelot. The compilers all agree in extolling her as the noblest of queens and best of women. Even so aggressively virtuous and clerical a romance as the prose *Perceval li Gallois*, though quite aware of the connection, regards Guinevere in a favourable light—indeed, as morally superior to Arthur! Nor can we quote the *Queste* as representing the opposite view; true, Lancelot is blamed for his relations with the queen, but Guinevere,

[1] The *Merlin* of course deals with a period anterior to this *liaison*, but as we possess it, it has been, as we saw above, redacted under the influence of a tradition of which the amours of Lancelot and Guinevere formed an integral part.

when she appears upon the scene, is treated with marked respect, and the reader has an uncomfortable suspicion that the writer objected to her rather as woman than as wife,—he objects to the sex as a whole, only forgiving Perceval's sister on account of her virginity. It seems clear that if the character of Guinevere has, among the Welsh, been handed down to posterity under the unfavourable light in which Professor Rhys tells us she is popularly regarded, this must be due *either* to a tradition emanating from an earlier and healthier state of society, when conjugal infidelity was not regarded with complacency, *or* to a later and more enlightened verdict on her relations with Lancelot, but in no case can it be due to the influence of those who told the story of these relations.

The second cause will, I think, account for the nineteenth-century presentment of Guinevere's character; we judge her on the grounds of her relations with Lancelot, which we regard as blameworthy, though not undeserving of sympathy—in fact, we do but emphasise Malory's verdict.

But this does not account for the Welsh tradition, which, as I have before pointed out, knows practically nothing of Lancelot; that must rest upon other grounds, and I believe it rests upon the tradition preserved to us in the Mordred story.

What this original tradition was, we can now only surmise; it belonged to a period of which but few and fragmentary traces survive, but I think that most probably the primitive story ascribed the rôle of lover to Gawain. I made this suggestion some four years ago,[1] and subsequent study has shown me nothing to induce me to alter my

[1] Cf. *Legend of Sir Gawain*, p. 76 *et seq.*

THE PROSE LANCELOT

opinion, though it has suggested sundry important modifications.

I think now that Gawain and Mordred really represent the two sides of one original personality; and that a personality very closely connected with early Celtic tradition.

What the exact nature of the relation between Gawain and early Irish mythic tradition may be we cannot yet say.: that such a relation exists is practically beyond doubt.[1]

Among the characteristic features of the early Irish heroes with whom Gawain is connected, we find the following: Adventurous hero and nephew on the female side to royal centre of cycle (Cuchulinn and Diarmid[2]); son to that uncle (Cuchulinn); lover of uncle's wife, eloping with her (Diarmid); deadly combat between father and son (Cuchulinn and Conlaoch). This latter incident I believe to be of greater importance in heroic-mythic tradition than has yet been realised. As I interpret it, the father and son combat in heroic tradition really represents the 'slayer who shall himself be slain,' the prehistoric combat of the '*Golden Bough*' (to which I have referred in chap. v.) influenced by the doctrine of re-birth, as set forth by Mr. Nutt in vol. ii. of the *Voyage of Bran, i.e.* it is a conflict of the god with his re-born and re-juvenated self, and as such has a very real place in Celtic tradition.

As we see above, we do not at present possess a version in which all these characteristics are united in one hero,

---

[1] On this point, cf. my *Legend of Sir Gawain*, Mr. Maynadier's *Wife of Bath's Tale* (both in Grimm Library), and M. Marillier's article in *Revue des religions* (July-August, 1899), already referred to.

[2] I have purposely omitted Tristan, as, though a Celtic hero, he is only indirectly connected with Irish tradition.

but they might very well be so united. I think that the earlier Gawain was at once Arthur's nephew and son by his sister,[1] adventurous hero of the court, lover of the queen, and eventually slayer of his father-uncle.[2]

Very probably in the original story there was some such device as the beauty-spot of Diarmid, which aroused involuntary passion in every woman who beheld him; or the love-potion of the Tristan story; a device whereby the earlier tellers of these tales secured sympathy for the lovers, without lowering the character of the husband, so that Gawain, no less than Diarmid and Tristan, would be regarded as a gallant and sympathetic figure.

But the peculiar line of evolution followed by the Arthurian story, the strongly ethical and Christian character which it early assumed (due probably to the heathen belief of the historic Arthur's genuine antagonists, the Saxons), made a change necessary, if Gawain was to preserve his position as leading hero of the legend, and I now think it most probable that that change was effected by divesting Gawain of the characteristics incompatible with his later position, and bestowing them on another personality, created for the purpose, since they could not altogether be dropped out of the story. It is significant that, as I remarked above, the earliest tradition gives Gawain no

[1] I am glad to find that M. Gaston Paris evidently holds this view, as in a note to his discussion of the tradition that Roland was Charlemagne's son as well as his nephew, in the *Histoire Poétique de Charlemagne*, he refers to Gawain as holding the same position.

[2] The above remarks of course refer to Gawain as connected with Arthur; originally he was probably independent. As our knowledge stands at present, the parallels between Gawain and early Irish tradition appear to belong mainly to the *Ultonian* cycle; while in the case of Arthur the parallels are rather to the *Ossianic*.

brother save Mordred, and Layamon remarks emphatically, '*he never had any other.*'

Further, I suspect, that exactly the same process took place with regard to Guinevere, and that we have a survival of it in the person of that mysterious lady, the false Guinevere.

I would therefore modify my original views on the subject, by saying that I now think that though Gawain was Guinevere's original lover, Lancelot did not succeed him in that rôle, in fact that Lancelot does not represent the original lover at all, that that tradition is now represented by the Mordred story, and that there was a period in the evolution of the legend, preceding the introduction of Lancelot into the cycle, during which the tradition of Guinevere's voluntary betrayal of her husband was dropped, and she was regarded in an altogether favourable light.

The invention of the Lancelot love-story, which I think we must regard as in its origin an invention, was probably brought about by two causes, the growth of *Minne-dienst*, and the popularity of the *Tristan* story.

To be absolutely accurate, I think we ought to consider it as *invented* to satisfy the demands of the first, and *developed* under the influence of the second. That it is, as some writers have held, a mere imitation of the *Tristan* story, I do not think, rather it is marked by certain complex characteristics which cannot be explained on the hypothesis of other than a dual source. Thus it is impossible not to feel that the relations of the lovers are dictated by the rules of a conventional etiquette rather than by the impulse of an overmastering passion. Even in the scene in which Lancelot first reveals his love to the queen, there is no touch of genuine passion or self-abandonment; the confession has been foreseen and expected, and you feel that Guinevere has carefully regulated her conduct in accordance with the etiquette prescribed for such an occasion.

In the *Charrette*, this artificial character is strongly marked; Lancelot's bearing becomes absolutely grovelling in its humility. The fact that he has been guilty of a momentary hesitation before mounting the cart is regarded by his capricious lady as a deadly offence against the rules of love, and resented accordingly, while Lancelot is so overcome by the assumed indifference of the queen that he promptly attempts suicide. Compare this with the story of Gawain and Orgeluse in the *Parzival*. Gawain is heartily in love with the lady, who treats him, not merely with indifference, but with absolute insolence—insolence to which Gawain opposes the most serene and unruffled courtesy, till the lady comes to her senses, when he reads her a well-deserved lecture on the correct behaviour due to a knight from a well-bred lady. Gawain is quite as well aware of the rules of the game as Lancelot, but understands how to play it with becoming dignity, and remain master of the situation.

There are moments in the Lancelot-Guinevere story when one wonders whether the whole business be not as platonic and artificial as the love-rhapsodies of the would-be poets of mediæval Italy, or of certain of the troubadours; but the night interview in the *Charrette*, the story of Lancelot's relations with King Pelles's daughter, and Guinevere's frantic jealousy, together with the final scene of discovery, forbid this charitable assumption.

Again, as I remarked above, the problem is complicated by the high character ascribed to Guinevere, and the absolute lack of any real condemnation of her relations with Lancelot. This is carried so far that even after the final discovery the kingdom of Britain is threatened by the Pope with an interdict unless Arthur will consent to take back his faithless wife; while throughout the war with Lancelot the sympathies of the reader are asked for the knight, not for the king. Nothing could well be lower than the morality of the *Lancelot* story as it now stands: the cynical indifference of what we may call the 'secular' sections, on the one hand, coupled with the false and wholly sickly pseudo-morality of the Grail sections on the other, cannot but be utterly distasteful to any healthy mind. For my own part, I must needs think the immense popularity of the *Lancelot-Grail* romances wholly undeserved.

Another point which is often overlooked is the discrepancy of age between Lancelot and the queen; the hero's birth takes place some considerable time after the marriage of Arthur and Guinevere. In the final war with Arthur we are told that Lancelot is twenty-one years Gawain's junior, this latter being seventy,[1] while Arthur is ninety years old! It is quite clear that we have here no tale of the genuine spontaneous love of youth and maiden such as we find in Tristan and Iseult, but rather the account of the *liaison* between a young knight and a lady, his superior in years and station.

All these discrepancies and difficulties in the *Lancelot* story can, I believe, be best explained on the lines above suggested. The original story of Guinevere's infidelity had been dropped out of the legend, a reminiscence only surviving in the account of Mordred's treachery. Shortly after the middle of the twelfth century the tone given to

[1] In some versions eighty.

courtly society by certain influential princesses, among them Eleanor of Aquitaine and England, and her daughter, Marie de Champagne, demanded the introduction into the popular Arthurian story of a love element, conceived after the conventions of the day. Doubtless the popularity of the older *Tristan* story was an element in the matter, but we must, I think, guard carefully against regarding the one as an imitation of the other; in colouring and characteristics the tales are, as I said above, diametrically opposed.[1]

Why Lancelot was selected as the queen's lover is a question which it is extremely difficult to answer with any certainty. When I treated the subject in my *Legend of Sir Gawain*, I suggested that he simply took the place of Gawain here, as elsewhere. That may have been the case, but the fact that, as I now think, we have distinct evidence of an intervening period, or rather of intervening stages, between the stories, somewhat militates against this idea.

[1] As far as English opinion goes, the popularity of Tennyson's version of the Arthurian tales has operated disastrously in confusing the question. Not long ago a writer contributed to a review an article on the subject, in which he contended for the essential identity of the *Tristan* and *Lancelot* stories, naming among other parallels the fact that in both cases the hero is sent to fetch home his lord's bride—an addition due to Tennyson; Lancelot in the genuine story being unborn at the date of the marriage. As regards the *Idylls*, it can only be said that whereas Malory's juxtaposition of half a dozen different compilations made confusion of a subject already more than sufficiently complex, Tennyson's edifying rearrangement of Malory made that confusion 'worse confounded.' Malory is highly valuable for the Arthurian legend in his proper place, when critically compared with other versions; and has a separate and independent position as an English classic. The *Idylls of the King* may perhaps also be considered an English classic, but is *entirely* outside the range of critical Arthurian scholarship, and should *never* be quoted as evidence for the smallest tittle of Arthurian romance.

THE PROSE LANCELOT

The choice may have been determined by quite simple considerations. It is noticeable that in each of the poems in which Chrétien mentions Lancelot previous to the *Charrette* he places him third in the list of Arthur's knights; in *Erec* the two first are Gawain and Erec; in *Cligés* they are Gawain and Perceval. None of the three here named would be available: Gawain from his relationship alike to Arthur and to Mordred, besides the fact that the character he early acquired as 'the Maidens' Knight' rather militated against the exclusive fidelity requisite for the post; Erec was already provided with a lady-love; Perceval was impracticable, not so much from the ascetic character ascribed to him, which was probably[1] a later accretion, as from his essentially uncourtly manners, and very slight connection with Arthur's household. It may very well be that at the 'psychological moment' Lancelot, by his new-won position in the cycle, was the one hero who approved himself fitted for the rôle, and thus reached in the character of the queen's lover his final evolution as an Arthurian knight.

Again, as I suggested in discussing the *Lanzelet*, it may be that some peculiarity in his relations with his mysterious protectress gave the required suggestion. With the knowledge at our disposal the question cannot be definitely answered.

But the central idea once conceived, the process of evolution proceeded merrily: doubts, hesitation, despondency, on the part of the hero, gracious advances on that of

[1] I am not quite certain on this point. Certainly the *Perceval* story is earlier than we commonly suppose, and I think we may find that it had reached the ecclesiastical ascetic stage at quite an early point in the evolution of the *Lancelot* story.

the queen; advances on the part of other ladies, jealousy on the part of Guinevere; despair and madness of Lancelot; reconciliation, suspicion, detection, danger, deliverance, all the well-known formulæ of such a love-tale are employed, well interspersed with the knightly adventures of Lancelot and other companions of the Round Table. Such a story could be expanded, *ad infinitum*, and there is no doubt that it was expanded to an inordinate length, as we shall find when the day comes for a critical edition of the various redactions of the prose *Lancelot*.

Meanwhile, what of the romance which had given the initial impulse to the formation of the Lancelot story, the *Tristan*? As a matter of fact the *Tristan* was in the unenviable position of a Frankenstein. It had created, or rather helped to create, a monster which was its eventual destruction. So far as incidents go, the *Lancelot* has borrowed but little from the *Tristan*; the episode of the blood-drops, which betray the nocturnal meeting of Guinevere and Lancelot in the *Charrette*, is generally admitted to be borrowed from the similar episode in the *Tristan* poems, while the version given by Hartmann von Aue of the abduction of Guinevere shows points of contact with that of Iseult by Gandîn, but the incidental parallels between the stories are in reality very slight. Turn, however, to the prose *Tristan*, and you find the influence of the *Lancelot* absolutely dominant. Following the example of Lancelot, Tristan believes himself to have lost the favour of his adored queen, flies to the woodland, where he goes mad; attempts suicide; Iseult pours out her woes in letters to Guinevere, who is regarded as the noblest of queens, and a recognised authority on love! Guinevere invites the lovers to Arthur's court; Lancelot places his castle of Joyous Garde at their disposal. The details of the beautiful old love poem, the poignant tragedy of Tristan and Iseult, are lost sight of. In a fragmentary form they still exist, but are buried out of sight underneath the great mass of Arthurian accretion. It is no longer the love of Tristan for Iseult which is the central interest of the story, but the rivalry between Tristan and Lancelot, which of the two shall be reckoned 'the best knight in the world.'

Dr. Wechssler, in his study on the various redactions of the Lancelot-Grail cycle, points out the manner in which the two versions of the *Tristan* have been worked over and modified so as to bring them more into harmony with the *Lancelot*.[1] But how thoroughgoing was this modification, and how disastrous to the older story, can only be understood by a first-hand study of the texts. An interesting point for future criticism to determine will be whether there was ever an earlier, and independent, prose *Tristan*, or whether the prose versions of this tale are not all posterior to and dependent upon the *Lancelot*. I do not think that any question can here arise as to the priority of the poetical relative to the prose form.

To sum up the conclusions arrived at in these pages, I would suggest that the order of Guinevere's lovers, so far as can be determined from the surviving Arthurian tradition, was as follows:

1. GAWAIN.—This being indicated by Gawain's close connection with kindred Celtic legends; traces of the relation surviving in the accounts given in the *Merlin* of Gawain as the 'queen's knight,' and in passages of

[1] Cf. Wechssler, *Über die verschiedenen Redaktionen des Graal-Lancelot-Cyklus*, p. 17.

Chrétien's *Perceval*, Wolfram's *Parzival*, and early English romances.[1]

2. MORDRED.—Representing a period when such a relationship was held incompatible with Gawain's character as chivalrous hero, and the more unamiable features of the primitive conception were transferred to another character who was regarded as Gawain's only brother. The later stages of this period are preserved in the *Chronicles*.

3. Intervening period wherein Guinevere undergoes same process as Gawain, and false Guinevere is evolved. The queen's character is regarded as irreproachable and Mordred as an unwelcome suitor. Strong traces of this period remain, both in the earlier metrical and prose romances, and complicate the subsequent presentment.

4. LANCELOT.—His introduction in this character being due (*a*) to social conditions in courtly circles, (*b*) to desire to create within the Arthurian cycle a love-tale which should rival in popularity the well-known and independent *Tristan* story. Mordred, however, remains in the story, and he, rather than Lancelot, should be considered as representing the original 'infidelity-motif.'[2]

---

[1] *Merlin*, Sommer's ed., chap. xxvi. p. 343; *Perceval*, l. 9546 *et seq.*; *Parzival*, xii. ll. 1306-7, xiii. l. 542 *et seq.*; also my *Legend of Sir Gawain*, p. 75 *et seq.*

[2] I have purposely excluded the Melwas-Meleagant story from this comparison. I am not clear that it was, in its origin, a tale of conjugal infidelity; it rather appears to me to be a *Pluto-Proserpine* abduction tale. The abductor *may* at one period have been Guinevere's lover; but, as we now have it, the queen is the innocent victim of violence. Further, it is evident that the abductor had ceased to be the lover *before* the introduction of Lancelot into the story (cf. *Lanzelet*). Therefore, if originally an infidelity story, we are met by the same perplexing gap in the tradition as we find in the Mordred version.

CHAPTER VIII

THE PROSE LANCELOT—LANCELOT AND THE GRAIL

We now approach the most difficult and complicated part of an exceptionally difficult and complicated question; rather, to be more accurate, we are now confronted with the union of two questions, each of them, in a high degree, intricate and obscure. We have not yet succeeded in solving the problems connected with the evolution of the Grail romances; we can scarcely be said to have begun the examination of the *Lancelot* legend; the union of the two might well appear to present such insuperable difficulties that the critic might shrink from grappling at close quarters with so formidable a task. And yet it may well be that this union of the two legends, which at the first glance appears so seriously to increase our difficulties, is precisely that factor which shall play the most important part in their final solution; that inasmuch as the *Lancelot* legend was the dominant factor in the later cyclic development of Arthurian romances, the disentangling of this particular thread will be the clue which sets free the other members of the cycle, and enables them to fall once more into their original and relative positions.

The elements composing the Grail problem are so well known that here I need do no more than briefly recapitulate them. The Grail romances are practically divided into two families: that dealing with the history of the relic—the *Early History* romances as they are very generally called; and that dealing with the search for the relic, the *Queste*, which latter family is again sharply divided into two sections differentiated from each other by the personality of the hero—the Perceval and Galahad *Questes*. I am not sure whether we ought not to go a step further and recognise a third clearly defined family, that of the Gawain *Queste*. Mr. Nutt in his *Studies on the Legend of the Holy Grail*[1] partly recognises this, but does not, I think, attribute sufficient importance to the matter, regarding Gawain as an understudy of Perceval. I incline to think that before the question is finally solved we shall require to study very closely the variants which regard Gawain as Grail hero, and compare them with the *Perceval* versions. I am not sure that we shall find the result quite what we expect!

So far criticism has confined itself to the question of the relation existing between the *Early History* and *Queste* versions, and that between the two main families of the *Queste*. In this latter case the general consensus of opinion is to regard Perceval, whose story is marked by certain definite and widely spread folk-lore features, as an earlier Grail hero than Galahad, whose *Queste* is strongly allegorising and mystical in character.

It is this latter *Queste* which here mainly concerns us, but we shall find that before we are in a position to examine it closely we must deal with certain features both of the Gawain and Perceval variants.

The *Gawain* versions will not detain us long. There is,

[1] Cf. references under heading 'Gawain.' They are scattered throughout the book.

correctly speaking, no definite *Gawain-Grail* romance, but we find records of Gawain's visits to the Grail castle scattered throughout the latter part of the *Conte del Graal*, *Diu Krône* (where he is really the Grail hero), prose *Lancelot*, and Dutch *Lancelot* (this latter, as we shall see, differing in very important particulars from the prose *Lancelot*). In each case these adventures are marked by peculiarly wild and fantastic features, sometimes apparently borrowed from the hero's feats at the *Château Merveil*, as recorded by Chrétien and Wolfram, sometimes entirely independent of those feats, but strongly reminiscent of Perceval's experiences in the Grail castle. In the distinctively *Lancelot* romances, where Gawain, Lancelot, and Bohort all attempt the adventures of Corbenic, Gawain is the first to do so, and his experiences are repeated, with a more fortunate result, in the case of the other two. The *Grand S. Graal*, which gives an account of the founding of Corbenic, and the establishment of its marvels, states that none are to escape with their lives till *Gawain* shall come, and he shall receive shame and dishonour.[1] This same romance makes Gawain a descendant of Joseph of Arimathea.

I think it is quite clear that the Grail castle as depicted in the later romances is really a combination of the features of two originally distinct accounts, the Grail castle of the earlier Perceval story, and the *Château Merveil* of Gawain legend. The marvellous features which the Galahad-Lancelot *Queste* emphasises have clearly been borrowed from the Gawain romances, and are therefore to be considered as younger than these.

Dr. Wechssler's study, *Über die verschiedenen Redaktionen*

[1] Cf. *Grand S. Graal*, ed. Hucher, pp. 271 and 289-93.

des Robert von Borron zugeschriebenen Graal-Lancelot-Cyklus, to which I have previously referred, is of value in helping us to the next stage of our investigation. The writer points out that the redactors of the prose romances we possess were familiar with two compilations, practically covering the entire ground of Arthurian romance, one of which, the earlier, was ascribed to Robert de Borron, the other, the later, to Walter Map; or rather, as the author is careful to write throughout, *pseudo*-Borron and *pseudo*-Map.[1] The original cycle, which the writer designates *A.*, consisted of *Livre del Graal*,[2] *Merlin, Suite Merlin, Lancelot, Queste*, and *Mort Artur*, but only traces of the *Borron* cycle remain, the romances as we have them belonging to the pseudo-*Map* redaction.[3]

Further, Dr. Wechssler claims to have detected clear traces of two subsidiary cycles formed by selections from the original; redaction *B.* consisting of the *Livre del Graal*, the *Merlin*, and *Suite Merlin*, and the *Queste* and *Mort Artur*. The redaction *B.* he considers the earlier shortened version of the pseudo-Borron cycle.[4]

A still later and shortened redaction was composed of the *Merlin* and *Suite Merlin, Queste* and *Mort Artur*; this also being attributed to the pseudo-Borron.[5]

According to Dr. Wechssler the distinguishing mark which separates the pseudo-Borron from the pseudo-Map cycle is the introduction into the former of the personages of the *Tristan* legend absent from the Map cycle.

[1] Dr. Wechssler's caution is quite right, nevertheless I think we may eventually find that Borron was really the author of some sort of a cycle.

[2] Dr. Wechssler contends for this, as the correct title, rather than *Grand S. Graal*.

[3] Cf. *supra*, p. 17.   [4] Cf. *supra*, p. 14.   [5] Cf. *supra*, p. 9.

This is very clear, and very interesting, but let us wait a minute before we examine it, and see how, in the hands of its own author, the theory works out. The study to which I have just referred was published in 1895; in 1898 another study appeared from the same pen, this time dealing exclusively with the Grail romances,[1] in which Dr. Wechssler practically adopted the standpoint of Professor Birch-Hirschfeld, that the Grail is *ab initio* a Christian symbol, but at the same time endeavoured to harmonise this view with that which regards the Grail as originally a heathen talisman, while, in the same way, he claimed to discover a *viâ media* between the conflicting variants of the *Queste*, presenting us, as the result, with a curious composite hero, who was named Galahad, but whose story was the story of Perceval.

I do not know if the author was himself really satisfied with the result of his ingenuity; I am convinced no other student of the Grail romances was; but the interest of the study for us lies in this, how did a scholar who three years before had published a really sound, solid, and valuable piece of criticism, such as that on the Grail-Lancelot cycle, come to wander so far astray in the quagmire of pure hypothesis and unfounded assumption? Simply and solely, I believe, because it had never occurred to Dr. Wechssler that the *Lancelot* romances *could* be associated with any *Queste* other than the Galahad *Queste*. He saw, and saw rightly, that the *Lancelot* story played a very important rôle in the cyclic evolution of the Arthurian romance; he saw that it was closely connected with a Grail *Queste*, and never suspecting that the hero of that

[1] *Die Sage vom Heiligen Gral, in ihrer Entwicklung bis auf Richard Wagner's Parsifal*: Halle, 1898.

Queste could be other than Galahad, while at the same time he recognised the priority of certain elements of the Perceval story, he endeavoured, with a fatal result, to combine the two, and evolve such a *Queste* as would suit the earlier redaction of the *Lancelot* story.

And yet the key to the truth was in his hand all the time, had he but known it. He knew M. Paulin Paris's '*Romans de la Table Ronde*'; on p. 87 of vol. iv. the writer quotes a passage from a MS. of the *Bibliothèque Nationale*, to which I have previously referred, but which is of such paramount importance for the question before us that I make no apology for repeating it here: '*Et le grant conte de Lancelot convient repairier en la fin à Perceval qui est chiés et la fin de tos les contes ès autres chevaliers. Et tout sont branches de lui* (c'est-à-dire se rapportent à Perceval[1]) *qu'il acheva li grant queste. Et li contes Perceval meismes est une branche del haut conte del Graal qui est chiés de tos les contes*' (MS. 751, fol. 144-48).

To this quotation M. Paulin Paris added the remark, 'Mais dans la *Quête du Saint Graal*, Perceval n'est plus le héros qui découvre le Graal et accomplit les dernières aventures. Galaad, le chevalier vierge, fils naturel de Lancelot, est substitué au *Perceval* des dernières laisses de Lancelot. La manie des prolongements aura conduit à ces modifications des premières conceptions. Et c'est la difficulté de distinguer ces retouches successives qui a donné à la critique tant de fils à retordre.'

The position could scarcely be more clearly stated to-day; one can only regret that this luminous hint of the great French scholar should have remained so long unfruitful. When the passage first attracted my attention, which it did

[1] Obviously added by M. Paulin Paris.

some years ago, I made a note of it as important for the theory of the early evolution of the *Perceval* story, but not till I had read Dr. Wechssler's study of the *Grail-Lancelot* cycles did its immense importance as evidence for the evolution of the Arthurian cycle, as a whole, dawn upon me. Yet here we have a piece of evidence of the very highest value, a direct and categorical statement that at one period, and that an advanced one (otherwise it would not be termed 'le *grant* conte'), of its evolution, the *Lancelot* legend was connected with and subordinate to the *Perceval* story, and that in its full and complete Grail-Queste form.

In other words, the distinction between the cycles respectively attributed to Borron and to Map is not only the presence or absence of the personages of the *Tristan* story (as Dr. Wechssler supposes), but the much more important and radical distinction that, in the first the *Queste* was originally a Perceval, in the second always a Galahad *Queste*. It is surprising that this distinction had not occurred to the original framer of the thesis, any one familiar with the genuine Borron romances must be aware that the *Queste* they pre-suppose *is* a Perceval *Queste*. Probably the disinclination, to which I have referred above, to connect Lancelot with any Grail hero save his own son had very much to do with the matter; further, I do not think that Dr. Wechssler had formed a clear idea of the process of evolution of the cycle he postulated, which he represents as progressing by contraction, *i.e.* the earliest form being the fullest, or why that cycle should have been connected with the name of Robert de Borron. In fact, he reserves the discussion of the questions concerning original formation for another study.

Now I would submit that the rational progress of evolution is by expansion, not by contraction, and that the name of Robert de Borron became associated with a cycle representing the *ensemble* of Arthurian romance because there was a smaller cycle which was really the work of the genuine Robert de Borron, which smaller cycle formed the germ of the later and more extended body of romance.[1]

Scholars have long ago recognised that the three works attributed to Robert de Borron, and which, as we possess them, probably represent prose versions of that writer's original poems, are closely connected with each other, and have every appearance of having been intended to form one consecutive work. These three are the *Joseph of Arimathea*, *Merlin*, and *Perceval*, which latter is only represented by one MS. and is what we generally call the 'Didot' *Perceval*.[2]

Now if we examine the Didot *Perceval*, as printed by Mr. Hucher in vol. i. of *Le Saint Graal*, we shall find that the last twenty pages, succeeding Perceval's achievement of the Grail Quest, are devoted to Arthur's expedition to France, his conquest of Frollo and war with Rome, succeeded by Mordred's treachery, the final battle and Arthur's departure for Avalon—in fact, precisely the contents of the *Mort Artur*, which, as we know, generally follows the

---

[1] On this point I need only refer to M. Gaston Paris, Introduction to the Huth *Merlin*, p. viii.

[2] I do not discuss here how far this romance represents the original Borron-Perceval poem. As it stands, it is certainly not Borron's work. The question is, are we to consider it the work of a later writer, or does it represent an early *Perceval* romance, worked over for cyclic purposes?

Queste, only related in a more concise and summary manner;[1] and one more in accordance with the *Chronicles* than is the case with the other prose romances.

I think it is quite clear that the *Perceval*, whether in the original form in which Borron wrote it or not, as we possess it, shows distinct traces of having formed the concluding portion of a cycle.

It is quite obvious that a genuine Borron cycle, such as suggested above, would contain the germ of later expansion. Thus the *Joseph of Arimathea* certainly appears to represent what we may perhaps call the first draft of the *Grand S. Graal*. *Merlin* was certainly expanded into the *Merlin* Vulgate and *Suite*. *Perceval* represents *Queste* and *Mort Artur*. Only the *Lancelot* is un-represented, and with that I do not think the original 'Borron' cycle had anything to do.

The introduction of the *Lancelot* probably belongs, as Dr. Wechssler suggests, to a subsequent writer, who borrowed the more famous name, to the pseudo-Borron; and from the quotation given by M. Paulin Paris, I should think it likely that, at first, the juxtaposition of the *Lancelot* and *Perceval-Grail* stories was purely external, and that they did not affect each other by contamination. The Didot *Perceval* may well have been the *Queste* of the earliest pseudo-Borron, whether or not it represents the *Queste* of the genuine Borron cycle.[2]

---

[1] Some years ago, when preparing my translation of the *Parzival*, I found in the *Gesta Comites Andegavorum* a summary of the closing events of Arthur's life closely agreeing with that of the Didot *Perceval*. The connection between Perceval and Angevin tradition has not, in my opinion, received sufficient attention.

[2] We have seen reason to believe that the original *Perceval* story did

But the growing popularity of the *Lancelot* story would render such a contamination inevitable, and I am strongly tempted to believe that in that perplexing romance, the prose *Perceval li Gallois,* we have the *Queste* of a later pseudo-Borron cyclic redaction. The perplexing features of this version are well known: the whole tone is highly ecclesiastic, there are numerous references to an earlier Perceval story, Lancelot plays an important rôle, yet Galahad is unknown, and there are certain mysterious folk-lore features not met with elsewhere. Hitherto no one has succeeded in satisfactorily placing this romance. I would suggest that it represents the *Queste* of a late pseudo-Borron *Lancelot-Perceval-Grail* cycle; and I am encouraged in this supposition by the fact that this romance knows the Questing-Beast, a mysterious creation only found in the *Suite Merlin* and the *Tristan Palamedes* romances. Now the *Suite Merlin* claims to be by Robert de Borron, and the introduction of the *Tristan* figures into the Arthurian story is, as we saw above, held by Dr. Wechssler to be the distinctive 'note' of the Borron-cycle.[1]

This conclusion is further strengthened when we examine the rôle assigned to Lancelot in these two romances. In each case he is one of the most distinguished knights at Arthur's court, but he is much less *en évidence* in the Didot

early affect the *Lancelot*, and this argument, which we used at first of the independent, becomes strengthened when we examine the cyclic form.

[1] If this be true, it would throw an interesting light on the conjunction of the *Queste* and *Perceval li Gallois* in the well-known Welsh MS. translated by the Rev. R. Williams. The compiler of the MS. may have had versions of the two *Lancelot* cycles before him and have taken the *Queste* from each, perhaps doubtful which was the right version.

Perceval than in the *Perceval li Gallois*. In the first-named romance he is represented as overthrowing all the knights of the Round Table, till the appearance of Perceval, by whom he is himself overthrown. He would thus appear to rank next to the hero of the tale and to be the superior of Gawain. So far as we can gather, the order of superiority runs thus: Perceval, Lancelot, Gawain, Yvain. But he is, apparently, not of those who start on the Grail quest; nor is there any indication of his *liaison* with Guinevere. But the author mentions among the knights '*le fiz à la fille à la femme de Malehot.*'[1] We do not know the lady of Malehault save through the medium of the prose *Lancelot*.

In the *Perceval li Gallois* (*Perlesvaus* Professor Heinzel prefers to call it), Lancelot is one of the three best knights in the world, the other two being Perceval and Gawain; he takes part in the Grail quest, but on account of his sinful relations with Guinevere is not worthy to behold the sacred talisman, which does not appear, even in a veiled form, during his stay at the Fisher King's castle, whereas it appears clearly to Gawain. The position, so far as Lancelot is concerned, is thus nearer to the presentment of the Galahad *Queste* than is the Didot *Perceval*. This last-named, we have seen above, shows clear indications of betraying a cyclic redaction; these indications, though differing in form, are not less clear in the *Perceval li Gallois*. The concluding passage runs thus: '*Après iceste estoire commence li contes si comme Brians des Illes guerpi le roi Artus por Lancelot que il n'aimoit mie et comme il aseura le roi Claudas qui le roi Ban de Bénoic toli sa terre. Si parole cis contes comment il le conquist et par quel manière, et si com*

[1] Hucher, vol. i. p. 421.

Galobrus de la Vermeille lande vint à la cort le roi Artus por aidier Lancelot, quas il estoit de son lignage cist contes est mout lons et mout aventreus et poisanz.[1]

In quoting this passage, Professor Heinzel remarks: 'Auch der *Perlesvaus* ist einem grösseren Romanwerk einverleibt, aus dem die Handschrift von Mons den *Perlesvaus* ausgeschrieben hat. Was ihm folgte muss ein Art *Lancelot* gewesen sein.'[2]

There is a further and interesting possibility before us. The compilers may—in one instance, I think, we can show reason to believe that they did—have incorporated the Chrétien *Perceval* (or a version closely akin to it) into their cycles as representing the *Queste*.

In the work of preparing these studies I felt that I ought to leave no available version of the *Lancelot* unexplored, and therefore undertook to read carefully the immense compilation generally known as the Dutch *Lancelot*. Well was it for me that I did not shrink from the task! I had not read far before I began to suspect that the text repre-

[1] Quoted by Professor Heinzel: '*Über die französischen Gralromane,*' p. 177. The parallel passage is on p. 279, vol. ii. of Dr. Evans' translation, *The High History of the Holy Grail*; but it is not included in the Welsh translation.

[2] Professor Heinzel's study did not come into my hands till the MS. of this chapter had been sent to the press. The support afforded to my theory by the above expression of opinion was most welcome to me. A point which deserves notice in connection with this romance is the appearance in it of the above-named *Briant des Illes*, and the story of the death of *Lohot*, King Arthur's son. So far as I know, no other prose romance knows either of these characters, but Chrétien refers to both in his *Erec*, ll. 6730 and 1732. I think it is possible that the name given by Wolfram von Eschenbach to Arthur's son, *Ilinot*, may rest upon a misreading of *Lohot*; the story connected with the latter is certainly curiously archaic in detail.

sented by this translation was, in every respect, a fuller and a better text than that used by Dr. Sommer in his Malory collation; in the *Queste* section in particular was this the case. In the succeeding chapters I intend to go fully into what is, I believe, in the interests of Arthurian criticism, a very important discovery. Here I will only say that I eventually found that the text of the Dutch *Lancelot*, of the printed version of the prose *Lancelot* Lenoire, 1533 (which, as I have remarked before, Dr. Sommer does not chronicle), and Malory's *Lancelot* and *Queste* sections all stand together as representing a much fuller and more accurate text than that of the prose *Lancelot* 1513, or the *Queste* MSS. consulted by Dr. Furnivall for his edition of that romance. Whether we have not here an important part of the *un*shortened pseudo-Borron-*Lancelot* into which the Map *Queste* has been introduced is a matter for careful investigation. The point to which at the present moment I would draw attention is, that the Dutch *Lancelot* incorporates a very considerable section of a *Perceval* romance, which bears a very close resemblance to Chrétien's poem, with this curious difference, that it gives an account of the achieving of the adventures named by the Grail messenger, which, so far as I know, is found nowhere else. This section, which occupies over two thousand lines, demands a special study, but for us its significance lies in this that it seems to point to the conclusion that in the evolution of a *Lancelot-Perceval* cycle (the existence of which I think we may hold for proven) the compilers allowed themselves considerable latitude in the *Queste* section. There were several Perceval *Questes* to select from, and they took which they preferred, even pressing the original, manifestly independent, *Perceval* romances into their service. I suspect that this variation in the Perceval *Queste* helped towards its suppression in favour of the Galahad variant, which had the advantage of existing only in one form, though the cause mainly operating was an entirely different one.[1]

So far then we have traced the evolution of the *Lancelot* story, and found that at one period of its development, and that an advanced period, it was connected with a Grail story, which regarded Perceval as its hero and knew nothing of Lancelot's son, Galahad. How then did the latter appear upon the scene, and in what light are we to regard the romances dealing with him?

I have studied the Galahad *Queste* closely, and have compared versions gathered from widely different sources, French originals, and translations, and I am distinctly of the opinion that we possess the romance practically in its original form. It is a homogeneous composition, it is not a compilation from different sources and by different hands. There is no trace of an earlier and later redaction, save only in the directly edifying passages, which in some cases appear to have undergone amplification. The difference between the versions is not that of incident or sequence, scarcely even of detail, but rather of the superior clearness and coherence with which the incidents are related in some of the versions as compared with others. I am strongly inclined to think that there is no peculiarity in any of the *Queste* MSS. which cannot quite well be ascribed

---

[1] I cannot at all agree with Dr. Wechssler's view that the Galahad *Queste* has been largely worked over; on the contrary it has been the least tampered with of all the Arthurian romances. I shall show this presently by comparison of texts.

to the greater or less accuracy of the copyist, or his greater or less taste for discourses of edification.

Nor is the *Queste* by the same hand as was responsible for the final moulding of the *Lancelot* story; though so closely connected with, indeed dependent upon, that story, it yet in many points stands in flagrant contradiction with it, and there is little doubt that the *Lancelot* would gain greatly in coherence if the *Queste* were omitted, and the passages preparatory to it eliminated from the original romance. These remarks apply also to the *Grand S. Graal* in its present form, though, as we shall see, this last named romance does not stand on precisely the same footing as the *Queste* with which it is now closely connected.

The following facts seem to stand out clearly. Both these Grail romances, the *Queste* especially, depend *entirely* for their interest on Lancelot. They are the glorification of his race as that from which the Grail Winner is predestined to spring. The genealogies, however they may vary (as they do in the different versions), are all devoted to this object. They are most closely connected with, and practically presuppose each other; yet admitting, as I think we must admit, that they do not represent the original form of the Grail story, they do not produce the impression of romances which have been worked over with the view of substituting a new hero for the one in whose honour the tale was originally constructed.

Nevertheless in the case of the *Grand S. Graal* we must, I think, admit imitation; even as in the original Borron cycle the *Joseph of Arimathea* was designed as an introduction to the life and deeds of the Grail Winner, Perceval, so in this, the latest form of the cycle, the introduction to the *Queste* is built upon and expanded from the *Joseph*. The introduction is based upon and follows the lines of the old introduction, but the *Queste* is a new *Queste*.

Let us be quite clear on this point. Galahad may have in a measure supplanted Perceval, but he has neither dispossessed nor robbed him. He has taken over no one of his characteristics, no one of his feats. Such traces of the Perceval story as remain are found in connection with Perceval himself; he, too, achieves the Grail *Queste*. He has undergone a change, and a change for the worse, but that was quite as much due to the evolution of the Grail as a Christian talisman as to the invention of Galahad. The hero of the Didot *Perceval* and *Perceval li Gallois* is as inferior to the hero of Chrétien and Wolfram as is the Perceval of the Galahad *Queste*. The truth is that Perceval is still the Grail hero, but he shares that character with another whose invention is due to special and easily discernible causes.[1]

The point of view of the writer of the *Queste* is not that of the compilers of the *Lancelot*. As I remarked in the previous chapter, the view taken by the *Lancelot* of the relations between the hero and the queen is frankly unmoral. Neither is blamed for his or her action, neither is apparently conscious of wrong-doing. In the *Queste*

---

[1] The worst fault of Dr. Wechssler's Grail study is that he predicates the distinctive traits of Perceval as being of Galahad—to whom they never in any sense belonged. Galahad is not Perceval's understudy, much less is he his original: he is an absolutely and entirely independent creation. The only quality they have in common is that of virginity, which is not of them, but of the monkish redactors of the legend. It is certainly no part of the primitive *Perceval* tale.

Lancelot's conscience is sorely vexed, and his sin insisted upon. The compilers of the *Lancelot* have a very courtly respect for women—the author of the *Queste* despises them utterly. The interest of the *Lancelot* lies in the relation between the sexes—the respective duties of knight and lady—the theme which inspires the *Queste* is their abiding separation.

Again, compare the treatment of the various characters of the story in the two respective sections. Next to Galahad and Perceval, the hero of the *Queste* is Bohort (Bors). But for a single youthful lapse he yields in nothing to those doughty champions of celibacy: his purity, alike of body and soul, is emphatically insisted upon; his confession fills the priest who receives it with a fervour of admiration; yet it is precisely this saintly youth who, in the section preceding and following the *Queste* (the *Lancelot* and the *Mort Artur*), is the confidant and go-between of Lancelot and Guinevere. It is Bohort who seeks Lancelot at the secret bidding of the queen, Bohort who carries love-tokens between them, who arranges meetings. It is he and Lionel who consult the queen as to the delicate question of Lancelot's future relations with the lady who has cured him from the illness caused by drinking the poisoned spring; he who is the confidant of Guinevere's indignation at the supposed love-affair between Lancelot and the maiden of Escarloet; and if he tries to prevent the last fatal meeting between them it is with no view of hindering a wrong to his lord Arthur, but solely because he has reason to suspect the trap laid for the lovers. The two presentments not simply fail to agree, but stand in flat contradiction with each other.

Lionel, again, is throughout the *Lancelot* a valiant

knight, warmly attached alike to his brother and to his cousin. Like Bohort he takes Lancelot's part on every occasion, with him he quits the court when the queen, in an access of jealousy, banishes Lancelot. When he is finally slain both Bohort and Lancelot are overcome with grief. But the *Queste* paints him in the most repulsive colours: violent, brutal, and unreasoning to a degree. He is so indignant with his brother for going to the rescue of a maiden rather than of himself (when both are equally in danger) that he does his best to kill him in revenge. He does kill an unoffending hermit, and a fellow knight of the Round Table who would intervene, and finally it needs a special interposition of Providence to part the two brothers before a fatal issue to the conflict forced on by Lionel has taken place.

Hector, Lancelot's half-brother, who in the later *Lancelot* story is one of the bravest and most distinguished knights of the court, is in the *Queste* held up to scorn and rebuke; while the author of this romance has no colours too black in which to paint the character of Gawain, who, though deposed from his position of chief hero, is, throughout the *Lancelot* proper, treated with the greatest respect. He is entirely loved and trusted by king and queen, and if his valour is in the long-run surpassed by that of Lancelot, the compiler is careful to preserve his honour intact by pointing out, first, that he never recovered from the severe wounds received in the war with Galehault, second, that he was over twenty years Lancelot's senior. The final conflict between them, the most deadly in which Lancelot was ever engaged, was fought when Gawain was seventy-two and Arthur ninety-two years of age; further, as we shall see presently, in some versions the conclusion is more of the character of a drawn battle than of a defeat for Gawain.[1]

It is, I think, quite clear that the Galahad-Grail romances are the work of another hand than that responsible for the main body of the *Lancelot* cycle; and the work of one who was at small pains to harmonise his story with the branches already existing. It is indeed doubtful whether the writer had any thorough acquaintance with the legend as a whole. It is noteworthy that the points of contact with what we may perhaps call the 'secular' section are all restricted to the *later* part of the story, that commencing with what M. Paulin Paris called the *Agravain* section. Between the *Grand S. Graal*, the Galahad *Queste*, and the later part of the *Lancelot* there are a number of what we may call cross-references, the precise value of which will be very difficult to determine. But they do not stray outside a certain limit—they are restricted to Lancelot,

---

[1] The passage which represents Gawain as admitting himself to be the slayer of eighteen out of the twenty-two knights who have lost their lives in the *Queste*, Baudemagus, his dearest friend according to the *Merlin Suite*, among them, should, I think, be printed at the end of the *Queste*, not at the beginning of the *Mort Artur*, where it is now generally found. It is entirely in accordance with the tone of the first named romance, and out of keeping with the latter. Moreover, both the Dutch *Lancelot* and the 1533 version print it in the former position. The compiler of the *Tristan* has generally been supposed to be the first to introduce the vilification of Gawain's character; in the light of Dr. Wechssler's suggestion it would be interesting to examine whether this presentment is to be found in the *Tristan before* its contamination with the later *Lancelot-Map* cycle. I think there were peculiarities in the original Gawain story, which, misunderstood by later compilers, helped to cast a false light on his character, but it is open to question whether it was the *Tristan* compiler or the author of the Galahad *Queste* who was the original propagator of calumny.

the Knight of the Round Table, the queen's lover, and father of the Grail Winner—they do not appear to know Lancelot the *protégé* of the Lady of the Lake. In this character the Grail romances ignore him, nor do they appear to know anything of his most famous adventure, the freeing of Guinevere from Meleagant.[1]

It is the later and not the earlier *Lancelot* story which is known to the writer of the *Queste*; and the more we study the romance the plainer this becomes. The *Lancelot* romance may really be divided into two great divisions, the *Enfances*, *Charrette*, and *Galehault* section, which is practically unaffected by the *Grail* tradition, though it shows evident signs of contact with the *Perceval* story; and the latter portion which (saving the *Mort Artur*, unaffected except by the addition of the concluding *Queste* paragraph, easily removed) has been redacted under the influence of the Galahad-Grail accretion.

Till the versions concerned have been critically examined we cannot determine the value or gauge the evidence of the matter common to the *Lancelot*, *Grand S. Graal*, and *Queste*. The most noticeable instances are the following: the keeping of the Grail at Castle Corbenic, the founding of which is related in the *Grand S. Graal*; the characters of King Pelles and his father, with regard to whom the evidence varies,—as a rule, the character of the Fisher King appears to be confined to the former, that of the Maimed King to the latter (the author of the *Queste*

---

[1] The *Queste* writer dwells upon instances of heroes betrayed through their love of women—Samson, Solomon, etc. If he had known the earlier *Lancelot-Borron* story, with the instance of Merlin's betrayal by the lady who brought up Lancelot, he would surely have made use of so very *à propos* an illustration.

appears to have no idea that the two characters are one and the same);—the daughter of King Pelles, and his son Eliezer. This latter is, I think, peculiar to the Lancelot-Galahad story, the Perceval versions do not know him. The adventure of the broken sword borne by Eliezer, told both in *Lancelot* and *Grand S. Graal*, and achieved, though without satisfactory explanation, in *Queste*.[1] The Boiling Fountain and Bleeding Tomb adventures, also told in the two first, partly achieved in the *Lancelot*, and achievement summarily announced in *Queste*. The Perilous Cemetery, origin stated in *Grand S. Graal*, vainly attempted by Gawain and Hector in *Lancelot*, final achievement barely recorded in *Queste*.

In these last instances the story may well have been in the *Lancelot*, and taken over by compiler of *Grand S. Graal*; the *Queste* makes very little of them; they only serve to keep up the connection between the 'secular' and 'religious' sections.

With regard to the Corbenic-Grail adventures, I am inclined, as I said before, to look upon them as due to the influence of the Gawain story, and as already existing, in a purely adventurous form, in the *Lancelot*, before it was formally united to the Grail Quest.

On the whole, I decidedly lean to the opinion that *Grand S. Graal* and *Queste* are by one and the same hand —the one based upon and expanded from an older poem, the other a practically new invention, the two being designed to replace the *Joseph of Arimathea* and *Perceval*

---

[1] I suspect this sword of being the sword of the original Perceval story, for which an edifying legend has been invented. It probably belongs to a very early stage of the tradition. I hope some day to make it the subject of special study.

of the earlier Grail cycle. As I said above, the author was very little concerned about the harmony of his work. So long as by a superficial rearrangement and interpolation of incidental adventures he could produce an appearance of harmony, he cared nothing at all about the more important questions of continuity of treatment, and preservation of tone and character. The result is that his work, which stands practically as he left it, is in flagrant contradiction with the story it is designed to complete.

But what was the motive which led to the setting aside of the earlier Perceval *Queste*, and what the causes which determined the particular form assumed by its successor?

I do not think they are difficult to detect.

During the later years of the twelfth and earlier years of the thirteenth century we see two stories in process of gradual evolution—the Perceval-Grail story and the Lancelot legend. One early took a decidedly mystical and ecclesiastical bent, the other became more and more worldly and secular. The two appear to have had an equal hold on popular imagination, they early came into touch with each other, but they never really blended. The *Lancelot*, as the younger, borrowed at the outset certain features from the *Perceval*, but it retained its own distinctive character; while the elder story slowly changed, the Grail, at first a subordinate element in the story, gradually but surely dominating the tale, which became more and more ecclesiastical, while the hero became more and more conventional.[1]

---

[1] Cf. the Perceval of Chrétien, and more especially the Parzival of Wolfram, with the hero of the Didot *Perceval* or *Perceval li Gallois*. I consider the two first represent the independent, the two latter the cyclic form.

But at a certain point it became evident that these lines of tradition could no longer remain parallel, they must coalesce, or the one must yield to the other. The Grail quest had become the most popular adventure of Arthur's court, one after another the knights were being drawn into the mystic circle; how could the most popular and most valiant of the knights of the Round Table, for this Lancelot had now become, remain outside the chosen group? It was plain that Lancelot must take part in the Grail quest; it was equally plain that the first knight of the court could not be allowed to come out of the ordeal with any detriment to his prestige; yet the Grail demanded purity of life, and Lancelot was the queen's lover. More, the queen's lover he must remain or forfeit his hold on popular sympathy.

How was it possible to preserve intact at once Lancelot's superiority and the purity of the Christian talisman? Only in one way: by giving him a son who should achieve the quest and then vanish, leaving Lancelot still *facile princeps* among the knights of the Round Table, with the added glory of having been the father of the Grail Winner.

But this son could not be the child of Guinevere. The offspring of a guilty *liaison* could not be the winner of the sacrosanct talisman; yet Lancelot must be faithful to his queen—how solve this problem? The story in its primitive form gave the hint for the required development. Who more fitted to become the mother of the Grail Winner than the fair maiden who filled the office of Grail-bearer?[1]

---

[1] It may be noted here that in Wolfram's version of the *Perceval* story—a version which, as we have seen, has certainly influenced the *Lancelot* legend — the Grail-bearer, Repanse-de-Schoie eventually becomes the mother of Prester John. The circumstance that the

The obvious propriety of such a relationship was bound sooner or later to strike the imagination of some redactor. The Arthurian story already possessed the machinery by which Lancelot could become father of the elect child, while remaining Guinevere's lover; Brisane had but to do for Elaine what Merlin did for Uther, and the difficulty was overcome. Moreover, *Helaine* was, in the old story, the name of the Grail Winner's father, nothing more easy than to bestow the same name on the new hero's mother. All this was only a question of clever adjustment of already existing factors.

Perceval, of course, was in possession, but the later development of his story, which had converted him from a genuine, faulty, but loving and lovable human being, true man and faithful husband, into an aggressively proselytising and persecuting celibate, had made it possible for him still to retain a place in the romance; he could act as second to Galahad, and, like him, disappear, the quest once achieved. But having thus disposed in Lancelot's interest of the two who might have seriously challenged his fame as a knight, Perceval, the real, Galahad, the vicarious (for I think we can only regard him as his father's representative), achiever of the quest, it became necessary to add a third, who should bring back to court the tidings of their success. It is quite obvious, from the point of view of the *Lancelot* story, that Perceval and Galahad *could not* be permitted to return. The third was easily found

details of the begetting of Galahad are found in the *Lancelot*, and not in the *Queste*, suggests the consideration that the author of this latter romance may have worked over the section of the *Lancelot* in question, so as to bring it into superficial accord with his story. Or he *may* have worked in conjunction with one of the later redactors.

in the person of Lancelot's nearest relative, the knight who, his shield unstained by the bar-sinister which marked that of Hector, had been gradually rising in popular favour; Bohort owes his position in the *Queste* to his position in the *Lancelot* proper.

The evolution of this character has not, I believe, attracted much attention hitherto, but it is one of the most remarkable features of the *Lancelot* story. In the earliest versions, represented by the *Lanzelet*, etc., he is not known at all.[1] When he first appears he plays but a small part, gradually his rôle becomes more and more prominent, till in the later portion of the prose *Lancelot* he has become a very efficient understudy to the hero, even surpassing in valour Gawain himself. Thus, on the return of the knights from one of their numerous quests in search of Lancelot, when they are called upon to rehearse their adventures, in order that a record of them may be made, it is decided that their rank, in order of merit, is Bohort, Gawain, Hector, Gaheriet, Lionel, and Baudemagus. Gawain and his brother, the representatives of the older stratum of Arthurian tradition, are the only two who can compete with the all-conquering race of Ban, and the bosom friend of that race, Baudemagus.

Finally he is represented as the father of a son who bids fair to rival his ancestors in valour. When a critical study of the Lancelot MSS. is seriously undertaken, I think we

[1] Chrétien does not appear to know anything about him: in the *Charrette*, for instance, had he known Bohort as represented in later legend, he would certainly have made him, and not Gawain, undertake the conflict with Meleagant, for which Lancelot threatens to be too late. The rôle of 'helpful friend,' played by Gawain in the earlier versions of the legend, is passed over to Bohort in the later.

shall find that the position occupied by Bohort in the story will afford a valuable indication of the relative age of the redaction.

I am quite prepared to find that among the objections which will doubtless be advanced against the theory here advocated one will be that it is too complete in detail, too 'cut and dried,' if I may use the term, to be free from suspicion. To this I would answer that I believe in examining the later stages of Arthurian romance we must follow a somewhat different process from that which we employ for the earlier. The Arthurian poems, being in a large measure independent, and never having formed part of a ' cyclic ' whole, may well be studied separately, in, and for, themselves, though of course we would not leave out of sight variants of the same story. But the later prose romances, those which have avowedly formed parts of a cycle, must be studied, not separately, but in conjunction with the other romances with which they were connected. They are in the position of the parts of a dissected puzzle, the study of one part by itself will never really help us to understand the whole, it is only by studying collective sections, and trying continually new combinations, that we can hope to find the original disposition of the parts.

It is no use to study the *Queste* romance by itself. If we wish to know how it stands with regard to the *Lancelot*, we must study it *with* the *Lancelot*, and if we do this certain points become absolutely clear. The *Queste* pre-supposes a very advanced stage of the *Lancelot* story; one at which the family of the hero, quite as much as the hero himself, is the subject of glorification.[1]

[1] On this point cf. what I have said before as to the development of the *Chansons de Geste*, p. 92 note.

The Galahad *Queste* is absolutely unthinkable without a previous knowledge of the *Lancelot* romances; as a matter of fact, it stands in closer relation to these than it does to any earlier Grail quest. The *Lancelot* romances, on the contrary, would be quite complete and far more coherent without the *Queste*. I have commented already on the striking discrepancies between the sections, but I have not so far dwelt at any length on the extraordinary lack of Grail references in the *Mort Artur*, the section immediately following the *Queste*. If we set on one side the introductory passage, which I have no shadow of doubt does not belong to the *Mort Artur* at all, but is the concluding passage of the *Queste*, there is no evidence of the influence of the latter throughout the whole of this last section of the cycle. Galahad is never mentioned; he was—and is not—as completely as if he had never been. Lancelot never thinks of, never refers to, his valiant son; his whole thought and care is for the queen, whom we were previously told he had renounced. I do not think it possible for any one to read the *Mort Artur* and believe that the *Queste* forms an integral part of the *Lancelot* story. On the other hand, cut out the *Queste*, suppress the few passages in the immediately preceding section of the *Lancelot* story which relate to it, and you have a tale as complete and coherent as is possible for any legend which has been the fruit of long growth and evolution, and has not possessed from the outset a clear and definite purpose and outline.

Admit, as I think we must needs admit, that the *Lancelot* and the *Grail* stories form two independent streams of tradition; recognise, as we must recognise, their diverse character,—one strongly secular, the other strongly ecclesiastical,—and I think we must own that if in their completed form they were to coalesce, that coalition could only be carried out under the conditions suggested above, which conditions we find fulfilled in the Galahad *Queste*. For me this romance is the last word of the *Lancelot* evolution, the final blending of two separate and important streams of tradition, the *grant conte* of Lancelot and the *grant conte* of Perceval and the Grail, the which is *chiés et fin de tous les contes*.

CHAPTER IX

THE DUTCH LANCELOT

In the previous chapters we have examined, so far as the material at our disposal permitted, the *Lancelot* legend in its gradual evolution from a collection of scattered tales, or *lais*, to the vast body of cyclic romance which was its final form. In this task we have restricted ourselves to those features which more intimately concern the personal character and fortunes of our hero; a choice which leaves untouched a large section of his adventures, such as his friendship with Galehault, and his winning of the *Dolorous Garde*. These are features which, affecting no romance or chronicle outside the *Lancelot* proper, cannot well be examined till more versions of this latter are available. In this, the concluding section of these studies, I propose, leaving the question of the nature and origin of the legend, to discuss the relation subsisting between those different versions of the text, on an examination of which I have based the three preceding chapters dealing with the prose *Lancelot*.

The texts in question are (1) the so-called Dutch *Lancelot*; (2) the printed edition of 1533 (Lenoire, Paris); (3) Dr. Sommer's summary of the prose *Lancelot*, based upon the printed edition of 1513, and compared by him with

Malory's text; (4) Dr. Furnivall's edition of the *Queste*; and (5) Malory's *Morte Arthur*.[1] This gives us practically four different texts for each section (Dr. Sommer having also used the *Queste*), two of which, the Dutch *Lancelot* and the 1533 edition, appear to me to be of far greater importance than has hitherto been suspected.

I propose to publish in an Appendix a detailed summary of the contents of the distinctively *Lancelot* portion of the **D. L.**, but the compilation covers such an extent of ground, and contains texts of such value to the student of Arthurian literature, that I think it will not be superfluous to give here a brief outline of its general character.

A noticeable peculiarity of the version is, that, contrary to all other known versions of the *Lancelot-Galahad-Grail* story, it is in verse and not in prose. The MS. containing it appears to be of the beginning of the fourteenth century;[2] but Dr. Jonckbloet gives reason to think that the version

---

[1] 1. Edited by Dr. Jonckbloet, 2 vols., 1850, will be referred to as **D. L.**

2. Edition in 3 vols., a complete copy is contained in the Douce collection in the Bodleian Library, referred to as **1533**.

3. *Morte Arthur*, edited by Dr. Sommer, vol. iii., *Sources of Malory*, the sections entitled *The Lancelot Proper*, *The Quest of the Holy Grail*, and *La Morte au Arthur*; all three are referred to as **S.**

4. *Queste del Saint Graal*, ed. Furnivall—**Q.**

5. *Morte Arthur*, Sommer (vol. i. text)—**M.**

6. The Welsh *Queste* (ed. Rev. R. Williams, 1876), which I have also consulted, being, in its available form, the translation of a translation, scarcely affords reliable ground for comparison; it is, moreover, a very free rendering of the text. Nevertheless, as it is well to make use of all available versions, I have, in the cases where the original text appears to be fairly represented, added this reading under the heading **W.**

[2] Cf. Jonckbloet, *Roman van Lancelot*, vol. i. p. lvii.

contained in it was decidedly older than this date, and there are certainly references to the *Lancelot* story in much earlier Dutch mss. Probably it is a compilation similar to that of Sir Thomas Malory, intended to combine the various romances of the Arthurian cycle with which the compiler was familiar, or of which mss. were at his disposal. In the first instance it was a translation, and I think we must hold a very faithful translation, from the French. Even as we have it we shall find that it agrees closely with parallel French versions. In its original form it consisted of four books, the first of which has unfortunately been lost.

Book II. begins with what M. Paulin Paris called the *Agravain* section of the prose *Lancelot*, *i.e.* the *Enfances*, *Galehault*, and *Charrette* portions are not included.[1] The first 36,000 lines follow the course of the *Lancelot*; at line 36,947 it takes up the *Perceval* at the point of the arrival of the Grail messenger, and for about two thousand lines goes on to give an account of the achieving of the adventures mentioned by her. In some points the compiler agrees closely with Chrétien and seems to have followed his version, in others he departs entirely from any known version of the *Perceval*. Sometimes his names agree rather with Wolfram than with Chrétien; *e.g.* the lady is Orgeloise simply, not L'Orguelleuse de Logres; and Gawain's challenger is Ginganbrisil, a form which Professor Yorke Powell pointed out some years ago as the probable source of Wolfram's Kingrimursel.

---

[1] To speak quite correctly it really begins rather before the *Agravain* proper. I have noted this further on. M. Paulin Paris remarks (*Romans de la Table Ronde*, vol. v. p. 296), with regard to the *Agravain*, that we find it 'le plus souvent copié isolément, ou bien complétement séparé des autres parties.' One of the useful hints of this scholar which might have earlier been taken into consideration.

L. 41,420, we have a visit of Gawain to the Grail castle, agreeing closely with that found in the Montpelier *Perceval*, and also, Dr. Jonckbloet informs us, with that contained in a German version of the *Perceval* preserved at Rome (cf. Jonckbloet, vol. i. p. xxiv.), adventures of Gariette and Griflette, and the fight between Gawain and Ginganbrisil, which ends in the victory of the former, and the king of Scavalon becoming Arthur's 'man.' This again is not recounted elsewhere.[1]

Ll. 42,540-47,262 contain the romance of *Morien*, son of Agloval, the hero of which bears a curious resemblance to Wolfram's Feirefis. In this romance occurs the episode of Lancelot's conflict with a monster, which I have examined in chap. iii. This concludes Book III.

Book III. opens with the *Queste*, the text of which I shall examine in detail further on; it extends to over 11,000 ll. The remainder of the book is occupied by a group of important episodic romances, some of which are found nowhere else. They are as follows:

11,161. *La vengeance de Raguidel.*[2]
14,300. An adventure of Lancelot, Bohort, and Dodinel, when the latter rescues a maiden tied up in a tree.

---

[1] In this connection it is amusing to find Dr. Wechssler (*Sage vom Heiligen Gral*, pp. 166-167) remarking complacently that the achievement of the adventures announced by the Grail Messenger '*wird nirgends erzählt.*' The Dutch *Lancelot* has been edited and available for *fifty* years. I must own that the result of my examination of this, and of the version of 1533, equally available, has been to seriously shake my belief in the soundness and reliability of foreign criticisms of the Arthurian cycle. It is quite clear that the material at our disposal, limited as it is, has not yet been properly examined.

[2] The romances not being named in the **D. L.**, I have adopted for convenience' sake the names given to them by M. Gaston Paris.

14,681. *Le Chevalier à la Manche* (van den riddere metter mouwen).
18,603. *Gauvain et Kei* (Hoe Keye Waleweine verriet).
22,271. *Lancelot et le cerf au pied blanc* (van der jonc frouwen metten hondekine).
23,122-26,980. *Torec.*[1]

Book IV. *Mort Artur*, 13,054 ll. The united three books thus comprising a total of over 87,000 lines.

It will be seen from the above brief summary that the **D. L.** presents many features of great interest for the student of the Arthurian story, but so far, with the exception of the studies published by M. Gaston Paris, to which I have just referred, it does not appear to have attracted much attention from scholars. It is especially to be regretted that Dr. Sommer did not use it for the purpose of his 'Malory' collation; had he done so, he would certainly have come, on many points, to a very different conclusion from that at which he ultimately arrived.

In the following comparison I shall confine my remarks chiefly to such decided variants as cannot possibly be ascribed to the mistakes or emendations of copyists; nor shall I include those minor verbal differences which, however important for a critical edition of the text, do not in themselves definitely prove a divergence of sources. The point I desire to prove is that the versions **D. L.** and **1533** represent a text radically different from that consulted by Dr. Sommer; and that, in conjunction with Malory, they may be held to represent a family of MSS. hitherto unregarded, or unsuspected.

---

[1] Abstracts of these episodic romances are given by M. Gaston Paris, in vol. xxx. of *Hist. Litt. de la France.*

As readers of Malory are aware, he gives no account of the birth or early adventures of Lancelot; the section dealing with that hero begins with Book vi., and takes up his adventures at a point well advanced in what, following M. Paulin Paris, I have called the *Agravain* section (l. 13,351 in **D. L.**). That Malory had before him any version of the earlier section of the *Lancelot* I very much doubt. It must be apparent to any careful reader that, in his view, the Lady of the Lake is connected rather with Arthur than with Lancelot; whenever she intervenes in the story it is to aid the former, rather than the latter. I incline to the belief that Malory's MS. only began at an advanced point of the story, and that he knew little, or nothing, of what had preceded it.

At the commencement of the Terriquen (**D. L.** gives the name as Tarquijn) adventure, **D. L., 1533,** and **M.** all represent Lancelot and Lionel as sleeping under the shadow of a '*pomier*' instead of a *perron* as in **S.**[1]

When Hector comes to the fountain he finds **D. L.** LX. shields and helmets, and XL. swords (the first letters have evidently been transposed and should read XL.). **1533.** Forty-five helmets, forty-five swords, and 'more than' forty-five shields. **S.** Forty swords, forty-five shields, and five spears: helmets are not mentioned. Here **S.** appears to have a confused version of the two preceding accounts.

In the account of the queens who carry off Lancelot **D. L.** and **1533** agree with **S.** in naming the ladies (the queen in **D. L.** is of Foreestan, *not* Sorestan); otherwise the accounts seem to vary. **D. L.** and **1533** do not say, as does **S.**, that the first-named is on her way

[1] Dr. Sommer says, and correctly, that the '*pomier*' must be the older version.

to Norgales through 'Sorelois,' but that her land 'borders on' these kingdoms. It is not the *three* but only the two last-named, Morgain le Fay and Sibile (Cybele) l'enchanteresse, who are learned in enchantments; and neither **D. L.** nor **1533** give any indication of their being the 'queen's ladies' as **S.** represents; they are simply travelling with her.[1]

The lands of the heiress of Rochedon were not seized by the *King* of Sorestan, as **S.** states, but by the *queen* who had been left her guardian (**D. L.** and **1533**). This is much more in accordance with the rest of the story. Otherwise these three versions agree against **M.**

Later on both **D. L.** and **1533** agree in speaking of Galehodyn as the *neveu*, not the *filz* of Gallehault, as in **S.** They are of course right.

In the account of the tournament there are a number of small variants. Judging from **S.**, who gives a very condensed summary, **D. L.** and **1533** are again more correct in details.

On p. 186 of **S.** the summary departs widely from **D. L.** and **1533**. Thus, according to **S.**, Lancelot, seeking for Hector and Lionel, has met with Bohort, Yvain, and four other knights at the 'Chastel du Trespas.' Lancelot

---

[1] This account of Lancelot being found asleep and carried off by three queens should be compared with that of Renouart found sleeping and carried off to Avalon by three 'fays.'

I assume throughout that Dr. Sommer's summary correctly represents his text, but I admit that I have my doubts on this point ; certainly in the *Queste* section he gives some most mistaken readings ; indeed, apart from the evidence of **D. L.** and **1533** the whole *Lancelot-Queste* section needs revision. It is unfortunate that some foreign scholars have been so ready to accept Dr. Sommer's statements without taking the trouble to verify them.

proposes that each of the *six* knights (*sic*) (there were of course seven) shall each ride forth separately and return to the castle 'a la feste de toussainz.' In **D. L.** and **1533** Lancelot has started *accompanied* by Bohort, Baudemagus, and Gaheret. *En route* they meet Mordred, naked, and being thrashed with thorns by 'Mathœus die felle' (Marchant li felon), rescue him, and ride to Chastel du Trespas, where Yvain is imprisoned, whom they also free. It is Yvain, not Lancelot, who suggests the separation and quest.

Again, in the fight between Lancelot and 'Terriquen,' both **D. L.** and **1533** agree against **S.** and **M.** in failing to mention Gaheret's (they have the correct spelling) horse, and saying that Lancelot rides off on his own. Whereas, later on, **S.** and **1533** agree in giving 'three varlets and three sommiers' and **D. L.** and **M.** agree in a 'foster' with four horses.

In the question of the final disposal of the castle **D. L.** and **1533** again fall into line against **S.** The latter says that the knights exchange Terriquen's castle for horses, though not very good ones. I suspect this of being a hasty summary which does not represent the text; **D. L.** and **1533** are so much more detailed. **D. L.** says that 'Die grave van den *Pale* (later on *Parke*, which is I think the correct reading) is rejoiced at the event as his '*neve*' was one of the prisoners. He gives all Arthur's knights very good horses. That he receives the castle is not told, though he afterwards appears as the owner. **1533** says that 'Keux[1] du Parc' has a 'brother' prisoner: delighted at his safety he gives them all horses, very good to Arthur's

[1] I do not think this is a proper name, but the equivalent of *Grave* = Count.

knights, not so good to the others. Out of gratitude they offer him the castle. If **S.** correctly represents the text of 1513, it is clear, I think, that **1533** gives the original reading, which has been condensed, but rightly understood, by **D. L.**, and confused in **S.**

In the account of the adventures at the castle **D. L.**, agreeing in the main with **S.** and **1533**, as against **M.**, yet in one point falls into line with this latter against the other two. Both **S.** and **1533** agree in saying that Lancelot ties his horse to a *tree*, **M.** says 'to a ringe on the walle'; in **D. L.** he ties his horse, when he comes to the '*meester torre, vor die porte al te hant*,' which seems to imply **M.**'s 'ringe.'[1]

I now come to a most extraordinary oversight on the part of Dr. Sommer. On p. 191 and again on p. 274 of his *Sources of Malory* he commits himself to the statement that **M.** is the only known source for certain adventures of Lancelot, his rescue of Kay, his riding off in Kay's armour, etc., and proceeds from this supposed peculiarity to postulate a lost '*Suite de Lancelot*,' of which this is a precious fragment. Now, not only are these adventures recorded both in **D. L.** and **1533**, but they are found in the summary given by M. Paulin Paris on p. 323 of vol. v. of the *Romans de la Table Ronde*.[2]

---

[1] No other version mentions, as does **M.**, that the ladies won their living by 'al maner of sylke werkes,' but the whole story looks so like a copy of Yvain's adventure at the Château de Pesme Aventure that I think it may have been in his source.

[2] Of course M. Paulin Paris's book, being greatly condensed and modernised, cannot be used for textual criticism; but the compiler was a scholar of very wide learning, and there are numerous notes and hints, which we, of a later generation, make a great mistake in disregarding.

The adventure with Kay does not, in the original, occur at this point, but follows after Lancelot's long imprisonment by Morgain; his freeing Lionel from the dungeon of the King of Estrangeloet; winning the hill guarded by Bohort; and discovering the tomb of his grandfather;—a sequence of incident in which **D. L.** and **1533** agree perfectly.

Of the following adventures contained in Book vi. **S.** consequently gives no summary. Throughout **M.** very closely agrees with **D. L.** and **1533,** but he omits to state, as do both these versions, that Lancelot's arraying himself in Kay's armour was due to the dim light of early morning. He believed himself to be donning his own, and was unaware of the error till his host detected it, when he refused to change, foreseeing the amusing complications which would result. This, having no bearing on the story, which is concerned with the *fact*, not with the motive, was probably omitted by **M.** Another slight variation in **M.**'s version is that he gives three knights and three pavilions, whereas the other two agree in giving two knights and four pavilions. Nor are the knights named as in **M.**, but this is most probably due to the English writer, who hardly ever fails to name his characters.

The four knights of the Round Table are the same in all three cases, and **M.** and **D. L.** agree in the order, while **1533** makes Yvain the last to joust. The two first are probably correct, as Gawain, being the most noted of the four, would probably be the last to try his fate. Both **D. L.** and **1533** agree in a feature omitted by **M.**, that Mordred was originally in the company of these four, but being severely wounded on a previous occasion cannot joust (**D. L.**); has been left at a castle that morning (**1533**). **M.** also omits to say that Segramore reveals their names to Lancelot, who, overcome with grief at having so ill-treated his friends, throws away his shield, and rides off weeping. This causes the four knights to suspect his identity, and they take the shield and carry it with them to court. I suspect that this was in **M.**'s original, as he makes Gawain say 'whan we come to the courte than fhal we wete,' which is the reason they give in the other versions for taking the shield; accordingly, they hang it on a pillar in the middle of the hall until it is recognised.

Immediately after this adventure **D. L.** and **1533** record one of which **M.** gives no hint, but which is important in view of a remark made by Dr. Sommer on p. 204 of his study. Lancelot, having overthrown these four knights, comes to two pavilions, in one of which is the lady who cured him from his illness at the Poisoned Spring;[1] as they talk a party of knights and ladies ride up, with them a fair child three years old (**D. L.**); two years old (**1533**). This is Bohort's son, Hélie le Blank, whom Lancelot is delighted to see. Now, Dr. Sommer tells us that, saving in the record of this infant's birth, the allusion to it in the *Queste*, and the mention of Hélie being at Arthur's court when Lancelot, Hector, and Perceval return from l'Île de Joie, there is no mention of him in the prose *Lancelot*. It seems clear that a large section of the *Agravain* must have been omitted in the versions consulted by Dr. Sommer.

Of the three subsequent adventures in Book VI., the final one, that of the knight who smites off his lady's head, and

[1] This lady, never mentioned by **M.**, plays an important rôle in the prose *Lancelot*.

is compelled by Lancelot to do penance for his crime by carrying the dead body from one court to another, is also in our two versions, but occurs at an earlier point in the story. In both he is to go first to Arthur's court, then to that of Baudemagus, and lastly to the King of Norgales. If all spare his life he may live. **M.**, departs from this by only directing him in the first instance to go to Arthur's court: it is Guinevere who sends him on to the Pope. The variant is probably Malory's own.

The other two adventures are not in either **D. L.** or **1533**. The Perilous Chapel, I suspect, was taken over from a Perceval section. Meliot de Logres, and the fetching of a piece of cloth from the chapel of a 'Perilous Cemetery' are both in *Perceval li Gallois* though not connected with each other. It is noticeable that **M.** never refers to the 'Perilous Cemetery' of the *Lancelot* proper, that of the upright swords, but drops out the reference to Galahad's achieving of it, which must certainly have been in his copy of the *Queste*. I think there may have been two Perilous Cemeteries, one of the Borron *Lancelot-Perceval*, the other of the Map *Lancelot-Galahad* cycles, and that this is the first and older.

The adventure of the Lady and the Hawk in chap. xvi. I have not been able to trace.

The events of **M.**, Book vii., are not recorded in either **D. L.** or **1533**, with this possible exception, that when the knights return to court after the adventures recorded above, and are called upon for an account of their doings, Gawain relates how he fought with Gariette, *not knowing that he was his brother*; which looks as if the story (not related in detail) might represent a version of the similar encounter in Book vii. It seems clear that, full as is the

THE DUTCH LANCELOT

account given in both these versions, the compilers still knew a great deal more than they included.[1]

Books VIII., IX., and X. of **M.** follow the prose *Tristan*, and not till Book XI. do we return to the *Lancelot*. This book opens with the adventures at Corbenic (**D. L.**, Cambenoyc, Cambenoyt, or Cabenoyt). **D. L.** fails to

---

[1] Here I take the opportunity of saying that I entirely dissent from Dr. Sommer's assertion that Gareth is the equivalent of the French *Guerresches* rather than *Gaheret*. It is this latter (in the **D. L.** *Gariëtte*) which **M.** renders by Gareth. I have paid a good deal of attention to this question, and have come to the conclusion that, although in the descriptive summary of King Lot's sons, found in the *Lancelot*, Guerresches (Gurrehes) is said to be the youngest, save Mordred, and Gawain's favourite, yet the adventures ascribed to Gaheret (variants, Gaheriet, Gariëtte, Garhiës) throughout mark him as the original of Gareth; a point which etymology alone would, I think, decide in his favour! This much is certain, wherever **M.** and the French versions can be compared we find Gaheret and *not* Guerresches. When Dr. Sommer takes it upon himself, as he does in the quotations from the French contained in the *Mort Artur* section, to arbitrarily change the *Gaheret* of all the foreign versions into *Guerresches*, because the latter agrees with his preconceived ideas, he is setting what I must consider as a most undesirable precedent; we cannot take these liberties with the texts and hope to arrive at a satisfactory and scientific conclusion. As pointed out in my review of Dr. Wechssler's Grail Study, once allow such a substitution, and what is to prevent us from a series of editions emendated to suit the personal views of each editor? I think myself that Gaheret and Guerresches may originally have been one, but that confusion arose from Mordred being sometimes considered as Lot's, sometimes as Arthur's, son, and that a tradition of *four* sons of King Lot having been established early in the evolution of the romantic story, the personality of the third was doubled to make up the correct number. This is only a suggestion, but there is certainly a confusion as to identity in the French versions, though there is no confusion as to the original of **M.**

mention that the lady of the bath is naked, and consistently calls the serpent of the tomb a serpent, never a dragon, in this differing from the other versions. **1533,** at this point, after relating the achievement of their adventures, has a curious remark : '*Ainsi prend fin le premier volume des vertus et glorieulx fais et gestes du noble et puissant chevalier Lancelot du Lac et des compaignons de la Table Ronde,*' and then continues, without any break of chapter, to relate the succeeding adventure with the Grail and King Pelles' daughter. So far from this passage occurring at the end of vol. i., the *Agravain* section does not begin till fol. xxxix. of the second volume of this edition. It is possible that when a critical edition of the *Lancelot* is prepared the above remark may be a guide to an earlier redaction, in which Lancelot was not the father of the Grail Winner. **D. L.** has nothing corresponding to this.

In the account given by **D. L.** of Bohort's visit to Corbenic, the fight with the knight who keeps the bridge for love of Elaine is omitted, but it was evidently in the source, as later on the knight arrives at court as vanquished, and his name is then given as *Brimol van Pleiche*, thus agreeing with **M.**, *Bromel la Pleche*, against the *Brunet du Plaissis* or *Plessis* of **1533** and **S.** **1533** records the combat.

On page 195 of the *Studies* we read that Dr. Sommer's source contained no passage to the effect of **M.**, p. 576, 30-32 : 'Mervelle not said sir bors / for this half yere he (Lancelot) hath ben in pryson with Morgan le fay, kyng Arthurs syster /.' But **1533** gives it : 'il a este en la prison ou il y a une dame plus dung an entier,' which is nearer the real duration of Lancelot's imprisonment.

This seems to indicate that **M.** had a fairly full MS. source, from which he selected at pleasure.

Dr. Sommer gives no summary of Bohort's Grail adventures, so I cannot tell if there be any interesting variants between the French versions, but both **1533** and **D. L.** contain two features, not reproduced in **M.**, which seem to indicate a knowledge of an older Grail tradition. In both the old man tells Bohort that he has seen '*la lance Vengeresse*' the '*wrake spere*,' he who sits in the Siege Perilous shall know the truth of adventure.'[1] (This, of course, might be Perceval equally as well as Galahad.) Galahad and Lancelot are not mentioned throughout.[2] The Maimed King and the Fisher King are one and the same person. All these points confirm my suspicion that the Corbenic adventure was originally taken over from an earlier, probably a Gawain, *Queste*.

In the events relating Elayne's visit to the court and Lancelot's madness, **1533** and **D. L.** in the main agree with **S.**, but with small variants. In both Elayne leaves the court of her own free will, but Arthur does not escort her; she speaks to Bohort before leaving. The knight encountered by Bohort is alone in **D. L.**, thus agreeing with **M.**; while in **1533** he does not meet him till after he has rejoined Lionel and Hector. The knights who go in search of Lancelot are in **D. L.** thirty-two in number, and

[1] It seems likely that this was in **M.**'s source, as we read that the old man has a spear in his hand, 'and that fpere was called the fpere of vengeaunce.' But the old man never speaks of it to Bors.

[2] As regards the mention of Galahad and Lancelot in **1533**, I find I have no special note. They are certainly not in **D. L.** and the two versions are in such habitual accord that I think I must have noted it had they differed here. Still, I think it only fair to point out my omission.

as later on we are told that twenty-five have returned, this does not seem to be a mistake for twenty-three, as we might otherwise think. **1533** does not give the original number as thirty-two, but agrees with **D. L.** as to those who return, which confirms this supposition.

In all that relates to Perceval and his first appearance at court, **D. L.** and **1533** agree on the whole with **S.** rather than with **M.**, but neither of them give any names of Perceval's brothers (save Agloval, who fetches him from his home), nor say how many there were. Lamorak is never mentioned (I believe this character belongs to quite a late redaction). In this and in the reference to Gawain's having slain Perceval's father, I think we have the influence of the *Tristan*.

In the account of Perceval's being driven from court by the mockery of Kay and Mordred, **D. L.** has a remark which again shows the influence of an earlier tradition: Perceval is described as '*Eene harde jonge creature, ende die wel simpel sceen te dien.*' Nowhere else is there any sign of the simplicity which is a primitive trait of Perceval's character. Later on, after the 'Patrides' adventure (which appears to be differently related from **S.** as it is from **M.**, Patrides and the lady having fled together, been overtaken, and imprisoned), both **1533** and **D. L.** agree in the words spoken by Patrides (**D. L.**) or the king (**1533**), *i.e.* that Kay and Mordred have driven from court one who should be a better knight *than all save Gawain*.

> '*Ghi hebt entrouwen, dat secgic u,*
> *Uter herbergen verdreven nu*
> *Den besten ridder dier in was*
> *Sonder Walewein sijt seker das.*'—ll. 36247-50.

(**1533** says 'When he is grown to manhood' he shall

be as good, etc.) This certainly points to an earlier stage of tradition, when Perceval and Gawain are the leading knights and Lancelot subordinate to both.

In view of what we now know, I think it is not an unreasonable hypothesis that these two versions, which agree so closely, represent an earlier pseudo-Borron *Lancelot-Perceval* redaction, which has been worked over in the interest of the later pseudo-Map *Galahad* version.[1]

Book XII. **M.** gives the account of Lancelot's frenzy and subsequent cure. Here **D. L.** agrees with **M.** in saying that Lancelot strikes the shield as if x. knights did it, whereas both **S.** and **1533** give XII. Later on **D. L.** is alone against the other three in saying that Lancelot has only his ankles fettered, whereas the other three versions give ankles and wrists. Nevertheless here I think **D. L.** is right, as when Lancelot rushes after the boar both **S.** and **1533** agree in saying that he breaks the rings on his ankles, and make no mention of those on the wrist. Again **D. L.** makes no mention of hunters, the horse Lancelot takes he finds tied at the castle gate. As later on, when he comes up with the quarry no hunters are mentioned in any version, I think it probable that they were not in the original, but introduced later by some copyist to account for the boar.

At this point **D. L.** departs abruptly from the other versions, taking up the Perceval story. It is impossible to say whether this be due to a *lacuna* in the source, which

[1] On p. 200 of the *Studies* there is a mistake. Dr. Sommer speaks of the fight between *Bors* and Perceval and their healing by the Grail. It should, of course, be *Hector*, not *Bors*. We may note here that in this instance the Grail is stated to be the dish out of which Our Lord ate the Paschal lamb in the house of Simon the Leper; there is no mention of its containing the Blood of Christ, or of its being borne by a maiden as in **M.**

the compiler filled up as he pleased, or whether this really represents an important (and apparently lost) *Lancelot* redaction. In the remainder of the incidents represented by this book **1533** agrees on the whole with **S.**, with this important difference, that it makes it quite clear throughout that there is a period of some years involved. The reader quite understands all the details of Galahad's arrival at the abbey, his age, etc. Very probably the compiler of **1513** (Dr. Sommer's source) condensed here, as elsewhere, thus causing the confusion noted on p. 205 of the *Studies*.

CHAPTER X

THE QUESTE VERSIONS

WE now reach a very important point in our investigation. The *Lancelot* section of Malory is not only so much condensed, but also so fragmentary in character, and, apparently, so capricious in choice of incident that a critical comparison between the version there offered and other forms of the *Lancelot* story can never be productive of a completely satisfactory result. It is one of those cases in which we must be content with probability, and renounce the hope of arriving at certainty. We have evidence enough to enable us to form an hypothesis as to the *original* character of the MS. used by Malory; of its actual condition, whether complete or incomplete, and, if the former, of the reasons which determined the compiler in his choice of incident, we cannot yet speak positively. I doubt if we shall ever be able to do so.

But with the *Queste* section it is different. As I remarked before, this part of the *Lancelot* cycle is far more homogeneous in structure than the sections preceding or following it: it is a romance within a romance, complete and rounded off in itself. Malory appears to have felt this; he condenses still, it is true, but it is condensation, not omission; he follows the sequence of incident accurately, begins with the beginning, ends with the end, consequently we are in a far better position for comparing his version with that of the other texts, and can hope to arrive at a really satisfactory result.

The first noticeable variant is in the passage 'for of a more worthyer mans hande may he not receive the order of knyghthode,' words spoken by the abbess to Lancelot. These are not in **Q.** but are in **D. L.**:

> '*Ende ic soude gerne sien dathi*
> *Van uwer hant ridder werde, wildi;*
> *Bedie van beteren man, sonder waen,*
> *En mocht i ridderscap niet ontfaen.*'—Book III. 61-64.

Also in **1533**: 'car de plus preudhomme que de vous ne pourrait il recevoir l'ordre de chevalerie sicomme il nous est advis,' vol. iii. fo. 67. Here then **M., D. L.** and **1533** agree together against **Q. W.** has 'for we think that a better than he could not receive that dignity,' thus referring the phrase to Galahad—a probable misreading of the original French.

In the account of the arming of Galahad, omitted in **M., Q.** and **D. L.** agree in saying that *Lancelot* buckles on one spur, *Bohort* the other, whereas **1533** gives *Lionel* and *Bohort*. This latter is, I think, the right version, otherwise Lionel, though present, would have no share in the ceremony. **W.** also omits Lionel, and makes Bohort only bestow a kiss on the youth, Lancelot buckling on the spur, in this case one only.

In the adventure of the sword in the stone we again find **M., D. L.** and **1533** in accord against **Q.** All three relate that Gawain attempts to draw the sword and fails. This must be correct, as **Q.**, though not saying that he makes the attempt, represents Arthur as telling him to *laissies ester* the moment he touches the hilt, words which both **D. L.** and **1533** place in Arthur's mouth after the attempt:

> '*Nu laet staen
> Gi hebet wel min bevelen gedaen.*'—ll. 231-2.

This latter phrase is evidently represented by **M.**: 'I thanke yow faid the kynge to fyre Gawayne /' **W.** records Gawain's (Gwalchmei's) attempt, but not the king's speech.

According to **1533** no other knight makes the attempt. **D. L.** records Perceval's failure, and says that after that none would essay the venture.

> '*Soe datmen vord daer niemanne vant,
> Die daer an wilde doen die hant.*'—ll. 255-56.

I suspect that **M.**, 'Thenne were there *moo* that durfte be foo hardy to fette theire handes thereto /,' should be corrected by the substitution or insertion of a negative (*no* before *moo* or *none*), it would read more coherently. **W.** relates no attempt after Perceval, but does not say definitely that no one essays the feat.

The result here is clearly, **M.**, **D. L.**, **1533** against **Q.**, with special agreement of **M.** and **D. L.**, **1533** and **W.**[1]

In the case of Galahad's message to his relations at Corbenic, every one of the versions gives a different rendering.

M. My graunt sir Kynge Pelles / and my lord Petchere / (a manifest error).

---

[1] There is no mention of Balyn's sword: this is clearly an interpolation of **M.**

Q. Mon oncle le roi Pelles / mon aioul le riche pescheoure.

D. L. Min here den Coninc Pelles—enten Coninc Vischere min ouder vader.

1533. Mon oncle le roy pescheur—et mon aieul le roi Pelles.

The greeting is omitted in **W.**

It is difficult to know what to make of such confusion, but of the four variants I prefer the last as possessing a certain *raison d'être*. The Fisher King was certainly the uncle of the original Grail Winner, and King Pelles is as certainly the grandfather of Galahad. It looks to me as if the compiler of this version had made an effort to combine the Perceval and Galahad stories, though his version as it stands is in contradiction to his text.[1]

D. L. text should be noted as compared with the

[1] This passage throws into strong relief the absolute unreality of the Galahad *Queste*. The hero knows all about the Grail, its keeper, where it is to be found, his own relation to it. He has grown up under its shadow as it were. Nor need he fulfil any test to gain it: in all the records of his adventures there is no temptation such as that undergone by Perceval or Bohort; he is as fit to become keeper of the Grail (for this and not Grail-*King* he practically becomes) when he leaves Arthur's court as when he finally, after a series of aimless adventures, arrives at Corbenic. Contrast this with the earlier versions: the hero knows nothing of the Grail; not till after he has beheld the Talisman and failed to accomplish the necessary test does he even hear the name; when he would make amends for his negligence he can no longer find the castle, and not till he has proved himself worthy through long-continued trial is the opportunity once lost again offered to him. Neither do the inhabitants of the Grail Castle know their deliverer; they hope that it may be he, since they believe none other might find the way, but they do not know him, whereas Galahad is well known to the dwellers in Corbenic.

statement of the earlier section, that the Maimed King and Fisher King are one, and that the personage thus named is *not* King Pelles but his father. The manifest uncertainty of the Galahad *Queste* as to the identity of this personage, and his relationship to the Grail Winner, as compared with the much clearer statements of the early Perceval story appear to me a proof of the lateness of the former. As to which of the four versions given represents the real view of the author of the *Queste*, I should not like to hazard an opinion—probably copyists altered according to their own particular view of the matter!

After the appearance of the Grail there is an interesting passage, omitted in **M.**, where Gawain remarks that each has been served with whatever food or drink he desired, which had never happened before save in the court of the *roi mehaignet* (**Q.**); *roi Perles* (**1533**, which generally adopts this spelling), *coninc Vischer* (**D. L.**). Here **Q.** stops, but **D. L.** and **1533** continue Gawain's speech, *nom-pourtant ils ne peuvent onques veoir le sainct vaisseau ainsi comme nous l'avons veu, ainsi leur a este la semblance couverte* (vol. iii. fo. 69). *Maer si waren bedrogen in dien, Dat sijt niet oppenbare mochten sien* (687-8). Nevertheless, since he has not seen it as clearly as he might, he will go in quest till it be wholly revealed to him.' I think the above passage is the source of **M.** '/ one thynge begyled vs we myght not fee the holy Grayle / it was foo precyoufly couered /.' The compiler omits, as I said above, Gawain's reference to the previous appearance, but adapts the latter part of his speech to the circumstances he is narrating. **W.** gives the passage practically in its entirety, but so freely rendered that we cannot use it for textual comparison. The king is called King Peleur.

Here again I think we may postulate an agreement between **M.**, **D. L.**, **1533** and **W.** in a feature omitted by **Q.**[1]

D. L. is alone against the other three in not giving the owner of the castle 'Vagan' the same name as his castle, but simply says: 'Nu was een goet man te Vagan' (l. 1146), which I suspect is the right version. **W.**, on the contrary, does not name the castle, but says it belonged to *Bagan*, 'a good and religious man.'

In the account of the adventure with the shield, both **D. L.** and **1533** give Galahad's remarks to his companions more fully than do **Q.** or **M.**, though the general bearing of the passage is well represented in this latter. In both the first Galahad tells his companions that if they fail in the adventure then he will attempt it; **1533**, 'et se vous ne le pouez emporter ie l'emporteray, aussi n'ay ie point d'escu'; they then offer to leave him the adventure, but he tells them they must essay it first. **D. L.**:

' Elst nu dat gi falgiert daer an,
Ic sal daventure proven dan—
In' brachte genen scilt met mi.'—ll. 1244-54.

With this **W.** agrees.

Here, again, **D. L.**, **1533**, and **W.** give a much clearer text than **Q.**; and **M.**, though condensing, agrees closely in substance with the two first.[2]

---

[1] Dr. Sommer's description of the swearing of the questers, on p. 210 of the *Studies*, is utterly wrong. In every version Arthur calls on Gawain to swear first, when Baudemagus interposes, saying that he who is to achieve the quest should be the first to swear. Consequently Galahad swears first, and is followed by Lancelot, Gawain, Perceval, Bohort, Lionel and Hélie le Blank. Baudemagus is in no instance the first to swear.

[2] Dr. Sommer's summary is again misleading, and entirely misrepresents the general character of the incident.

THE QUESTE VERSIONS

In the adventure with Melians de Lile, **D. L.** and **1533** again all agree against **Q.** in stating that he is son to the King of Denmark (**W.** King of Mars), thus motiving Galahad's lecture on the duties of his high station. It was certainly in **Q.**'s original, as he says: '*Puis ke vous estes— de si haute lignie comme de roy*,' though Melians has not told him his parentage.

M., D. L., 1533, and **W.** are here superior to **Q.**

In avenging Melians on the knight who has overthrown him, **M.** and **D. L.** agree in saying that Galahad smites off the whole left *arm*, as against the '*poing* senestre' of **Q.** and **1533**. **W.** says he cuts off his *nose*!

In the symbolic interpretation of Melians' adventure, **1533** gives the fullest and clearest version. The right-hand road represents the Way of Our Lord, wherein His knights 'cheminent de iour et de nuyt la nuyt selon l'arme et le iour selon le corps,' **1533** (vol. iii. fo. 74), which is intelligible. **Q.** exactly reverses this: 'entrent de jours selon l'arme, et de nuis selon le corps.' **M.** gives, 'For the way on the ryʒt hand betokeneth the hyghe way of our lord Jheſu Cryſte / and the way of a true good lyver /'; **W.**, 'On that road go the souls of the innocent,' thus evading the difficulty. **D. L.** is here very confused, and does not seem to have understood the passage.

In the adventure of the Castle of Maidens, **M., D. L.,** and **1533** again agree in saying that Galahad meets seven maidens, against one in **Q.** **M.**'s '/ Soo moche peple in the stretes that he myghte not nombre them /' is evidently a rendering of **1533**: 'tant de gens que il estoit impossible de les scavoir nombrer.' **D. L.** has exactly the same phrase, but gives '*joncfrouwen*' instead of '*gens*,' thus for once agreeing with **Q.**, which gives *puceles*, against the other two. **W.** here gives 'maidens,' but in the first instance has 'a youth.'

A little later, **1533** and **D. L.** throw light upon an apparent contradiction between **M.** and **Q.**, noted by Dr. Sommer.[1] The old man of whom Galahad inquires the meaning of the adventure is, as Dr. Sommer remarks, the same who has given him the keys; but **M.** says he asks a '*preest.*' Both **1533** and **D. L.** agree in saying that Galahad asks the old man who brought him the keys, when he comes to him the second time, if he be a priest, and is answered in the affirmative. Again, the three agree in giving seven years as the time the customs have been established, against the two in **Q. W.** here agrees in both points with **1533** and **D. L.**

It is plain that we must reckon this entire adventure among the agreements of **M., D. L., 1533,** and **W.,** though in one particular **D. L.** and **W.** agree with **Q.**

In the account of the fight of Gawayne, Gareth, and Uwayne, with the seven brethren, both **D. L.** and **1533** give Gariët (Gaheriet) as the equivalent of Gareth.[2]

When Lancelot is sleeping before the Grail chapel, **1533** clearly states that the servant of the knight who has been healed takes Lancelot's sword and helmet, as well as his horse, whereas **Q.** only mentions the horse; but says later that Lancelot finds himself 'tot desgarnis de ses armes et de son cheval.' **D. L.** also only mentions the horse at the moment, but a little later on states that Lancelot is 'sonder scilt ende helm ende part,' thus practically agreeing with **1533. M.** differs from both in

[1] *Studies*, p. 212.

[2] Cf. Dr. Sommer's remark on p. 212. I cannot recall a single instance in which the equivalents to **M.** give any other reading.

THE QUESTE VERSIONS

saying that it is *sword*, helm, and horse of which the squire deprives him. **W.** here agrees with **M.**

M. and **D. L.** agree in omitting the parallel between Lancelot and the bad servant, in the Parable of the Talents, which is given by **1533** and **W.** But it is a noticeable feature of both **D. L.** and **1533** that though they give as a rule a fuller account than **M.**, both of them shorten very considerably the improving and 'sermonising' sections which are such a feature of **Q.** On the other hand, both give the adventurous sections in a more accurate and detailed manner.

Perceval's interview with the recluse, in Book XIV., is clearer in **D. L.** than in either of the French versions, and has some special features of interest.[1] Thus in **Q.** Perceval asks, who was the knight who overthrew him. He does not know 'ne se ch'est chil qui vint en armes vermeilles a court' (*when* he does not say); the recluse answers, 'Yes,' and she will tell him the 'senefianche.' In **D. L.** the passage runs thus: Perceval asks,

> ' " *Oft gi wet wie die riddere es*
> *Dien ic soeke berecht mi des,*"
> *Si gaf hem antwerde daer of;*
> " *Hets die gene die quam int hof*
> *In sinxen dage, ende die dan*
> *Die rode wapine hadde an.*"
> " *Nu seldi mi wel berichten des,*
> *Wat betokenessen dat was?* " '—ll. 3229-36.

This seems to me a preferable rendering.

W. here hovers between the two versions. The aunt

---

[1] On p. 212, Dr. Sommer states that **Q.** does not, at this point of the story, say what becomes of Perceval. This is wrong; **Q.** distinctly says he leaves Lancelot *to return to the recluse*.

tells Perceval who Galahad is in answer to his question, as in **D. L.**, but volunteers the explanation as in **1533**.

Later on Perceval tells her:

> '*Hoe hi gevonnen hadde sijn lant,
> Ende sijn broder daer in es bleven
> Met sinen liden, mit sinen neven.
> "Dat wet ic wel," seit si saen,
> "Die heilegeest deet mi verstaen,
> Dies ic harde blide was."*'—ll. 3442-47.

There is no parallel to this in the other versions, but it agrees with what we find in *Morien*; and I think it probable that the Dutch compiler, who seems to have been very familiar with the *Perceval* story, may have introduced it.[1]

The castle at which Perceval is to seek a kinsman is not named in **D. L.**, but **M.** Goothe, **W.** Goth, and **1533** Got, agree against **Q.** there.

In Perceval's adventure with the Fiend Horse, the text of **1533** is again preferable, being clear and detailed throughout, *e.g.* whereas when the lady asks Perceval what he does under the tree, **Q.** makes him answer, 'Qu'il ne *sent* ni bien ne mal mais s'il eust cheval il se leva d'illuec.' **1533** gives 'qu'il ne *faisoit* ne bien ne mal' mais si j'avoye ung cheval ie m'en iroye d'icy.' **W.** here agrees with **1533**.

After the fight with the dragon, **M.** tells us that Perceval 'cafte donne his fheld / *whiche was broken* / .' **Q.**, agreeing in the first part, omits this feature; but both **D. L.** and **1533** say the shield was not broken, but *burnt*: 'Der

In his summary of the conversation on p. 213, Dr. Sommer again misrepresents his text—*all* agree in saying that Perceval asks his aunt about his mother and 'parens,' not that the aunt asks Perceval!

verbernt was wech ende wede' (3886); 'Qui estoit tout brulé' (III. fo. 83). As we have previously been told that the dragon was breathing forth flame, this is manifestly correct. **W.**, describing the fight, says, 'his shield and breastplate were burnt all in front of him,' and that he 'threw the shield from him burning.' **M.**, who is condensing here, omits the fiery breath, hence, I suspect, the *broken* instead of *burnt* shield.

I think we may take this again as agreement of **M.**, **D. L.**, **W.**, and **1533** against **Q.**

The 'drois enchanteres vns multeplieres de paroles' of the French versions, with which **M.** closely agrees, is in **D. L.**:

> '*Hets een toverare sijt seker des*
> *Die can dinen van vele spraken*
> *Ende van enen worde hondert maken.*'—ll. 4294-6.

An amplification probably due to the exigencies of rhyme;[1] though as **W.** gives, 'He was a necromancer, who of one word would make twelve without ever saying a word of truth,' the original source may have had something similar.

M., **D. L.**, and **W.** again agree against **Q.** and **1533** in giving a shorter version of Perceval's prayer, and omitting all New Testament references.

The adventure of the dead hermit, in Book xv., is, again, better told in **D. L.** and **1533** than in **M.** or **Q.**

The adventure of Perceval on the rock agrees closely with that of Mordrain in the *Grand S. Graal.* There also are two ships—in one a man who encourages, in the other a woman who tempts, him. In both cases the woman accuses the man of being an enchanter; in both her ship is covered with black silk, and she departs in a tempest. Cf. Hucher, *Le S. Graal*, vol. ii. pp. 354, *et seq.*

Thus **Q.** omits to state the nature of the supposed transgression, which is clearly set forth in the other three:

> *'Maer hine es niet, donket mi,*
> *Na sire ordinen gebode,*
> *Noch na onsen herre Gode;*
> *Want hi niet heden den dach*
> *In sulken abite sterven ne mach,*
> *Hine hebbe bi enegen onmaten*
> *Sine ordine nu gelaten.'*—ll. 4780-87.

This is evidently the source of **M.**'s 'this man that is dede oughte not to be in suche clothynge as ye see hym in / for in that he brake the othe of his ordre / .' **W.** gives the same reason at greater length.

Later on **M.** seems to have had before him a reading nearer to **Q.**: in the morning, 'il trouverent sans faille le preudhomme *de vie*,' which **M.** understood as *alive*, since he says, 'he laye all that nygt tyl hit was daye in that fyre and was not dede / ,' though immediately afterwards he says that the Hermit came and found him dead. **D. L.** and **1533** say, 'Ende alse dat vier utginc si vonden Den goeden man doet tien stonden,' ll. 4915-16; 'ilz trouverent sans nulle faulte le preudhomme mort.' The miracle consisting in the fact that his garments (*e.g.* the linen shirt) were untouched by fire, so that he evidently had died from the previous ill-usage, not from the burning—a result which he had predicted. **W.**, on the contrary, says that 'when the fire was extinguished the man was as lively as he was before. And then he prayed Jesus Christ to take his soul to Him, and He received him, without injury to the shirt or himself.' The whole adventure should be carefully compared, and the superiority of these three versions will be clearly seen. The two first are,

I think, the correct version of the incident, but **W.**, though rendering freely, gives a fuller account than is often the case.

The list of Celidoine's descendants agrees in **D. L.** and **1533**, while **M.**, though varying from the other three, leans rather to these two than to **Q.** :

D. L.	1533.	M.	Q.
Marpus.	Narpus.	Nappus.	Warpus.
Nasciens.	Nasciens.	Nacyen.	Chrestiens.
Cham.	Ch'm le gros.	Hellyas le grofe.	Alain li gros.
Helyas.	Helyas.	Lyfays.	Elias.
Jonas.	Jonas.	Jonas.	Jonaaus.
Lancelot.	Lancelot.	Lancelot.	Lancelot.
Bans.	Ban.	Ban.	Ban.

I think here the second name is certainly Nasciens, and that the mysterious *Cham* of **D. L.** and **1533** (a personage whom we do not know) ought probably to be *Alain*. Such a mistake might easily be made by a copyist, if the MS. before him were not clear and he was unfamiliar with Grail traditions. I think it very likely that **M.**'s source was much the same as that of **D. L.** and **1533**, and that he dropped out *Cham*, but the comparison of the four versions is interesting. The list is omitted in **W.**

The black and white knights are treated by **D. L.** as purely visionary and symbolic, and no names are given.

The incident of the black knight, who issues from the lake and kills Lancelot's horse, differs in **1533** from the other four versions. Instead of striking the horse at once he rides past Lancelot without touching him, then returns, striking the horse *en route* and disappearing in the lake. I suspect that this is the right version; the knight is evidently a water-demon, and having his dwelling in the lake should return there.

At the commencement of Book XVI., when Gawain and Hector meet, they ask if any tidings have been heard of the principal questers. Here there are some interesting variants: **Q.** mentions Lancelot, Galahad, and Bohort, but says these *four* are the best of the questers; **D. L.** only mentions these, but says rightly these *three*; **1533** first mentions Lancelot alone, then Galahad, Perceval, and Bohort, and reckoning all together, says these *four*, and with this **M.** and **W.** agree.

There are but few interesting variants in the account of Bohort's adventures; the symbolic interpretations are, as usual, much less insisted upon, indeed **1533** gives no such explanation either of the disinherited lady, or of the 'lily and dry wood' vision, though Bohort is assured of Lionel's safety. The fight between the two brothers is also more briefly told: we do not hear that they lie long unconscious after the flame descends, but Bohort is told at once to join Perceval. Here **W.** agrees with **D. L.** and **1533**.

D. L. differs from all the other versions in naming the damsel who warns Bohort of her mistress' suicidal intention. She is called Pallada.

In Book XVII., in all concerning the mysterious ship, the text of **D. L.** and **1533** is far superior to that of **Q.** The inscription in **D. L.** runs thus:

> '*Hort man, die wils gaen hier in,*
> *Besie di wel, ende oec merc*
> *Dattu sijs geloves vol ende sterc.*
> *Want ic els niet dan gelove ben*
> *Hier bi hoede elkerlijc hem:*
> *Falgiert hem eneger maniren*
> *Van gelove, ic sal hem falgiren.*'—ll. 7910-16.

1533 says the inscription is in 'langaige dit *Caldeu*,' and says 'si tost q tu guerpiras ta creance ie te guerpiray en telle maniere que tu ne auras de moi ne conseil ne ayde,' and proceeds to explain (which no other text I have consulted does) that if he who enters fail in faith he will fall into the water. This should be compared with the passage in Hucher,[1] where the inscription on the ship agrees closely and is also said to be in Caldiu. The warning as to the nature of the penalty is omitted here, but the penalty is incurred exactly as 1533 foretells.

M. evidently had the warning of **D. L.** and **1533** before him when he wrote 'for and thou faile I shal not helpe the /.' **W.** gives the warning in more general terms, due perhaps to the translator.

Perceval's speech on entering the ship is again best given by **1533**. Here, he says, he will enter 'pour ce que se ie suis desloyal que ie y perisse comme desloyal, et se ie suis plain de foy et tel comme bon chevalier doit estre que ie soye sauvé,' *i.e.* he submits to the test in all humility. **Q.** says: 'Car iou sui plain de foi et teus comme chivalers doit estre,' thus omitting the qualifying phrases, and giving the speech quite a different meaning. **W.** closely agrees with **Q**. **D. L.** also, though less abrupt, practically agrees with **Q.**; while **M.** must have had the version of **1533** before him: 'for yf I be a nys creature or an untrue knyghte there shalle I perysshe'—a reading he could not possibly have derived from either of the other two.

In the account of the scabbard of the sword we have a most interesting variety of readings, but, comparing one with the other, it appears certain that here again **1533** is in the right.

One side of the scabbard is said by **D. L., 1533** and

[1] *S. Graal*, ii. p. 444.

M. to be red as blood, with an inscription in letters black as a coal; while **Q.** says the scabbard is 'black as pitch'—an evident confusion with the inscription. **W.** says the sheath is 'rose-red,' with letters of gold and silver.

The name is given differently in each instance: **Q.**, memoire de *sens*; **D. L.**, Gedinkenesse van *sinne*; **M.**, meuer of *blood*; **1533**, memoire de *sang*. **D. L.** and **1533** go on to say that 'none shall look upon that part of the scabbard which is made of the Tree of Life but they shall be reminded of the blood of Abel.' **M.** omits the latter part of this sentence, thus making great confusion.

Now, comparing these versions together, the right reading becomes perfectly clear. The scabbard is red, for it was made (at least one half of it was) of the wood of the Tree of Life, which, as we are distinctly told, turned red at the death of Abel; and the inscription '*memoire de sang*' was intended to keep this event in mind. The confusion, in the case of **Q.** and **D. L.**, clearly arose from the MS. at the root of the first having had the reading san*s* for san*c* or san*g* (a reading often met with); a careless copyist, heedless of the sense of his transcription, wrote *sens* and this was correctly translated by the compiler of **D. L.** as *sinne*; a reading which, however unintelligible in itself, would probably not strike the compiler (who was certainly an intelligent writer with a very good knowledge of French) as absolute nonsense, inasmuch as it was connected with the 'calling to mind' of the death of Abel. **Q.**, who omits this qualifying passage, does make nonsense of it. In **M.**'s case the mistake was in the first word, and probably arose from a confusion between *m* and *uv*, which may very well be due to Caxton; otherwise **M.** appears to have had the same version as **1533**, which, alone, has preserved it free from error. **W.** omits the inscription altogether.

The 'erle Hernox' in **M.**, Ernous in **Q.**, is in **D. L.** and **1533** Arnou*t* and Arnou*l*. Ernoulf in **W.**

Both **D. L.** and **1533** state that the maiden who shall cure the lady by her blood must be not only a virgin and a king's daughter but *Perceval's sister.* This is neither in **Q.** nor in **M.**, and may perhaps indicate that, as I have suggested, these two versions belonged to an original *Perceval-Lancelot* redaction, from which they introduced occasional additions to Perceval's share of the *Queste*, as in the previous allusion to his having recovered his kingdom in **D. L.**[1]

In the account of Lancelot's visit to Corbenic, after being struck down at the sight of the Grail, **Q.** says he is discovered seated (seant) before the door, while the other three all represent him as lying (lyinge—licgende—gisant), which is certainly more in harmony with the general situation. **D. L.** says that when Lancelot recovers and knows he has lain unconscious fourteen days he bethinks him:

> '*Hoe hi hadde gedient den viant*
> *.xiiij. jaer, ende pensede te hant,*
> *Dat hem onse here daerti dede*
> *Die macht verlisen in sine lede*
> *.xiiij. dage.*'—ll. 9919-23.

Whereas **Q.** only says 'qu'il avoit servi l'anemi.' A meaningless phrase, as it stands. **M.** agrees with **D. L.**

[1] As I said before, this *may* be due to the influence of *Morien*, but we must not overlook the fact that this poem certainly has some curious points of contact with the *Parzival* of Wolfram von Eschenbach, which also knows of the hero (or more accurately here, his son) regaining his kingdom, which he also does in *Perceval li Gallois.*

with the exception that he says *twenty-four* instead of *fourteen*, in which he is certainly correct, as Lancelot's *liaison* with Guinevere had begun long before the birth of Galahad. The number may have been altered by the compiler of **D. L.** for the exigencies of the rhyme, which would not admit the original form. **1533** omits the passage altogether, condensing considerably at this point.[1] **W.** does not specify whether he were lying or seated, but agrees with **D. L.** in giving fourteen years, which rather looks as if that number may have been in the source of this latter.

In the account of the questers at Castle Corbenic **D. L.** and **1533** alike clear up a passage which, as it stands, is obscure in **M.** and utterly unintelligible in **Q.** Nine stranger knights arrive at the castle,[2] three being of Gaul, three of Ireland, and three of Denmark. When they separate the next day, **Q.** has this unintelligible passage —Galahad has asked the strangers' names—'et tant qu'il trouuerent estrois de gariles, que claudins li fieus le roi claudas, en ert li uns et li autre de quel terre qu'il fuissent, erent asses gentile homme et de haut lignage.'[3] **M.**

[1] The scribe of the original MS. may have had to condense on account of space here, which is contrary to the usual practice of **1533**; but in a printed edition it is not easy to decide the real value and significance of such omissions.

[2] **1533** *ten*, representing the number as thirteen, Galahad taking the place of Our Lord. This is a point on which we might expect to find different readings, according as the compiler held, or did *not* hold, Judas to have been present at the Institution—a question on which a difference of opinion has always existed.

[3] This is the passage to which I referred in connection with the Yvain sources, p. 76. This son of King Claudas is, no doubt, the same who played such a valiant part in the war between Lancelot and his father, related at great length in the *Lancelot*.

renders, without any mention of names being asked, 'But the thre knyghtes of Gaule, one of them hyghte Claudyne, kynge Claudas sone / and the other two were grete gentylmen' (which should surely have given Dr. Sommer a clue to the right rendering of the passage).

D. L. runs thus:

> '*Ende alsi buten den castele quamen*
> *Vragede elc oms sanders namen,*
> *Soedat si worden geware das,*
> *Dat van den drien van Gaule was*
> *Claudijn Claudas sone die een,*
> *Ende si vonden van den anderen tween*
> *Dat si waren van groter machte*
> *Ridders, ende van groten geslachte*'—ll. 10601-8.

1533 has, 'Si trouverent que des trois de Gaulle Claudius le filz au roy Claudas en estoit ung et les autres estoiet assez vaillans.' It seems clear that **M.**'s text is that of **D. L.** carelessly abridged.[1]

---

[1] This arrival of the nine knights at the Grail Castle, and their share in the Grail revelation, is a striking proof of the unreality of the Galahad *Queste* quâ *quest*, on which I have remarked elsewhere. Who are these knights? What claim have they to be admitted to a feast so holy that even King Pelles and his son are excluded? Practically they are as much achievers of the Quest as Galahad himself. The fact is the writer is so taken up with the religious symbolism of the relic that in exaggerating and insisting on symbolic details he loses sight of the real point of his story. I very much doubt whether any one but the Grail Winner himself ought to reach, or was ever contemplated as reaching, the Grail Castle, much less be witness of the full explanation of the relic. To this it may be objected that Gawain reaches it; but Gawain was certainly at one time looked upon as the Grail Winner, and I believe it is only in this character that he ever found the castle. The accessibility of Corbenic is a *very* weak point of the Galahad *Queste*.

Both **D. L.** and **1533** conclude the *Queste* section with the passage relating the death of the twenty-two (twenty-four) questers, eighteen of whom fell by the hand of Gawain; the writing out of the knights' adventures, and the preservation of the record in the abbey of Salisbury where Map found them, this latter item being omitted by **1533**. This passage is, as a rule, now found at the beginning of the *Mort Artur* section, but, I think, it is clear that its proper place is at the end of the *Queste*; as I have pointed out already, the light in which it represents Gawain is entirely in keeping with that romance, while it does not agree with either the *Mort Artur* or the *Lancelot*, both of which regard Arthur's gallant nephew with genuine respect. Further, the drawing up of a record of adventures is better placed at the end of the section dealing with the adventures to be recorded than at the beginning of another. **M.**'s words, 'alle this was made in grete bookes / and put up in almeryes at Salysbury / coupled with his total omission of any corresponding passage at the commencement of the next book, seem to prove that in his source, too, it stood at the end of the *Queste*.[1]

---

[1] I cannot agree with M. Gaston Paris's suggestion that this passage, which he takes as part of the *Mort Artur*, refers to an earlier *Queste* redaction. A *Queste* giving a full account of the fate of so many of the knights engaged would be of portentous length, and there is absolutely no sign of this Galahad *Queste* having existed in another form. I regard it as a summing up, by the author, of the general results of the expedition, a *postscriptum* which enabled him to have a final fling at his *bête-noire* Gawain. The addition of Baudemagus's name may have been his work, or that of a copyist, and designed to give point to his accusation. Whether the tradition that he should be killed by Gawain arose from this passage, or was incorporated in the *Merlin* from

THE QUESTE VERSIONS

What now are the results we may deduce from this examination of four versions of the Galahad *Queste*? First, I think it is clear that the verse translation in **D. L.** and the prose **1533** both offer a text very decidedly superior to that edited by Dr. Furnivall, and, if Dr. Sommer's extracts are to be relied on, that represented by the majority of the printed editions of the *Lancelot*. Second, it is equally clear that the text used by Malory stood in close relation to these two versions. Many variants attributed by Dr. Sommer to the English compiler, are, it is now certain, due to his source, in the treatment of which he shows little sign of intelligence or invention, but rather a tendency to compression at all hazards, sometimes omitting the very part of a phrase which was required to make the whole intelligible. The general tendency of our examination, therefore, goes to establish the practical agreement of **D. L., 1533** and **M.**, as against **Q.** and **S.** The version given by **W.** is so free a rendering, and omits so many details, that it is scarcely possible to place it. It seems clear that the *original* source must have belonged to the same MS. family as the former three, but whether the

another source we cannot say. The Baudemagus tradition demands study. In the *Merlin* he is represented as but six years older than Gawain, whose dearest friend he is, but in the *Charrette* he appears as quite an old man, whose son, Meleagant, is the contemporary of Gawain and Lancelot; while in the prose *Lancelot* and *Queste* he appears as the devoted friend of the family of King Ban, sharing the adventures of these young knights on an equal footing. The whole presentment is hopelessly confused. The frequent reference to the Arthurian records, as kept in the 'almeryes' at Salisbury, appears to me to be a parallel case to the allusions in the Charlemagne Romances to the records at S. Denys. I suspect there is as much, or as little, truth in the one ascription as in the other.

agreement was with **1533**, rather than with **D. L.** and **M.**, or *vice versa*, it is impossible to say.

But how do these three stand as regards each other? On the whole **1533** appears to represent the better text, and it also appears to have preserved signs of an earlier redaction, yet I do not think it is the direct source of the other two. We often find **D. L.** and **M.** agreeing in details of numbers and names, as against the other version; certainly in the case of such a name as Brimol van Pleîche, Bromel la Pleche, the agreement must be due to a French source common to both. I should be inclined to postulate some such scheme as this.

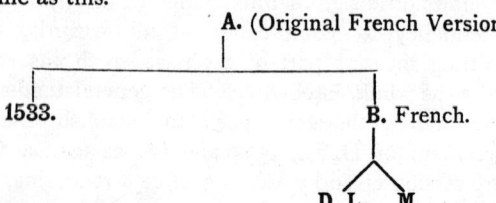

As will be seen from the summary of **D. L.** appended to these studies, both this version and **M.** show, in the *Lancelot* section, a certain *plus* of incident as against **1533**, though these incidents vary in each case. The relation cannot, therefore, be exactly determined, but I think there can be no reasonable doubt that for the *Lancelot-Queste* section of his compilation Malory used an *Agravain-Queste* MS.

That he had *two* MSS., one for the *Lancelot*, another for the *Queste*, as Dr. Sommer[1] suggests, is highly unlikely. It

---

[1] Cf. *Studies*, p. 214. Dr. Sommer uses as an argument for this the difference of spelling in the name of *Corbenic*, but this proves nothing. **D. L.** has at least four ways of spelling this word, and some-

THE QUESTE VERSIONS

would be too curious a chance that he should in each case hit on a version so closely corresponding to that of the two with which we have compared his reading.

This appears to me practically to dispose of the argument, that Malory had before him a number of episodic romances, an argument often brought forward;[1] the 'Turquine' episode in Book VI., the whole of Book VII., and the adventure with the damsel of Escalot being instances in point. Turquine certainly came out of the *Lancelot*, as did the lady of Escalot; Book VII. may have been an episodic romance, as also the handling of Urre of Hungary; though this latter, as we shall see, may equally well be an amplification of an adventure found in the prose *Lancelot*.[2]

Again, it very greatly limits the probability of Malory's having elsewhere worked with a free hand, inventing and rearranging, when we find, as we have done, that numerous small details, hitherto ascribed to him, are faithful reproductions of his source. We are justified in cherishing very serious doubts as to the originality of any marked deviation from the traditional version of an adventure which we may find in his compilation.

These arguments, of course, apply most strongly to his

times a variant occurs in the space of a few lines. The general character of the name is always preserved, and in MSS. that have been frequently copied, to say nothing of printed, the substitution of one letter for another is too frequent to call for remark.

[1] Dr. Wechssler in his *Lancelot* study announces solemnly, '*So viel aber steht für uns fest, dass Malorys Quelle für sein sechstes Buch nicht die Branche eines Cyklus, sondern ein selbständiges Originalwerk gewesen ist*' (*Gral-Lancelot*, p. 35). But we now see it was beyond any doubt part of a cyclic work.

[2] Cf. Appendix, p. 237.

version of the *Charrette* adventure, the problem of source of which, so far as Malory is concerned, is absolutely unaffected by the evidence we have collected. This alone is certain, there is *no proof whatever* that he knew anything of the first part of the *Lancelot* romance, his treatment of the Lady of the Lake seems to show that he was absolutely ignorant of it. He was *not* in the habit of departing unnecessarily from his source, his variations as a rule are slight, and their motive can generally be detected; when, therefore, we find him giving an entirely different account of the abduction of Guinevere from that given elsewhere, the probabilities are all in favour of his reproducing a separate source, and all against his original invention. So far as the matter stands in the light of the latest evidence, the question remains unsolved, with a decided balance in favour of the theory advanced by M. Gaston Paris, and against that advocated by Professor Foerster.[1]

Leaving the question of Malory, what may we hold to be the result of this examination on the problem of the *Queste* itself? Is the form in which we possess it practically the original form, or are we to postulate a series of successive redactions? I think that every one who has carefully

[1] I take this opportunity of strongly protesting against the tone assumed by Professor Foerster on the question of Malory. He has not himself examined the question of the sources, but has simply accepted all Dr. Sommer's far too hasty and inadequately founded conclusions. When he says, on p. lxv. of the *Charrette*, '*Der überall seine Quellen und zwar nur seine Quellen und obendrein noch treu wiedergebende Malory ist ein Phantasiegeschöpf der Walliser und Engländer*,' he is simply dogmatising in an unwarrantable manner on a question with regard to which he has no *locus standi*. Exaggerated as the statement is, and is meant to be, it is infinitely nearer the truth than are many of Professor Foerster's own hypotheses.

studied the variants given above must have been struck by the fact that in no case is the question one involving a variety of incident or even an alteration in sequence. It is the same story in every case, told in the same order, in the same words, only certain copies give a fuller and more coherent version than others. In fact, as I said above, the variations are the variations of the copyist, not of the compiler. The one point in which we may postulate either omission or addition, *i.e.* the greater or less fulness, the presence or absence, of the 'improving' sections, is precisely a point in which we might expect a copyist of a more or less didactic turn of mind to assert himself; it was so easy to expand or to contract such passages. And it is a curious feature that precisely in those versions in which the *story*, as a whole, is the best told (**D. L., 1533,** and in a minor degree **M.**), we find the edifying passages in their shortest forms; while **Q.**, the text of which as compared with the others is decidedly poor, gives them at the greatest length.

Of any previous redaction of Galahad's adventures there is no trace; there are no lengthy interpolations as in the *Conte del Graal* MSS.; there is no conflict, such as we find in other romances, between an earlier and later form; in sundry passages we have allusions to unrelated adventures: we are told that the heroes ride so many days, weeks, or years, and meet with many and strange adventures, but in no copy do we find any hint of what these adventures may have been; yet had there existed an earlier and fuller form, some fragments of it must surely have been preserved.

And this argument becomes more convincing the more closely we look into it. Above we have compared *four* versions of the *Queste* (*five* if we include **W.**), but one of these, Dr. Furnivall's edition, does not represent one MS. only, but is founded on a critical collation of two, and contains a specimen of the opening columns of twelve MSS. of the *Bibliothèque Nationale*; while Dr. Sommer states that he has examined four other versions and found that, saving details of style, all agree in incident and sequence. We may therefore take it as certain that one of the four variants represents at least *five* MSS., while scholars of standing assure us of the practical identity of sixteen more!

Now, side by side with these *Queste* versions, we have compared four versions of the prose *Lancelot*, and of these four no two agree perfectly throughout, and all differ from the summary given by M. Paulin Paris.

D. L. and **1533**, which on the whole correspond well with each other, yet have their distinctive differences, *i.e.* **D. L.** contains adventures not related by **1533**; **M.**, while on one side condensing arbitrarily, on the other gives two adventures known to neither of the first; and **S.** omits an important section altogether. The summary in *Romans de la Table Ronde*, while agreeing on the whole with the two first, deviates from both in the later sections.[1]

The practical identity of *all* the versions of a romance transmitted in so large a number of MSS. as the *Queste* is, I believe, unique in the Arthurian cycle. Such a phenomenon, for it is nothing less, can, I think, only be explained in one way: there was but one version of the story, and that version took shape, *not* at a period when *oral* transmission was the rule, but at a later date, when the story could at once find expression in literary form. I do not believe that any story, the earlier stages of which were developed

[1] Cf. Appendix, p. 241.

THE QUESTE VERSIONS

orally, is ever, when committed to writing, found so entirely free from variants.[1]

Can we decide what special form of the Perceval *Queste* the Galahad variant was intended to supersede? I think not: it is noticeable that the writer never gives any adventure which finds an exact parallel in the older romances, yet he not only knew the Perceval story, but knew it in various forms. The allusions in Book XIV., though slight, are remarkably instructive: he knew that Perceval was the son of a widow, and that his mother died of grief at his departure (Chrétien, Wolfram, Didot *Perceval*); that in his wanderings in search of the Grail he came to the dwelling of a female recluse, who proved to be a near relative (only related by Wolfram); that he has a sister (Didot *Perceval*, and *Perceval li Gallois*). Thus in these few allusions he is in touch with the whole cycle of Perceval romance! When, therefore, we find that he never elsewhere assigns to Perceval any of the adventures traditionally connected with him, but gives him a new series which are duplicated elsewhere, one can only conclude that it is done of set purpose.

Of the parallels given above, the existence of the sister appears to me to be the most important, judging from the prominence of the rôle here assigned to her. She only appears in the two forms of the Perceval *Queste* which show traces of having formed part of a cycle; and inasmuch as *Perceval li Gallois* represents the mother as living to see her

[1] The passage quoted by Dr. Wechssler (*Gral-Lancelot*, p. 60, *et seq.*), and which he considers belongs to an earlier version of the *Queste*, is manifestly only a condensed variant of the ordinary *Queste* into which an allusion to Tristan and Pallamedes has been clumsily introduced.

son return, and regain his kingdom, the correspondence is closer with the Didot *Perceval*, but the question can hardly be settled.

As a *Grail* romance the *Queste* is extremely poor. The utter confusion of the writer as to the identity of the Fisher King and Maimed King; the inter-relation of Grail Winner, owner of Grail Castle, Fisher King and Maimed King; the neglect of the most obvious conditions of the quest, such as ignorance on the part of the predestined Grail Winner; his giving proof of identity by fulfilment of a test; the inaccessibility of the Grail castle to all but the elect knight—all show a most extraordinary carelessness on his part, were he intending to write a Grail romance pure and simple. Ignorance we cannot postulate. He knows too much about Perceval not to know more about the Grail! It is evident throughout that the main anxiety of the author is to keep himself in touch with the *Lancelot* rather than with the *Grail* tradition. He is extremely careful to introduce references to that portion of the *Lancelot* story with which he is familiar; to explain that the adventures foreshadowed in *Grand S. Gaal* and *Lancelot* have been really fulfilled, and so long as he can demonstrate his hero to be a worthy upholder of the glories of the race of King Ban, he cares very little if he fails to fulfil the necessary conditions of the original Grail Winner. This latter may know from the first what the Grail is, where it is, his own predestined relation to it, his final winning it may be reduced to an absurdity by the presence of eleven or twelve others all equally worthy of beholding the sacred talisman, but that matters nothing to the author; he has contrived to bring the Grail into more or less harmony with the *Lancelot* legend; he has crowned the most popular of Arthur's knights with reflected glory as father of the Grail Winner, he has put the last touch to the evolution of the *Lancelot* legend, and in so doing he has achieved the task which he set himself to perform. The *Queste* is in all essential features not a *Grail* but a *Lancelot* romance, and as such primarily it should be judged.

CHAPTER XI

THE MORT ARTUR

This, the final section of the *Lancelot* cycle, offers less opportunity for criticism. The versions of **D. L.** and **1533**, though still closely in accord with each other, differ much less from the summary given by Dr. Sommer, and show less affinity with Malory.[1]

So far as Malory is concerned I differ from Dr. Sommer, who says that 'he cannot have derived his account from the prose *Lancelot*.'[2] On the contrary I think there is little doubt that Malory had the latter portion of the *Lancelot* before him, but dislocated it by the introduction of the *Charrette* and *Urre of Hungary*[3] episodes, which he most probably knew in an independent form; though of course, as I have suggested above, it is quite possible that some *Lancelot* MSS. may have included the latter. But considering the clear proof that the English compiler

---

[1] This seems to point to the fact that the *Agravain* section of the *Lancelot* is that which offers the most important variants, and is the most likely to reward the careful critic. The final section is practically based upon a romance foreign to the original *Lancelot* story, and which has been incorporated into it; consequently we may expect to find all the versions in pretty general agreement as regards the *Mort Artur* proper.

[2] Cf. *Studies*, p. 220.   [3] Cf. Appendix, p. 237.

was following an *Agravain* MS. for the earlier part of his *Lancelot* adventures, and that he includes the Astolat and Patryse stories, which are a part of the ordinary *Mort Artur*[1] section, I see no reason to doubt that his *Lancelot* MS. represented *all* the latter part of the cycle (as we know he had, and followed, an alternative version of the **M. A.** proper). I have carefully compared both **D. L.** and **1533** with the abstract given in the *Studies*, and give the following as the most important of the variants, but I should like to make it clearly understood, both as regards this and the previous sections, that the instances I quote by no means represent *all* the points of contact and departure to be noted between the different versions. I have many others in my notes, and a critical edition will certainly very much strengthen the case I have here stated in outline.

As we have before noted, **D. L.** and **1533** agree against **S.** in incorporating with the *Queste* the passage generally given as the opening of **M. A.** Otherwise all three versions are in practical agreement as regards the events leading up to the tournament at Winchester. **D. L.** does not mention Hector when Lancelot inquires on which side his kinsmen are fighting, but only Bohort and Lionel. **1533** agrees here with **S.**

According to **D. L.** and **1533** Gawain and Gaheriet take no part in the fighting at Arthur's desire: he fears they may fight with Lancelot, and ill-will arise from it. **S.** does not mention this, so I cannot say if it be in the **1513** edition or not.

S. says, 'The people think the two knights' (Lancelot and his comrade) 'cannot be the sons of the lord of the

[1] Referred to in future as **M. A.**

castle of Escalot.' This does not agree with the other versions: the people think they *are* the lord's sons at first; then *Gawain* says, one of them cannot be. **D. L.**:

> '*Ende man waende daer wel dat Lanceloet
> Ware een vanden broderen van Scaerloet.*'—ll. 851-2.

and Gawain proceeds to say, 'This knight with the red sleeve is not he whom I thought, no one ever saw such valour by one of the "Kinder van Scaerloet."' Arthur asks what knight he may be. **D. L.** makes Gawain say simply he does not know, 'but he is certainly a good knight'; while **1533** goes on to add 'if Lancelot had not been left at Kamalot he would have said that this was he.' This does not at all agree with **S.**

Both **1533** and **D. L.** agree against **S.** in saying Lancelot's wounds will take six (not seven) weeks to heal.

When Gawain and Gaheriet follow Lancelot, **S.** says they meet a *wounded* knight; in **1533** the knight is dead. **D. L.** omits the incident.

When Gawain returns to Arthur, **S.** represents the king as saying 'it was not the first time he took trouble without results, nor will it be the last.' **1533** and **D. L.** here add '*through that knight*,' which is evidently correct.

S. simply says the second tourney is fixed at Tanebor, 'du lundi dapres en ung moys'; whereas the other versions carefully specify the wherabouts of this place, 'dat een casteel es, Staende in den inganc van Nortgales.' **D. L.** spells it 'Caneborch.'

Again, according to **S.**, Lancelot, unable to go to the tourney, sends greeting to the queen and Gawain, 'from the knight who wore the red sleeve'; whereas **D. L.** and **1533** say 'the knight who won the tournament at Winchester' and make no mention of the sleeve, which, considering the relations between Lancelot and Guinevere, seems to me the better version. Neither do these mention that Guinevere tries to persuade Bohort to return to Camelot.

When Gawain comes to Escalot S. represents him as admiring the maiden's beauty and envying the knight 'with the red sleeve.' **1533** says, more correctly, 'the knight who wins her love'; he has not yet learned to whom the sleeve belonged.

In the account of what happens after Gawain's return to court, and Guinevere's learning the truth, all the versions agree on the whole, and it is noticeable that **M.**, though making Bohort a more energetic defender of his cousin's good faith, yet correctly reproduces all the main features of incident and speech. I think any one comparing his version closely with two or three others can hardly fail to come to the conclusion that it is the prose *Lancelot* and no other account he is reproducing.

According to **S.** Lancelot's kinsmen only remain for a week at court; according to **1533** and **D. L.** it is 'that week and the next.'

When they leave the court on the second occasion after the tournament of Tanebor, neither **D. L.** nor **1533** say (as **S.** does) that the queen tries to persuade Bohort to remain, though they agree in making her regret his departure.

After Lancelot's return to court when Bohort lectures Guinevere on the mischief done by women, with reference to David, Solomon, etc., **D. L.** omits the reference to Tristan, while **1533** amplifies it by saying 'it is not five years since Tristan died for love of Iseult.'

D. L. omits all reference to Lancelot's being wounded in the wood, condensing considerably at this point, and gives no account of the arrival of the dead body of the maiden of Escalot.

In the account of how Lancelot learns of the queen's danger from Madoc de la porte, all three versions differ. According to S. he meets a knight from Kamalot who tells him of the queen's plight, and at once resolves to rescue her. *The next day* he meets Hector and reveals his intentions; and a few days after both meet Bohort, who asks if they know the news. **1533** says that as the first knight rides off, Hector appears from a cross-road; he is on his way to defend Guinevere.

In D. L. it is not said how Lancelot first learns the news, but he meets Hector and Bohort together, and on their asking him if he has heard, replies in the affirmative.

I suspect M. had a version akin to this last before him as he makes *Bohort* Lancelot's informant.

In the account of the final detection of Lancelot and Guinevere, S., as I have before pointed out, goes wrong, by substituting *Guerreshes* for *Gariët*. All the texts I have consulted agree in stating that it is this latter who sides with Gawain, and refuses to be a party to the betrayal.[1]

D. L. omits the fact that Arthur hears of Lancelot's victory at the tournament of Cahere; and also the remark

---

[1] As I have said before, there can be no doubt which of the two is the prototype of Gareth; also, subsequent study has shown me that, outside the *Lancelot* proper and the romances which have been modified for cyclic purposes, we rarely find any mention of Guerresches, whereas we often meet with Gariët. I am strongly of opinion that originally the two characters were one, and that in that earlier form the knight was Gaheriet or Gariët.

of Bohort that only Morgain or Agravain can have betrayed him.

In the details of the detection all three versions agree closely.

In the account of Guinevere's trial **S.** again diverges from the others. We read[1] 'Arthur decides to punish Guinevere with death. He will have her tried at once. **P. L.** introduces here, and a little later, a certain "roy Yon" who counsels moderation. The trial takes place; Arthur, with Gaheriet, Mordred, and Agravain, doom the queen to the stake.' I do not know if this accurately represents the text **1513,** it certainly differs widely from the reading of **D. L.** and **1533.**

D. L. does not mention Yon; **1533** simply introduces him as telling Arthur that the trial cannot take place that evening, while both agree in saying that *Gawain* (whom **S.** does not mention at all) warns the king not to proceed to extremities, threatening to give up all his lands if the queen be burnt. Mordred and Agravain doom the queen to death, Arthur *alone* specifies the nature of that death.[2]

In the account of the fatal fight at the stake, **D. L.** represents Lancelot as slaying both Gawain's brothers, while **1533** agrees with **S.** in saying that Bohort kills Guerresches and Lancelot Gaheriet. **M.,** it will be remembered, agrees in this with **D. L.** It may be noted that all three, **1533, D. L.,** and **M.,** while making no remark about Guerresches, especially lament Gaheriet: the

[1] *Studies*, p. 254.
[2] Throughout this section it must be borne in mind that **S.** systematically replaces the *Guerresches* of his text by *Gaheriet*. This latter sides throughout with Gawain.

two first say that Lancelot knows Gawain will never forgive him for this, and **M.** speaks of him as 'the noble knyghte,' making the identity with Gareth quite clear.

The castle at which the queen and Lancelot stay *en route* for Joyous Garde, called *Scalee* by **S.**, *Scalle* in **1533**, and *Calet* in **D. L.** does not, I think, belong to Keux the seneschal, as **S.** supposes; **D. L.** does not mention him, and **1533** speaks of '*ung Keux*,' a friend of Lancelot's, which cannot be *Kay*. Both here, and in the '*Keux* du Parc' of the Turquine adventure, I suspect that we have not a proper name at all, but a misreading of 'Queus'=*count*. In the latter instance **D. L.** renders *Keux* by *Grave*.

On p. 255, **S.** must surely have misread his source, as he says that Lancelot sends messengers to *King Ban of Benoyc*, asking his aid. King Ban was of course dead long before; **D. L.** and **1533** say to *the barons* of Benoyc, which must be the right reading

Again, the summary of the battle, **S.**, p. 256, differs very materially from **D. L.** and **1533**. **S.** says Gawain fights like a madman and kills thirty of Lancelot's men with his own hand, wounding others, Lionel among them. The next day there is another battle, in which occurs the incident of Arthur being unhorsed by Bohort, and remounted by Lancelot. Now in the other two versions Bohort and Gawain wound each other so desperately at the first onslaught that they are carried off the field half dead, and it is *Hector* who overthrows Arthur.

Later on, after the return of Guinevere, when **S.** represents *Hector* as challenging Gawain, the other two versions give *Bohort*.

After the kinsmen return to Benoyc we find **D. L.** in

apparent contradiction with the other version's. **S.** says that he makes Bohort king of Benoic and Lionel of Gannes, while he himself keeps the crown of Gaule, *because Arthur gave it to him.* **1533** seems to agree with this latter phrase, as it says, 'et pour ce que le roy Artus me donna le royaulme de Gaule ie le tiendray.[1] **D. L.** on the contrary says:

> '*Ende vanden conincrike, dat secgic u,*
> *Van Gaule sone doe ic niet nu,*
> *Ende ne houder gene tale af,*
> *Om dat mi die coninc Artur gaf;*
> *Want al haddi mi gegeven vor nu*
> *Al die werelt, dat secgic u,*
> *Ic gavese hem al weder te hant,*
> *Bedie ic ne soude en geen lant*
> *Nu ter tijt van hem willen houden.*'—ll. 7407-15.

Now in the earlier portion of **D. L.**, after the war with Claudas, we are told that Lancelot has made Bohort king of Gannes, Hector of Benoyc, and Lionel of Gaul, an arrangement which exactly agrees with that which **M.** takes from the English **M. A.** In this earlier passage Lancelot gives as reason for not taking the crown that he prefers to remain a simple knight, and **1533** represents Bohort and Hector as following his example and declining the offered kingdoms.

I think the lesson of this discrepancy is that the *Lancelot* and the **M. A.** were fundamentally independent of each other, and each contained an account of the crowning of the race of Ban. When brought into close contact this caused a contradiction of statement which **D. L.** and

[1] It is of course possible that a negative may have dropped out here.

1533 evaded each in their own way. **S.** gives no clue to what happened on the earlier occasion.

The number of knights Arthur takes with him on his last expedition agrees in **D. L.** and **M.**, sixty thousand, against forty thousand in the two French versions.[1]

In both **1533** and **D. L.**, Guinevere does not, as in **S.**, ask for a *week's* respite, but for a *day*, and Mordred himself suggests she shall have the week. *Labor*, whom **S.** calls simply 'a faithful knight,' is in both these versions a near kinsman—*neve, cousin*. **D. L.** gives as a reason for Guinevere's rejection of Mordred's offer that she suspects his true relation to Arthur. This is not in **1533**.

In the account of the fight between Lancelot and Gawain, all three versions apparently differ at the outset. Gawain will send the challenge by a squire. **S.**, squire refuses, fearing Lancelot's wrath; **1533**, refuses, fearing to bring about Gawain's death; **D. L.**, goes at once.

The issue of the fight too is different in **D. L.** and **1533**. In **S.**, Gawain receives a mortal wound in the head and retreats. In **1533**, Lancelot appeals to the king: it is vesper-tide, and a fight for treason must be concluded by nightfall. Arthur, seeing Gawain is getting the worst of the battle, stops it at once. **D. L.** apparently condenses a similar version, but makes Arthur appeal to Lancelot, who says that he will be dishonoured if he leave

---

[1] On p. 260, Dr. Sommer makes a strange mistake. We are told that Bohort fights against Ywain; to this Dr. Sommer appends a note of exclamation, and a footnote to the effect that Ywain has already been killed by Gawain, as related in the *Queste*. Of course it was not the '*Chevalier au Lion*,' but his bastard half-brother, '*Yvain li avoutres*,' who was slain on that occasion. The text of **Q.** is quite clear.

THE MORT ARTUR

his foe in possession of the field, but Arthur entreats him to do so for his sake, and Lancelot retires. Both agree in saying that Gawain is over twenty years Lancelot's senior, and is now eighty-two years old![1]

D. L. represents the war with Rome as lasting twenty years, which would make both Arthur and Gawain well over a hundred at the time of their death!

After the news of Mordred's treachery **D. L.** makes no mention of Gawain being carried in a litter on the return journey, or of his desire for Lancelot's forgiveness; nor does he warn Arthur against fighting with Mordred. This is, I suspect, due to the compiler's desire to condense, as **1533** agrees in the main with **S.** The warning against Mordred appears, however, to be fuller in the former, *e.g. Studies*, p. 265. Gawain is represented as saying briefly, 'Avoid, if possible, fighting with Mordred, for it will cause your death,' which is in **1533**, 'Car ie vous dy vrayement que se vous mourez par une homme q̄ vive vous mourrez par lui et madame la royne,' p. 154, which certainly seems to point to an earlier redaction of the **M. A.**, where Guinevere was a partner in Mordred's treason.[2]

---

[1] On p. 261, Dr. Sommer again falls into a curious error of identity. We are told that King Karados assists at the council between Arthur, Lancelot, and Gawain, when the fight is determined upon. Dr. Sommer reminds us in a note that Karados had been previously slain by Lancelot! That was, of course, the giant of that name, brother to Turquine; *this* is the famous Karados '*Brief-bras*,' sometimes regarded as Arthur's nephew. Dr. Sommer's apparent lack of familiarity with the minor characters of the Arthurian cycle is inexplicable.

[2] On p. 263 the parallel passages quoted from **M.** and the English **M. A.** make mention of *Baudemagus* as one of Lancelot's councillors, whereas at the end of the *Queste* his death at the hand of Gawain is

In the description of Arthur's death there are some interesting variants. Both **1533** and **D. L.** account for Lucan's death by the weight of Arthur's armour; it is that, and not the vehemence of the king's embrace, which really kills the sorely wounded knight.

They again differ in the details of the final scene. **S.** says 'a boat full of ladies arrives; they land, go ashore, put Arthur, his horse, and armour into the boat, and row off.' **D. L.** says they call Arthur, who rises, takes his horse and armour, and goes into the ship. **1533** says the mistress of the party is Morgain; she calls Arthur, who rises at sight of her, she takes him by the hand (which would seem to imply her landing), and bids him bring horse and arms and enter the boat, which he does. Dr. Sommer evidently regards the entire account as absurd, but I not only accept it, but regard the versions of **D. L.** and **1533**, which would merit his strictures more fully than that in which he finds such difficulty, as representing the earlier and more primitive form of the story. There is no doubt that Arthur was conceived of as living and ruling in Avalon. This account of his practically voluntary departure for the mysterious island is much more in accord with that idea than the version which represents him in the extremity of mortal weakness, and subsequently dead and buried. Arthur's tomb is *not* compatible with Arthur in Avalon, and I strongly suspect that the earlier redaction

recorded. Cf. this with my remarks on the Baudemagus legend, p. 184. I do not think this story of his death was a genuine part of the cyclic *Lancelot*, but belonged to another line of tradition known to the author of **Q.** from the Merlin *Suite*, and unintelligently quoted by him. This, which is a real discrepancy, as there is but one Baudemagus, Dr. Sommer does not remark upon!

of the **M. A.** made no mention of it; it is certainly omitted in the corresponding section of the Didot *Perceval*, which only says he departed to have his wounds healed in Avalon, and has not since been seen; but Bretons claim to have heard his horn, and seen his armour, and believe he will return.

There is a curious discrepancy in the accounts of Lancelot's death, which seems to point to two distinct versions of that event. **S.** says he died August 5th, but does not say how long he was ill. **D. L.** says he fell ill on May 15th, and died after four days. **1533** says he fell ill May 15th, was ill four days, and died August 5th! Evidently a combination by some unintelligent compiler of the two previous accounts, but it is unusual to find such an obvious *bévue* in so otherwise admirable a version as that of **1533**.

All three agree that Lancelot is buried in Galehault's tomb, and that Bohort becomes a hermit in his stead.

From the above comparison it seems clear that though offering less striking and interesting variants, the Dutch version and that of **1533** yet maintain, on the whole, their previous agreement as against **S.**; while **M.**, which here possesses an alternative source the English **M. A.**, yet occasionally betrays the same curious agreement with **D. L.** which we have noted before. The result appears to confirm the conclusion previously arrived at, that **D. L.** and **1533** represent a common French original, and that **M.**'s source, whether complete or incomplete, was a MS. belonging to the same family.

CHAPTER XII

CONCLUSION

WE have now reached the final stage of our *Lancelot* studies, and it only remains for us to gather up the threads of the previous investigation, and to endeavour to formulate the results at which we have arrived. We have seen that the *Lancelot* legend was one of remarkably speedy growth. We find no mention of the hero's name before the latter half of the twelfth century, yet within ten years of that first mention he is the most famous of Arthur's knights, and the lover of the queen.[1]

We have examined the legend (*a*) in the form of a loosely constructed biographical romance, composed of episodes originally foreign to each other; (*b*) in detached episodic poems; (*c*) in its final form as the most important member of a great prose cycle; and we have found that in all this mass of literature the only really distinctive and individual trait on which we could lay our finger was the story of the hero being stolen as a child and brought up by the mistress of a water kingdom.[2]

Into the question of the character of the Lady of the

[1] Cf. chap. i. p. 5.
[2] (*a*) chap. ii., the *Lanzelet* of Ulrich von Zatzikhoven; (*b*) chaps. iii. and iv., *Le cerf au pied blanc*, *Le Chevalier de la Charrette*; (*c*) chaps. vi., vii., and viii., the prose *Lancelot*.

Lake we have not entered deeply; we have seen that she touches on the one side the mysterious queen of the Other World, on the other the scarcely less enigmatic Morgain le Fay, King Arthur's sister. The subject was too wide in extent to be adequately treated in this series; it demands separate study, but the result, so far as the *Lancelot* legend is concerned, was to lead us to believe that the root of that legend was a *lai*, presumably Breton, dealing with the theft of a king's son by a water fairy; a theme which afterwards underwent considerable expansion, in the course of which the characters of the hero and of his patroness alike became greatly modified from the original conception.

The final and best known form of the story was mainly influenced by the introduction of a *motif* foreign to the earlier and tentative development, *i.e.* that of Lancelot's love for the wife of his lord. This *motif*, however, we saw reason to believe, did not really represent the earlier tradition of Guinevere's infidelity, but was a practically new development introduced under the dual influences of a special social condition and the high popularity of the earlier *Tristan* story. As to the reasons which determined the choice of Lancelot as the queen's lover, we found ourselves unable to express any decided opinion.[1]

But from its very earliest stages the *Lancelot* story came into contact with another and highly popular tale, the legend of *Perceval*. The earlier and later biographical forms (*Lanzelet* and the prose *Lancelot*) and the episodic romances (*Le cerf au pied blanc* and *Morien*) show traces of contact, direct or indirect, with this story; while the precise statements of certain MSS.[2] make it quite clear

[1] Cf. chap. vii., *The loves of Lancelot and Guinevere*.
[2] Cf. pp. 97, 124, 129.

that even at an advanced stage of its evolution the *Lancelot* legend formed part of a cycle of which the most important member was the story of *Perceval and the Grail*.

This continued contact with the *Perceval* story, with the resulting developments, appears to be the most important factor in the evolution of the *Lancelot* legend, and one which has hitherto been overlooked.

So far as the evidence at our disposal permits us to trace it, the course of development seems to have been the following. Gradually the legend of the *Grail*,[1] originally foreign to the *Perceval* story, completely dominated that story and changed the character of the hero, who became transformed into an ascetic celibate; while, on the other hand, the growing popularity of the *Lancelot* story had reacted prejudicially on the position alike of Perceval and the still earlier hero Gawain as knights of King Arthur's court. Eventually the two competing centres of romantic interest were *Lancelot* and the *Grail*, and it became necessary to combine them in such a manner that the latter, while still retaining its sacrosanct character, should yet contribute to heighten the fame of the popular 'secular' hero.

Such a combination was possible, under certain conditions, and an ingenious writer, perceiving this possibility, turned it to account by inventing the Galahad *Queste*, which, poor and inadequate as a *Grail* romance, yet as a contribution to the *Lancelot* cycle had a very certain and decided value. It put the final touch to the evolution of the hero by enabling him to take part, under circumstances which should vicariously increase his fame, in the great

---

[1] I do not here intend to imply any opinion as to the *original* nature of the Grail, only to refer to the undoubted fact that *as connected with Perceval* it is more or less religious in character.

CONCLUSION

adventure of the Arthurian cycle, the Grail Quest; it also restored superficially the unity of the cycle, which had been injured by the cleavage between the *Grail* and the other sections, caused by the growing popularity of Lancelot as compared with Perceval.

While Gawain and Perceval were the leading heroes of the Arthurian cycle, a Perceval *Queste* was natural; but as soon as these two were supplanted in the popular favour by Lancelot, the Perceval *Queste*, as an integral part of the cycle, became more and more inharmonious. A change in the interest of the *later* Lancelot development was inevitable, and that the change took place precisely at the psychological moment is, I think, proved by the practically universal welcome accorded to the Galahad *Queste*. With unanimous consent the Perceval *Queste* appears to have been discarded *as a part of the cycle*, although in its *independent* form it still retained its popularity.

Naturally all the branches of the cycle into which the new *Queste* had been adopted were more or less affected by it; in some cases the references to the coming Grail Winner were more or less vague, and would apply as well to the later as to the earlier hero; in other instances they were amplified but not altered, thus introducing confusion into the text (this is, I suspect, the case with the *Merlin Suite*). The romances that represented the *Early History*, as introduction to the *Queste*, were naturally the most affected, and at the present moment it is extremely difficult to decide whether the *Grand S. Graal* be a *direct* amplification of the *Joseph of Arimathea*, constructed with a view to the Galahad *Queste*, or whether, in its existing form, it depends upon an intermediate version the *données* of which would agree with the cyclic *Perceval*.

O

In any case the 'net' result was, I believe, the substitution of the name of the supposed author of the *Queste*, Walter Map, for that of the traditional author of the earlier *Perceval-Grail* story, Robert de Borron; and to ascribe to Map that cyclic redaction of the Arthurian romances which had previously been ascribed to de Borron.

I think that much of the difficulty hitherto experienced in determining the order and date of the various Grail romances has arisen from our very natural tendency to regard these romances as a group apart, and to compare them exclusively with each other; whereas they should be treated as members of the cycle, and compared with the other branches of the cycle. More especially is this the case with the Galahad *Queste*; treated as a *Grail* romance proper, it is inexplicable, and appears to represent no possible step that can be postulated in the *natural* evolution of the Grail legend. We could imagine the honour transferred from father to son (as a matter of fact it is *Lohengrin* and not Galahad who should be the successor to Perceval); but this sudden break in the tradition by which the honour passes to the race of King Ban, no relationship between Perceval and Lancelot being previously hinted at, is, considered in itself, most perplexing. On the other hand, treat the *Queste* as an integral part of the *Lancelot* cycle, and it not only explains itself, but gives us valuable assistance in 'placing' the earlier versions.

At the same time it is obvious that the theory here advanced only applies to the *later* stages of the Grail tradition; it does not touch the problem of the origin of the Grail itself, or its first connection with Perceval.

In the course of our investigation we found it necessary to devote especial attention to the work of Chrétien de

CONCLUSION

Troyes, endeavouring to ascertain the exact position which, in the evolution of the Arthurian romantic cycle, should be ascribed to this famous poet. It became clear that a very considerable portion of the matter with which he dealt belonged by its nature to the domain of what we call folk-lore; and by reason of that nature could not have been *invented* by the poet, but must have ante-dated, in some instances by many centuries, any possible *literary* rendering. Judged by the rules laid down by scientific authorities on comparative religion, and story-transmission, Chrétien could not have been an *inventor*, but only a brilliantly successful re-teller of stories long known and popular. Instead of standing at the *source* of Arthurian romantic tradition, he was swept into the current at a comparatively late period of its evolution. To solve the complex problems of Arthurian romance we must go behind Chrétien: it is the period preceding, not following, his work in which the solution of our puzzles must be sought.

To this Chrétien himself bears witness. The position claimed for him by certain modern scholars is not that which he claimed for himself; he never professed to be telling a story no one had ever heard before, though he may have flattered himself, not without reason, that he was telling it better than it had ever previously been told. He was dealing with heroes and adventures already well known to his public. The manner in which he introduces, or refers to, incidental characters makes it abundantly clear that he expected his readers to understand his allusions. Especially is this noticeable in the case of Perceval, who has been claimed, with more zeal than discretion, as one of his most famous creations. He alludes to the hero in a manner that makes it quite evident that this story was well known, and the name familiar, to the public, some decades before Chrétien himself undertook to tell it.

As practical results arising from these studies I would claim:

- *a* That we, in future, place the evolution of the *Perceval* story at a much earlier date than we have hitherto been willing to assign to it.
- *b* That we admit the possibility of very important variations in the tale, some of them being anterior to Chrétien's version.
- *c* That we recognise that this story of Perceval was of capital importance in the general evolution of the Arthurian cycle.
- *d* That in the mutual relations between the *Perceval-Grail* and *Lancelot* stories we have the key to the final shaping of the entire cycle.

These principles admitted, and I think the evidence adduced goes far to prove their soundness, it is obvious that in order to establish and appraise the above relations at their full value, we must have complete and critical editions of *all* the principal texts. As matters stand at present, the only texts which can be said to have been in any sense critically treated are the Didot *Perceval*, and the *Parzival* of Wolfram von Eschenbach for the older story, and the *Charrette* for the younger. We have been waiting for years for a critical edition of the *Conte del Graal*, and when we get it will the editor have taken into consideration the various additions to Chrétien's text, and the version of the Dutch compiler, or will it be Chrétien's portion of the poem alone? In that case it will not help us very far. We need sorely a critical edition of the curious *Perceval li Gallois*, with its blending of wild, folk-lore features with late proselytising and allegorising tendency, its baffling parallels to the German *Parzival*.

And if we are at a loss for material to adequately criticise the earlier story, what of the later? Considering the highly mythic, prehistoric character of so much of the Arthurian tradition, the disappearance of so many of the intermediate stages, and the consequent difficulty in fixing the *earliest* form of any characteristic feature, it would seem that our best plan would be to start from the *final* form assumed by the cycle and work gradually backward, since for a certain period, at least, we might hope to find solid ground beneath our feet. But the most important text for this final form of the Arthurian cycle, the prose *Lancelot*, remains unedited. And indeed it might well seem to be a work beyond the powers of any one scholar; the number alike of MSS. and of printed editions is so large; they are so scattered, no important library but can show one or more *Lancelot* texts, and we cannot afford to leave even *one* of all this mass unexamined. The great discrepancy between the printed texts which the foregoing comparison has shown us; the pregnant hints as to earlier redactions, which the passages I have quoted from M. Paulin Paris and Professor Heinzel assure us may be found in the MSS., are all indications of the vast extent of the task which confronts us.

Yet this much is certain, until it is boldly grappled with, and scholars are in possession of a complete critical edition of the *Lancelot* in which all the varying adventures shall be carefully chronicled, and all the traces of earlier redactions duly noted, any studies such as these in the preceding pages, be they the work of scholars of the very first rank, will always be liable to the necessity of revision, or the risk of subversion, by the accidental discovery of some hitherto unknown factor.[1]

This appears to me to be the great and pressing question which confronts Arthurian scholars; we desire our work to have a permanent value, yet we are leaving undone that which, to all appearance, is the surest means of securing such permanence.

A work of such magnitude can, I think, only be grappled with by a body of scholars, a chief editor, assisted by a group of sub-editors. The great extent and diffusion of the material (the *Lancelot* MSS. are, as I said before, practically scattered all over Europe), render it impossible for any one man to hope to complete the task within a reasonable term of years. I do not know what may be the principles regarding the choice of publications by the *Sociètiè des anciens textes Français*, whether their aim be the introduction to the public of MSS. of which unique copies alone exist, rather than to publish critical editions of more easily accessible texts; but if the latter should lie within their province, I cannot imagine any publication that would be more warmly welcomed by Arthurian scholars, or that would be of greater interest and more enduring benefit to the students of mediæval literature, than a full and complete edition of the prose *Lancelot*.

---

[1] Dr. Sommer's study on Malory is a case in point. It is a work of great extent, carried out with the most painstaking perseverance, yet because he omitted to consult such accessible texts as the Dutch translation and the Bodleian *Lancelot*, and assumed the general unanimity of the printed versions, a very important section of his work is largely deprived of value, and urgently requires revision.

APPENDIX

THE DUTCH LANCELOT[1]

(Opens with short introduction alluding to Meleagant, thus pre-supposing the *Charrette* adventure.)

Line 20. Eight days after Whitsuntide A., his knights, and twelve tributary kings are hunting in a forest. Guinevere and her maidens ride to see hunt escorted by Kay, Segramore, Dodinel, and Lancelot. Knight rides up and seizes queen's bridle. Her knights resent this. K., S., and D. are overthrown. L. is about to joust when maiden rides up and demands his aid, he is pledged to her. L. asks permission to fight first; overthrows and badly wounds knight, and follows maiden. Wounded knight is tended by queen's people.

Line 245. Queen sends K. after L., whom he finds fighting with two knights; K. gives him his horse; returns to queen.

Line 352. Queen is hungry. Dodinel and Segramore go to find food. Come to a pavilion with knight, he and S. fight, D. looks on. Maid on mule rides up, calls D. to go with her. Knight flies and S. is left alone.

Line 444. SEGRAMORE meets one of A's horsemen pursued by two (**1533,** *three*) knights, rescues him and overthrows knights. Comes to a pavilion; dwarf stands at door, strikes S.'s horse with stick. S. chastises him. Lady appears and reproaches

---

[1] The parallel with the edition of 1533 begins vol. ii. fo. xxxix.; with the abstract of M. Paulin Paris, vol. v. chap. cxxii. That is, somewhat earlier than the beginning of the *Agravain* section proper.

S., he is struck with her beauty. Enters pavilion and finds Calogrenant prisoner. He had come there and blown horn at maid's request, two armed knights appeared and overthrew him. S. blows horn. Red Knight appears; they fight, well-matched. A knight arrives, carries off maiden. R. K. begs truce that he may pursue them. S. will do so too. Cal. is released (**1533**, *R. K. remains to guard C.*). S. pursues ravisher, comes to hill and fair meadow, ten pavilions by a fountain. Knight with thirty companions appears and demands joust. S. overthrows him and asks news of maiden. Knight will tell him if S. will grant first request asked. Leads him to pavilion with maid and four knights. Maid will return with S.; has been brought against her will. A knight throws knife at S. who cleaves his head with sword. Others attack S., who slays first, and others fly. Rides off with maid to ten pavilions, ten knights ride out, S. must go with them to their lord or joust; chooses latter. They ask his name, he is *Segramore die Wonderlike*. Another knight appears, S. must leave maiden or joust. He is Brandalis, rejoiced to meet S., would entertain him. S. says he must return to queen who waits by 'Elfin Spring.' B. will escort maiden to her *ami*. S. rides off to house of Mathamas (his original destination), finds him and knights in hall, and demands provisions for queen. M. and his men treacherously attack S., finally overpower and throw him into dungeon, where he is wellnigh starved, but M.'s daughter takes pity upon him, and brings him food.

Line 1050. DODINEL and maid meet knight and lady richly dressed, with dwarf. D. greets dwarf, who makes no answer but tries to kiss maiden, who throws him to the ground. Knight tries to kill maiden, but is unhorsed by D. and sent prisoner to queen. He is Maroc van den Ynsen Roken, 'twixt Ireland and Scotland. (**1533**, *Marruc le roux, no island named.*[1])

---

[1] Is this perhaps the Sir Marrok of the were-wolf story?—**M.**, Book XIX. chap. ix.; also vol. iii. of *Arthurian Romances Unrepresented in Malory*.

APPENDIX 217

Line 1267. LANCELOT meets a black rider unarmed with knight's head on saddle-bow, asks L.'s name, bids him give him his armour, L. has pledged himself so to do (reference to adv. in earlier part of prose L.). L. does so. Knight is 'Griffoen van den quaden passe.' He rides thus past the Elfin Spring. Queen sees him in L.'s armour with head at saddle-bow and thinks L. is slain. Kay and other knights pursue him, and are overthrown, Kay taken prisoner. Queen and maidens remain at spring weeping.

Line 1425. LANCELOT meets maiden, who hails him as best knight in the world, thinks he is Gawain[1] (*1533, knows him for L.*), whose presence in land of Strangore is much desired. Leaves him, and L. and attendant maiden come to house, where they are well received.

Line 1480. DODINEL comes to a deep river crossed by narrow plank. Maiden crosses safely, plank will not bear weight of an armed man. D. falls into water and is nearly drowned. When he reaches bank maid has disappeared. Castle near at hand, knight comes out and challenges D., who is too exhausted to answer and is taken prisoner.

Line 1565. QUEEN and maidens return to court in great grief, tell A. what has chanced. (*1533, Queen's account does not agree with facts of story. She says 'prisoner has gone after knight.' What prisoner? Probably Segramore's, but she says they have heard nothing of S.*) Ten knights will go in quest of L. Gawain chooses his companions: Ywein, Garhies (*Gariët* general spelling), Gurrehes, Mordrec, Hestor van Maris, Acgloval ('twas he brought Perceval to court), etc. (*Neither D. L. nor 1533 give ten names, the latter adds to those mentioned Les Hardi [le Laid Hardi?] and Brandalis.*) They take an oath to seek a year and a day. They ride to the 'Swerte cruce' (here we have story of Joseph of Arimathea and King Agestes [Agrestes] from *G. S. Graal*). Gawain harangues them, they will separate, and search forest for a week. Hear loud cries,

---

[1] **D. L.** always has the form *Walewein*.

maiden meets them, and says best knight on earth is being slain. Leads them to a valley where one knight fights against ten. Gawain and companions rescue him and put others to flight. Knight has two swords. Gawain asks reason. Knight explains. He is Eliezer (1533, *Helye*), son of the rich Fisher who holds the Grail. One sword is that with which Joseph of Arimathea was wounded (here adventures of Joseph as in *G. S. Graal*); it is broken and can only be mended by him who achieves adventures of the Grail. Ywein begs E. to accompany them in their search for Lancelot, he would doubtless fulfil the test. E. refuses, must return to his father. They separate, agreeing if they find L. to send him to E. (which they do not do).

Line 2335. AGLOVAL rides five days without special adventure. Meets wounded knight who prays his aid. A. jousts with and overthrows pursuer. Makes him ask pardon of first. Spends night in castle of second, who is Griffoen van den quaden passe. A. tells him name and quest. G. conceals share in adventure, tells A. he will find Kay at a hermitage. When A. has ridden away sets K. free, and tells him to go to hermitage, not saying whence he came. K. does this, meets A., hears of quest and follows him.

Line 2565. GAWAIN rides three days without adventure. Comes to castle of Mathamas where Segramore is imprisoned. Being weary rides past without greeting. M. pursues him, they joust, M. is overthrown. S. is released and M. sent prisoner to court.

Line 2685. HECTOR[1] seeks in forest up and down for eight days; ninth, comes to where Dodinel fell into water, crosses safely and rides to castle. Knight attacks him and is overthrown, makes feint to yield and tries treacherously to stab H. H. smites off his head. Folk of castle receive him gladly, tell him of D. who is freed. Maiden explains knight was her '*ami*

---

[1] This name is spelt *Hestore* throughout. On the whole the spelling of proper names in **D. L.** is very erratic, and varies greatly.

and hated D. who had overthrown him at a tourney, she had been forced to fetch him hither on pain of death. H. tells D. of quest; he will join. Leave castle and ride to trysting-place. All meet, have heard nothing of L. Part in great grief, knowing it will be long before they meet again.

Line 2925. GAWAIN rides fifteen (1533, *twelve*) days without adventures. Comes to an abbey where he leaves his arms and takes others. Spends Sunday there. On Monday rides forth, comes to a spring, unhelms to drink, maid rides up, knows him, and takes him to castle. Lord of the castle arrives with thirty knights. A great tourney to be held on the morrow two miles hence. Mabonars (1533, *Marbortas*), the king of Galehout's race (1533, *Galehout's cousin*), has summoned it at Castle 'van der Molen,' will give hawk to best knight and circlet to his lady. Maiden prays G. to help her lover Taganas (1533, *Tanaguis le blanc*). On the morrow go to tourney. Argument between maiden and 'a king's niece' as to whose knight is the best. At first G. overthrows all adversaries. Then Red Knight appears, prolonged struggle, G. is unhorsed, R. K. rides away, G. follows, overtakes him at forester's house. It is Hector, who is much grieved at what he has done. G. forgives him, and they continue quest together. Third day (1533, *time not mentioned*), come to ruined chapel and churchyard wherein is marble tomb with inscription to effect that only the 'keytive' knight who has failed through 'luxurien' to achieve adventure of the Grail can fulfil this. Enter churchyard, find burning tomb with twelve others round it, upright sword on each. G. will test adventure, enters enclosure, is attacked by swords, beaten to the ground, when he recovers consciousness is outside. Tries again, with even worse result. H. also tries, fails; letters appear on the door that none shall dare adventure till the 'son of the dolorous queen' come.[1] They leave

---

[1] This adventure of the Perilous Cemetery is one of the 'crossreferences' to which I have referred earlier. It is mentioned both in *G. S. Graal* and *Queste*. The wording here is not very clear, but it

chapel and ride till they come to two roads by a cross on which is written 'whoso takes left-hand road shall not escape without much dishonour; of right-hand nothing shall be said save that there is much danger.' H. insists on going to left though G. would dissuade him. They separate.

Line 3535. GAWAIN comes to pavilion where six knights are at meat, he greets them, they make no response. G. seats himself and begins to eat, they order him to stop, and on his refusing attack him with swords and axes. G. slays one, cuts off arm of another, rest flee. Rides away, comes to a valley where he sees castle surrounded by deep water, goes towards it. Hears cries from a tower, enters and finds maiden in bath of boiling water (**1533**, *does not say water is boiling, and states that she only expects aid from Lancelot*), prays him to lift her out; he fails, she tells him he will not go hence without shame, and that only 'the best knight in the world' can help her. G. goes to castle, is well received. As they sit in the hall out of the chamber whence the king came (**1533**, *he sees 'entrer parmi une verriere'*) there comes a dove with censer in beak.[1] All are silent and kneel till dove has passed through hall and entered a chamber. Then tables are prepared and all sit down in silence. G. wonders much. Out of chamber where dove entered comes the fairest maiden G. has ever seen, holding above her head a vessel in the shape of a cup. The vessel 'ne was van houte ne van stene, ne van metale negene.' All kneel as she passes, save G., and the tables are filled with the best food on earth. When she has passed all but G. have

does not, I think, mean that Lancelot has already failed in the Grail adventure, but that he shall come to the cemetery after he *has* failed; which is fulfilled in *Queste*. At the same time we must remember that in *Perceval li Gallois*, which knows nothing of Galahad or the *Queste*, Lancelot fails for the same reason, and more completely, as the Grail does not appear at all in his presence, so this *may* refer to the earlier story.

[1] It may be noted that Chrétien knows nothing of a dove connected with the Grail, whereas Wolfram does.

APPENDIX

been provided with food; he doubts if he has done amiss. After the meal all leave the hall, doors are closed, and G. is left alone. He lies down beneath a window. A man (dwarf?) appears and tells G. to go into a chamber where none shall see him, would strike him, but G. takes staff out of his hand, warns him he shall not depart without dishonour. (**1533**, *G. is only told 'fuyez vous en d'icy, vous n'y devez m'y estre, car en vous a trop villaine chose.' G. sees bed through open door, and enters chamber of own accord.*) G. goes into the chamber, sees a fair bed and sits down upon it. Hears a voice warning him if he sit unarmed on 't bedde van aventuren' he will surely die. Arms himself; a sword (**1533**, *lance*) with fiery blade enters room, smites him so sorely he cannot defend himself: becomes unconscious, on recovery feels that blade is being drawn out of his wound. Lies till daylight. (**1533**, *Quant il fut ennuyte si que l'en y veoit mauvaisement fors que de la lune qui luysoit a plus de quarante fenestres qui tout estoient ouvertes; lors regarde monseigneur G. en une chambre qui estoit pres de lui.*) Sees a great serpent enter the hall, making fearful noise, out of its mouth come small serpents. Leopard attacks serpent, fierce battle. When serpent finds it cannot slay leopard returns to hall (chamber?), where the small serpents attack it. They slay each other. A great wind rises, which sweeps hall clean. G. hears women weeping, rises and sees twelve maidens come weeping and kneel before door where dove went in. They depart, and an armed knight comes and bids G. go and rest on a bed in another chamber, he may no longer stay here. G. refuses, they fight fiercely all day, at last fall exhausted. It begins to thunder, the whole palace trembles, G. is deafened by the sound, knows not if it be day or night (**1533**, *if he be living or dead*). A great wind rises (**1533**, *soft and sweet*), and he hears voices, two hundred at least, singing so sweetly, nothing on earth can be like to it. He cannot understand all the words, only 'Glorie ende lof moete hebben ewelike die coninc van hemelrike.' The palace is filled with a sweet smoke. Opens his eyes and sees the maiden of evening before with vessel, preceded by two censers (**1533**, *and two cierges*), places vessel on silver table, ten censers give sweet smell around it. Voices sing 'Ere, bliscap, ende lof moete hebben ewelike, Die soete here van hemelrike.' Maiden carries vessel back to chamber. Hall grows dark and windows fly open (**1533**, *and close again*). G. can see nothing, but feels he is healed of his wounds, rises and looks for knight with whom he had fought, but can find nothing. Hears people enter and feels himself taken by hands and feet, bound, carried out of hall, and laid on a cart. Daylight comes, he is still in the cart, to which a wretched horse is harnessed; feels himself shamed. A maiden (**1533**, *une vieille*) comes and drives the horse out, as they pass the gateway the people mock at and pelt G. When bridge is passed maiden looses his bonds and tells him to leave the cart, he has been there long enough. G. asks name of castle, it is Cambonoyc.[1] He curses the day he was born and made knight to be thus shamed. Rides all day, at evening comes to hermitage, where he is kindly received. Hermit asks his name, and is rejoiced at hearing it. Where has he spent the night? G. will not say at first. (**1533**, *G. shows shame at being praised. H. comforts him; no man but knows misfortune. G. says no man has had such ill-luck as he for fifteen days. H. asks how, and G. tells all.*) When he does tell, H. keeps silence for a long time, then tells him he has seen the Holy Grail, his own sin prevented him from being fed by it. (**1533**, *quant vous ne luy feistes honeur bien vous deistes mesadvenir.*)[2] G. asks meaning of serpent; it is A. his uncle. He shall leave his kingdom in charge of his kinsmen

---

[1] I have before remarked on the uncertain spelling of this name in **D. L.**, the above is the more usual form.

[2] From this it appears that Gawain's failure at the Grail castle was in no way due to any defect of *character*, but to his omission of the reverence due to the Grail, of the sacrosanct nature of which he was ignorant. This explanation appears to me to be peculiar to the *Lancelot* version, which otherwise, as I have pointed out, regards Gawain with great respect.

APPENDIX

and go to fight a knight whom he cannot overcome; on his return his own kinsmen shall fight against, and slay him. It shall come about through G. himself. He must swear not to reveal what H. has told him to any one. G. spends night there, and in morning rides forth to seek Hector.

Line 4260. HECTOR rides till eventide, meets a dwarf, who warns him, but will give no explanation. H. rides on and comes to a stone on which it is written, that no one enters this land save to his shame. Then meets two maidens who lament over him. Comes to a castle surrounded by water, over which is a bridge. A maiden sitting under a tree greets him kindly, and tells him there is a knight at the bridge who jousts with all comers, and throws the vanquished into the water. H. overthrows knight and crosses bridge. The gates are closed, none may enter save by swearing to put an end to the evil customs of the castle. H. swears and enters. Asks what are the customs. There is an evil knight there who fights with all who comes; if victorious he drives them naked through the streets; also he has dishonoured more than one hundred (**1533**, *forty*) noble maidens. H. bids them lead him to knight. They take him to a fair garden, well planted with trees, in the midst of which is an open space. They show him an ivory horn hanging on a tree, if he sound it the knight will come.[1] He does so and a 'hunch-backed and ugly' (**1533**, *grant*) knight, on a white horse, appears unarmed, and asks H. his name. If he will swear to renounce evil customs H. will tell him, not otherwise; knight prefers to fight. Folk tell H. it was a ruse coming to him unarmed, had he made terms and disarmed, he would have been overpowered at once. Knight returns in red armour. After fierce fight H. slays him and learns he must now deliver lady of the castle, who is in a cave guarded by two leopards (**1533**, *lyons*). This he does; slays leopards and releases lady, who is joyfully received by

---

[1] Certain details in this adventure recall that of the 'Joie de la court' in *Erec*.

the people. She is Argale van Grakenlant (**1533,** *Grindelain*), and Lancelot's cousin. The knight was Margarij (**1533,** *Maugart le Roux*); she is concerned to hear of L.'s disappearance.

Line 4812. YWEIN rides three (**1533,** *four*) days without adventure. Fourth meets a maiden who laughs as she sees him. Y. asks reason, she will tell him if he will promise her a gift that will cost him little. Y. promises. A knight has threatened to take her horse, because his *amie* reproached him with having done little for her honour. Will Y. give her the knight's horse? She knows Y. and his fame, and therefore laughed for joy on meeting him. He consents and they ride together. Knight comes out from his pavilion and demands Y.'s horse. Y. will fight for it. They do so and the knight is slain (**1533,** *apparently not, the lady only thinks he is dead*), and his horse is given to maiden, who goes her way rejoicing. Y. rides till evening, when he meets a maiden lamenting loudly; a knight has taken from her the hawk her *ami* gave her, *he* will think she gave it willingly and slay her for jealousy. Y. bids her lead him to tent of knight who stole hawk; she does so, and Y. bids her go in and take it. Knight objects, they fight. Both are wounded, knight mortally; prays for hermit that he may receive last sacraments. Y. sends maiden, and himself finally returns with hermit, who tends him for fifteen days till wounds are healed.

Line 5070. MORDRET, Gawain's youngest brother, rode all day with nothing to eat, weary, because he was young, only twenty; fair-haired and good to look upon, but evil at heart. Description of brothers: Gawain fairest, courteous to all, especially the poor [1] (**1533,** *fist voluntiers bien aux meseaulx plus que a autres gens.*) His strength doubles, at certain times, as

---

[1] I think this is probably the explanation of A.'s vision, when he sees G. after death surrounded by the souls of poor men 'who have helped G. to conquer the heavenly kingdom.' Cf. Sommer, *Studies*, p. 266.

APPENDIX 225

he fights (not specified, **1533** says, *toutes heures du iour*), so that none can overcome him, he will either conquer or be slain. A good knight in all things, and faithful to his lord. Courteous to all women, and not given to boast of his deeds. Agravain, handsome and valiant, but of bitter tongue; 'Lancelot slew him as ye shall hear' (*omitted in* **1533**), Garhiës (later on Gariëtte) (*Gaheriet*, **1533**) more courteous than any of the others 'save Gawain' (*omitted in* **1533**). His right arm was longer than his left, so that he did great deeds of knighthood (**1533** adds, *most gentle of all, and most relentless when wrathful*). Gurrehies (**1533**, *Gueresches*) very valiant, fond of deeds of knighthood, never took any rest. Handsome in face and more fastidious in dress than the others. Much loved of ladies. Gawain's favourite, and youngest save Mordret.[1] Mordret was valiant, but an evil knight, save for first two years of his knighthood. 'He did more harm in his life than all his brethren did good, for fifteen thousand [2] valiant knights were slain in one day because of him, and he himself died there too' (**1533** *omits this*).

Line 5250. MORDRET spends night at castle of a lady (**1533**, *widow*), who treats him well. Next morning he rides on his way, comes to two pavilions; at door of one is a horse ready saddled, and armour. Dwarf comes out with bow and arrow, and shoots M.'s horse dead. M. would chastise dwarf, but owner arrives and challenges M. They fight, and knight is slain. M. takes horse and goes on his way. Comes to a tent where is a fair maiden; she will lodge M. if her lover does not object; if he does, M. must go. They fall in love; M. prays her favours and is not refused. Lover arrives; M. may stay when he tells his name; would do anything for

---

[1] These passages illustrate the difficulty previously referred to, of identifying the original of Gareth. I believe it can only be done by comparing the parallel adventures in **M.** and his source.

[2] In the account of the final battle all versions I have consulted give one hundred thousand on each side killed; the above is much more reasonable.

Gariëtte's brother. Two knights come, with squire bearing venison. M. is well treated. He prays maiden to come to him when her lover is asleep. After some demur, she does so. Lover awakes, finds M. and maiden together, reproaches him; he cannot be G.'s brother, or he would not have acted thus. They fight; M. being the younger and stronger, makes him swear to pardon lady. Next morning he rides away.

Line 5530. AGRAVAIN comes to a fair tent, where there is a dead knight on a bier, a maiden and wounded knight beside him. A. asks explanation. Dead knight was brother to the other. On their way to A.'s court they came to the 'Keytiven berch.' A knight, Dryas (1533, *Druas*), attacked them, they were unarmed; one was slain, the other fled. Dryas sent the body after him. He slays all who come to this place. A. says he will avenge him; is warned if he slay D. not to sound ivory horn dwarf will proffer, or D.'s brother, twice as fierce as he, will come from the other side of the mountain. A. goes forth, comes to a fountain; is challenged by D., slays him and gives head to knight, who is much rejoiced, even more when he knows A.'s name. A. returns; finds dwarf and maiden lamenting over D.'s body. Dwarf offers A. horn, which he blows loudly, all know D. is slain. His brother Sornahan (1533, *Sornehault*) arms and comes to avenge him. They fight, both are thrown. A. is unconscious. S. is about to slay him, when maid rides up, demands a boon, which S. grants: it is A.'s life. S. will keep him in prison though maid warns him Gawain is in the land, and will avenge his brother. S. has a wall built all round the mount, with notice that whoever would enter must first fight with him.

Line 6095. GURRËES (1533, *Gueresches*) rides through thicket forty miles long, ten (1533, *forty*) wide; finds knights ill-treating old knight, rescues him. His son had accidentally slain his cousin, his sister's son (1533, *a maiden*); in revenge the brothers have slain son, and would have slain him, but for G. G. goes with him to castle, most kindly received. Offers his love to daughter; she asks who he is, when she hears, says he is too

APPENDIX 227

rich and well-born for her. Asks him name of knight who bears certain arms; it is Lancelot. G. would fain know what has become of him. Peasant comes lamenting, he had fled from armed knight and wolves had slain his ass in forest, has lost means of living. G. was the knight; prays his host to give peasant horse for his sake, which he does. During night nephews attack castle, are repulsed; pray for peace. G. advises host to make peace as they are such near kinsmen; he consents. G. leaves castle, comes to fountain in plain, where three ladies are seated, one sixty years old, one forty, one less than twenty; youngest very poorly dressed. G. asks cause of her grief; her husband is very jealous because she had praised Lancelot unduly, has taken away her rich clothes, and forced her to eat with the servants. Oldest lady is in woe because she has been forced to promise her daughter to knight of low birth, who has murdered one wife already. Asks G.'s advice. He tells her to keep her word, and he will free the daughter. They go to castle together; knight arrives and claims maiden, mother gives her up. As they ride off G. says *he* loves maiden, will fight for her, follows and slays knight. Beseeches maiden's love, but she refuses; she loves another, and G. restores her to her mother in safety. Will not stay, but will at once seek castle of lady with jealous husband. She receives him well; her husband is away, but returns shortly, and though angry, allows G. to stay. Meanwhile another knight arrives, Segramore. Husband, very wroth, plots to slay them; but page overhears and tells lady, who warns them. They prepare, and when host would pick quarrel with S., slay him to joy of lady and her relatives. Next morning G. and S. depart, come to thirteen pavilions, must joust ere they go farther. Each unhorses his adversary; may depart with honour. Owner of pavilions is Count Wigans (1533, *Gimas*), hearing Gawain was in the land, has come out to seek jousts. Ride on, meet sister of Agloval, seeking her brother; S. will escort her. G. goes on alone.

Line 7840. GURRËES comes to four tents, in first a meal

spread; second, four coffers, and a dwarf sleeping; third, two maidens; fourth, maid and knight. G. eats, and goes to sleep in last tent by maiden. Knight awakes, drags G. out of bed; G. seizes sword and smites off knight's head (**1533**, *cleaves him in two*); lady much grieved, it was her husband. G., smitten with her, forces her to ride with him. Come to a forest; knight challenges G. and is slain. Next day four brothers of lady overtake them, but are overthrown by G. Come to Abbey of White Nuns. Lady takes veil, she is of high birth; Lancelot, Lionel, and Bohort are her kinsmen. G. rides on, comes to Sornahan's Mount, is overthrown, and shares fate of Agravain. S.'s niece treats the prisoners well.

Line 8540. GARIËTTE meets a maiden seeking Lancelot, and they ride together. Her brother-in-law has seized her lands, and she seeks one of A.'s knights to fight with him. G. promises to do so. Come to an abbey, see maid's uncle, who encourages G. Reach pavilions of Count Glimas (cf. *supra*), joust, and G. overthrows count himself, whom he sends prisoner to Gawain. Count treats them well. Next morning they go on; meet six knights, with knight and maiden, whom they are treating very cruelly. Knight is Brandalis of the R. T.; by his oath of fellowship G. must aid him first. Gosennes van Strangeloet comes up and frees maiden, who is so much hurt she lives but six days. G. returns to maid he is escorting. They ride on and come to tent where is a dwarf (**1533**, *three pavilions, dwarf in first*), he will lodge them if his master permits; G. promises to leave if he objects. Knight comes with two maidens; ill-treats dwarf. G. interferes, overcomes knight, and makes him ask pardon of dwarf. G. has already slain his nephews (**1533**, *he was one of the knights who had taken Brandalis.*)[1] Next morning they ride on, and come to land of lady of Roestoc, where fight is to be fought. Rejoiced to see G. for sake of Gawain, who had fought for her against Segurades, 'alse hier voren

---

[1] There is a *lacuna* of a few lines here in **D. L.**, so this may well have been in the text.

gescreven es,' l. 9366. (This evidently refers to the earlier part of the *Lancelot*, and makes it probable that the Dutch compiler had also translated the first part of the work.) Fierce fight between G. and Gindan, the brother-in-law. Latter, seeing he is over-matched, jumps into river and is drowned; maiden regains her land. G. departs; meets a maid who reproaches him with cowardice: he did not free captive maiden, and has allowed his two brothers to be in prison. G. explains conditions of his vow, and asks about brothers. She tells him, and he rides to Sornahan's Mount, overthrows him, and frees Agravain and Gurries. S. *did not know who they were*. (This is a contradiction of previous statement, that maiden tells him A.'s name and threatens him with Gawain's anger.) Brothers stay three days till wounds are healed, then ride forth. First night lodge with hermit; second, with rich man, who warns them not to seek Lancelot in that land; there is civil war, the duke's six sons have rebelled against him because he made his daughter and her husband his heirs; they have slain these two. The three agree to help duke, ride to castle, overthrowing two knights on their way. Duke accepts their aid, but does not know who they are. Great battle, Agravain is taken prisoner, but exchanged for two of the sons.

Line 10735. ARTHUR and court are much distressed; do not know how adventure of the Grail is to be achieved if Lancelot be dead. (It is not explained how they know of the Grail, nor is it clear whether L. is to achieve it personally, or through agency of Galahad.) Lionel returns, and is much distressed at news. Questions wounded knight, who proves to be Bohort. (The reason for B.'s attempt to lead away the queen is given in the earlier section of the *Lancelot*, so far as **D. L.** is concerned it is not explained.) Maiden comes from Lady van Galvoye to beg aid, wants Lancelot or Gawain, if both absent, will have B. B. and L. go with messenger. Queen gives B. a ring for Lancelot; if any one find him it will be B.

Line 11167. QUEEN has dream L. is faithless to her. Very

ill. When better sends her niece to 'Moustier Royale' to find Lady of the Lake, and bid her come to Guinevere.

Line 11520. LANCELOT, six weeks before wounds are healed, then sets forth, and finds maiden lamenting, her sister had been carried off, and her lover slain in defending her. She has been to A.'s court, but they are too sorrowful to give aid. L. will help her if she will go errand for him. She leads him to tower, knight too wounded to resist, frees damsel. Maiden must now go to court, say she has seen a knight who had eaten with L. 'and slept in same bed' (*not in* 1533). All greatly rejoiced. A. gives maid a castle.

Line 11870. LANCELOT rides with sister, comes to a fountain, where two knights and two ladies are at a meal. They ask L. to join them. One maiden falls in love with L. L. drinks from spring, two vipers have poisoned it, is very ill, and is nursed by maiden. While still ill, Bohort and Lionel find him, and he sends his hair, which has fallen out, to queen, who is much rejoiced. (Love complications between maiden and L. Lionel again sent to queen, this time for advice. Maid swears to remain virgin for L.'s sake; L. will be her knight.) When cured L. and maiden ride on, come to castle of the six brothers, who make up false tale as to their cause. L. believes them, and fights for them. Duke is killed, and the three sons of King Lot taken prisoners. L. is much distressed, bids them be well treated, and rides off, hiding his name.

(Here follows his slumber in forest with Lionel, when latter is carried off by Tarquin; L.'s being taken by the queens; released by daughter of Duke of Rochedon, and attending tourney. All this has been commented upon in chap. ix.)

Line 14580. LANCELOT at the Grail Castle. This has also been previously noticed.

Line 15353. LANCELOT leaves castle, and comes to another 'surrounded by water' (*detail omitted in* 1533). Knight challenges him; lost in thought, L. does not hear, but rides over bridge, and is thrust from horse into water; gates closed, must spend night in wood. Sits by spring, three (**1533**, *four*) knights ride up, with maid who cured L. of poison; have carried her off against her will. She says were L. there they would not have dared. Knights say L.'s father was a coward, he must be one too; would do violence to lady. L. appears and rescues her, slaying one knight. They ride to castle of lady's kinswoman, where they spend the night. Next day L. will go to castle where he lost his horse. Host would dissuade him; failing, rides with him. Asks does he know Hector. Tells him H. is his brother (as H. is previously represented as one of A.'s most valiant knights, it is difficult to understand how L. comes to be ignorant on this point). The knight at castle is H.'s uncle. Would not joust with L., but thinks this is not he. Is overthrown. L. is welcomed by lady of the castle, who tells him H. is her son and his brother. L. next comes to forest, with hermit's cell and chapel at entrance, with notice warning knights to go no further. Hermit begs L. not to attempt the adventure; it is 'Der Verlorenen Forest'; has seen a hundred knights (1533, *two hundred within half-year*) enter, but none have ever returned. L. insists on going on (1533, *stays night with H.*). Meets maiden, who warns him he goes to his death. Comes to a clearing where is a company of knights and maidens dancing and singing; feels compelled to join them. Squire leaves him and returns.

Line 16260. YWEIN stays at hermitage till wounds are healed, then rides forth. Meets dwarf, maiden has stolen his brachet; will Y. get it back for him? Promises to do so. Maid and knight ride up. Y. bids dwarf take dog; does so. Y. and knight fight fiercely; finally find it is Bohort, rejoiced to meet each other. Dwarf tells them L. is well, was at tourney lately (1533, *also gives news of intended tourney at Kamalot*). They separate. Y. goes to an Abbey of White Nuns, is healed of his wounds. Rides forth. Meets lady thrashing a dwarf, bids her stop; she will, if Y. will do what she wants; promises. He must kiss her; so ugly he hesitates. She reproaches him; he is certainly not Y., she will go to court and complain of him. Y. calls her back. She will let him off if he will fetch sword, shield, and helmet from tent near by. Dwarf warns Y. she is most treacherous lady in land. Y. will go. Rides with her, takes arms, leaving his own in their place. Maidens rush out of tent weeping and tearing their hair. He has dishonoured all maidens in the land, will come to shame. Y. asks explanation. They will not answer; he waits till evening, and as no one comes rides on to a hermitage, where he is well received. H. asks if custom still maintains that no man may sit at R. T. unless he be wounded. Custom given up since Lancelot, Galehaut, and Hector were admitted unwounded. Now each knight must vanquish one at least in week following, or forfeit seat (**1533**, *must have done so in preceding week*), (ll. 16770-875). Y. asks of shield; belongs to a giant who had wasted the land, but for love of a maiden had promised to remain in castle unless one did him shame. After a year (**1533**, *longuement y avoit été*), becoming weary, had sought chance of release, so had hung up shield, setting twelve maidens to watch it (**1533**, *the people of the land had set the watch*). Now he will be free, land wasted and maids dishonoured. Y. rides on, bearing shield; all flee from him (**1533**, *two maidens only*). Finds two maids by spring; they bid him eat with them, does so. Knight comes up, would fight with Y. for having released giant. Is overcome. Y. sends him to giant to tell him who it is who has taken the shield. Knight goes, giant strikes off his hand for tidings (**1533**, *giant gives him his choice: he may lose his hand for the shield or his head for the helmet*),[1] and rides through land destroying and slaying wherever he goes. Y. rides on, seeking shelter; no one will have him. At one castle fights with father and son. Sleeps under tree. Is wakened by sound of giant, who makes more

---

[1] This adventure of Ywein and the giant's shield should be compared with *Meraugis de Portlesguez*, ll. 1418 *et seq.* There lady has taken dwarf's horse; and it is the eye, not the hand, which the messenger loses. I believe the above to be the older version, as, though L'Outredotez is always spoken of as a knight simply, Meraugis once refers to him as a *giant*, which must have come from another version.

APPENDIX

noise than twenty (**1533**, *twelve*) knights. Y. calls him, but he is too angry to hear. Y. mounts and rides after him. Comes to 'Castel van den Trepasse'; five (**1533**, *fifteen*) knights fall upon him, kill his horse, and make him prisoner; will deliver him to giant.

Line 17470. BOHORT comes to lady of Galvoye. She has been deprived of a castle by a knight, and needs champion; fight to be fought at King Pelles's court. Come to Corbenic. King and daughter rejoiced to see B.; tell him of L.'s great deeds. Fights with and overcomes knight. Sees Grail. Does not sleep in 'palace of adventures.' Next morning comes to a hermit, who knew his father and King Ban. Tells him how his father had built this chapel in memory of a victory gained over King Cerces, and given it a golden (**1533**, *silver*) crown won from king's steward. B. leaves, meets maiden, who reproaches him for having left Grail castle without testing adventures, should have slept in hall. (*Here* **1533** *gives adventure of a lady whose brother has been taken prisoner while seeking a sparrow-hawk. B. frees him.*) Returns to Kamalot.

Line 18070. GAWAIN meets the maid who cured L. of poison, and was rescued by him. Assures him L. is well. They ride together to court.

Line 18130. LANCELOT at the '*caroles*' sits on throne in centre of ring, and has crown placed on head. Enchantment ceases. Maid explains it has lasted ever since King Ban came there on his way from A.'s wedding. With him was a youth, his nephew, learned in necromancy. Fell in love with maiden sitting on throne, and for her sake wove spell that dance should continue till fairest and bravest knight on earth came.[1] Also made chessboard of gold and silver, which plays of itself against all men. At last clerk and maiden died, but spell was not broken. L. plays with chessboard and wins; enchantment ceases for ever. Chessboard is sent as present to Guinevere.

---

[1] This appears to be a reminiscence of Merlin and Vivienne. Cf. *Merlin*, Sommer's ed., chap. xix.

L. leaves castle, meets knight, who threatens him, but flies when L. would fight. Comes to a high tower where party of knights lie in wait for him. They attack him, overthrow and bind him, and cast him into pit infested with serpents. Maid releases him. Her father was nephew to Duke Karles whom L. has slain. Squire warns his lord of L.'s escape; he arms his knights and attacks L., who takes refuge in maiden's room. L. slays nineteen (1533, *more than twenty-four*). Father jumps out of the window, and breaks his neck. L. tells maiden all are slain. She seeks father's body, cannot find it, so thinks he has escaped. L. throws corpses out of windows. They go to rest, and maiden has dream which terrifies her much. Next morning they ride out together; hear cries for help, find knight ill-treating lady, and bids him stop, when he strikes off her head and throws it in L.'s face. (This is the adventure in **M.**, Book VI., and has been commented upon earlier.)

Line 19179. LANCELOT rides back to maiden, finds her gone. Meets knight, who asks if he has seen knight and maiden (1533, *two knights and maid*), asks for his maiden. She has been carried off by four knights. L. pursues. Finds them about to burn her. L. slays twenty (?), rescues maid: this was meaning of her dream. Knights were her brother and three of his followers. Come to house of lady, where they stay fourteen days, till L. is cured from bites of serpents in the pit. Ride together. Come to 'Castle of the Charrette.' Lad meets them; rejoiced at L.'s coming. Daughter of Duke of Rochedon, who freed L. from prison of queen, is to be married against her will to brother of Queen of Foreestan; it was he who slew her betrothed, his own nephew. L. enters church, challenges knight, who flies; lady receives her lands again. Morgain le Fay is there, bids L. unhelm, 'in the name of her whom he loves best.' They reproach each other, and M. threatens L. with punishment. L. and maid depart as quickly as possible, fearing M.'s spells.

Line 19525. How knight with dead maiden fulfils L.'s commands, and body is buried.

APPENDIX

Line 19595. LANCELOT comes to Kamalot; lodges with hermit for tourney. Sends maiden with letter to queen. She receives heritage for the one lost. King Ider, jealous of L. King and queen say he could overthrow all R. T. Knights very angry at this, except Gawain (1533, *and Bohort*). Queen sends message to L. to come secretly and discomfit knights. L. is recognised by King Bagdemagus, who will aid him. L. comes in red armour, does great deeds till he beholds queen, when he nearly swoons, and is carried off the field by K. B. R. T. knights get best of it. Queen sends message by Bohort to tell L. to come secretly that evening (maid of poison cure is there; queen is at first jealous, then satisfied). Ider praises Red Knight, says L. would not have done so well. Queen makes King B. challenge A. to another tourney in three days. L. spends each night with queen. Third day she arms him in white, Bohort in red. L. not to enter field till after tierce. He overthrows and wounds Gawain and Gariëtte, and scatters knights of R. T. A. bids him unhelm, is joyful at recognising L. Sunday, great feast made in his honour. Chessboard is brought, all play and are beaten save L. Clerk writes down on oath all L.'s adventures in book, which was found after king's death. All others tell their story. A. says L. has done more for honour of R. T. than all the rest put together; they are very jealous. Decide to go forth and seek all who have not returned from quest. Gawain will seek his three (1533, *four*) brothers. (Confusion here; when we last heard of Agravain, Gurrëes, and Gariëtte they were prisoners. How did latter return for tourney? **D. L.** probably saw this, and only mentions three brothers, including Mordred, while 1533 says four, which is certainly wrong.) Bohort will seek Hector and Lionel. (1533, *Will join quest; they shall not go without him. H. and L. are not mentioned.*) Queen and L. talk over adventure of churchyard as told by Gawain. She is sure L. is knight meant to achieve it, and is very sad; he will fail through his sinful love for her. L. says he has more bliss from her love than from any feats of arms, all he has done has been inspired by her. King Bagdemagus is made knight of R. T.

Line 21596. LANCELOT, Bagdemagus, Gariëtte, and Bohort set forth; Gawain will follow when wounds are healed. Come to castle of 'Witten Dorne,' meet knight on horseback, naked, beaten, and ill-used by one hundred men; it is Mordret. Lord of the castle is Matheus die felle (**1533**, *Marchant li felon*). G. releases M., attack castle, slay lord and scatter his people. Ride fifteen days till they come to castle where Y. is in prison. Host refuses lodging; hates A.; has one of his knights in prison. They attack castle, and release Y. Are told of the giant, he will come on the morrow, host had meant to give Y. up to him. B. asks boon of L., that he may fight giant. L. unwilling, but consents. Great fight, giant is slain. Next morning all ride forth (seven). Y. suggests they should separate. All ride different ways, meet again at castle on All Saints Day.[1]

Line 22120. LANCELOT rides fifteen days, meets maiden, asks her of Lionel. She tells him, and promises to lead him to Tarquin's castle, if he will promise to go with her wherever she pleases afterwards. He agrees. (Adventure with Tarquin has been commented upon in chap. ix. p. 154.)

Line 22600. LANCELOT. Maiden leads him to knight who steals horses; maid rides first, L. after; knight attacks maid and is slain by L. Rests eight days till wounds are healed. Then would find Hector. (**1533**, *Meets old man who tells him H. had slain knight there previous day, shows him road.*) Adventures at castle (cf. chap. ix. p. 155). Finds at castle squire from A.'s court, bids him lead his horses into 'ten Verlorene foreeste' and wait for him at cross. Comes with two knights whom he dismisses, rides into forest, meets maiden who says she is seeking him to achieve an adventure. Emissary of Morgain's leads him to tower; drugs him. M. comes, blows powder up his nostrils, which deprives him of his senses; when he recovers he is in prison. Sees man in outer hall illuminating, begs brush and colours, and paints on walls of prison history

[1] Cf. this with *Studies*, p. 186; also remarks, *supra*, p. 153.

of his love for queen. M. sees this, and resolves to show it to A.

Line 23146. GAWAIN comes first to Tarquin's castle, now owned by 'Grave van den Parke,' who tells him of L.'s feat. Then to hermitage, finds King B. sick, has heard of L. slaying owners of Castle Vaguel. Tells him of *rendezvous* for All Saints. L. will surely be there. B. had helped Gurrëes against four knights and been badly wounded. G. offers to stay with him, but B. will not allow it.

Line 23260. Tryst at castle. All meet save L. and Bohort. Gawain says 'twould be great shame to return to court without them, will seek till S. Mary Magdalene's Day, then quest will have lasted a year and a day. All separate, agreeing to meet again at castle. 'Some ride all year, some are taken prisoners' (*omitted by* 1533), finally only Mordret, Agloval (1533, *Agravain*) and Bagdemagus return. Much perplexed. Decide to send messenger secretly to court, to know if anything has been heard of questers. Finding nothing is known, swear to ride till they find their comrades.

Line 23388. LANCELOT lies all winter a prisoner, when summer comes (1533, *two winters, one summer, second spring*), scent of flowers and sight of roses remind him of Guinevere. Tears out bars of window and escapes, leaving insulting message with porter for M. Meets maiden, who tells him Lionel is prisoner in castle of King Vagor of Estrangeloet. Challenged by king's son; unless he can find some one to take his place will be overcome. L. will go. Meets wounded knight on litter, if L. will lodge in his castle will meet one of A.'s knights who lies sick there. He himself has been wounded by shot from maiden's bow, and iron cannot be pulled out till best knight in world comes. Has been to A's court, but useless till L. returns. A. is much distressed at absence of Gawain and L.[1] Go to castle, L. asks to be

[1] It is quite possible that we have here the story of Urre of Hungary, which may well have been given at greater length in one of the *Lancelot* MSS. Also the source of Malory's version of Lancelot

allowed to try to pull out shaft. Knight says it is no use to try unless he be L. Does not reveal name. Would see sick knight, it is King B., wounded in a tourney. Rejoiced to see L., tells him of quest. L. leaves next day, and B. tells knight who he was. Knight follows in litter. L. comes to the castle 'dat fremde eylant,' meets squire, who tells him Lionel is there, L. says he is one of A.'s knights. Will fight instead of Lionel. King receives him well; Lionel is joyful. A lady had accused him falsely to her husband, they fought, and husband was slain, he was king's son. Brother challenged Lionel, who being too badly wounded to fight at once had been imprisoned lest he escape. L. fights and is victorious, peace is made, and the two cousins ride off together. Knight in litter follows on their tracks. They come to an abbey, 'Celice' or 'die cleine aelmoesene' in die 'Mersce van Scollant.' (Here follows long story as to origin of abbey.)

Line 24454. LANCELOT hears at abbey of castle near by,[1] 'die verbodene berch,' a knight had built it for love of his lady, only a narrow footpath leads to it. At abbey shields of knights of R. T. overthrown by knight of castle; them he keeps in prison, all others he slays. L. sees shields of Gawain, Ywein, and others (1533, *does not mention Ywein*), and decides to rescue them. At foot of hills finds hermit, who foretells his success. Finds cross with inscription, for forty (1533, *twenty*) years all who came have been vanquished, 'save one, and he doubtless was of David's line' (*omitted in* 1533). Goes on, finds pavilion with dwarf, who warns him not to fight, shows him a horn he must blow. Prisoners in castle warn him; sees Gawain, wounded in the head. Knight appears. Fierce fight, finally L. gets the better of his foe, who is Bohort (1533, *names*

---

being wounded by a maiden, Book XVIII. chap. xxii., where the prose *Lancelot* gives one of his squires.

[1] M. Paulin Paris omits this adventure in his summary, which only records the *Lancelot* sections. It is thus apparently lacking in the MS. used.

APPENDIX

B. in middle of fight, apparently forgetting that no one knows who he is), he had overcome knight of castle two years (**1533**, *one year*) ago, and been forced to take his place (by whom?). He may imprison his comrades but must slay all others; did not know their names, would not ask them. (How, then, did he know they *were* his comrades?) He is much ashamed and apologises to knights; all are rejoiced to see L. Stay there that night. L. has wonderful dream. Old man appears, and bids him ride without delay to 'ten Vreschlichen woude,' where he will find a wondrous adventure. He is his grandfather. L. rises, arms, and rides away at once. 'Comrades depart together' (*omitted in* **1533**).

Line 25150. LANCELOT meets dwarf, who warns him of great adventures. Comes to hermitage by a fountain, where is a bleeding tomb guarded by two leopards (**1533**, *lyons*), whom L. slays. Sees head in fountain, water is boiling, but takes head out and lays it in tomb; it is his grandfather's body, treacherously slain by a kinsman on a Good Friday. Fountain will not cease boiling till one comes who can bring adventure to end, which he cannot, on account of his sin with Guinevere.[1] L. rides on, comes to forest full of wild beasts. Rescues boy from bear. Rides in search of lodging. Moon rises. Sees white hart with gold chain round neck, guarded by six leopards (**1533**, *lyons*), marvels much; swears not to leave forest till he has learnt meaning. Comes to two pavilions, asks lodging. Must joust with owner; does so, and slays him; twelve maidens make great lamentations, carry off body on bier; he was a great king. L. is much distressed. Knight comes and asks lodging. Had kept Easter at A.'s court. All sorrowful because of absence of L. and G.; but joyful news has come that he who shall achieve adventure of Grail is born of Fisher

---

[1] This is one of the adventures referred to previously, cf. pp. 137-139, *Grand S. Graal*, vol. iii. p. 303 *et seq*. It is worth noting that it is only in the passages parallel to *Grand S. Graal* that L.'s relations with queen are spoken of as sinful.

King's daughter.[1] He seeks fountain of Sycamores, where a valiant knight has overthrown Gawain and Ywein; twelve have made a vow to seek it. Boy knows road, will lead knight to it. On the morrow they separate; knight, Sarras van Logres, comes to fountain, fights with Belyas the Black, and is overthrown. L., who has followed secretly, comes up, overthrows B., gives S. his horse; tells him his name, and bids him return to court, saying he and all questers are well, and will be at court for Pentecost. S. rides off, meets wounded knight seeking L.; directs him. Comes to court on a Sunday; all are rejoiced at news. A. will hold great feast in their honour.

Line 26045. Maid sent by queen to Lady of the Lake comes to court of King Claudas; who asks tidings of L. and kinsmen. Maid says they are best and bravest knights alive, and will certainly come and slay him, and take back their lands. Claudas imprisons maiden, and sends messengers to court to see if her tale be true. One is so impressed that he becomes A.'s man; other returns and tells C. what he has seen. First tells queen fate of maiden; she writes to C. bidding him free her. C. returns insulting answer. Queen, much distressed, longs for L.'s return.

Line 26630. LANCELOT. When Sarras has left him, another knight appears, like Belyas. They fight; knight flies, pursued by L. to castle near at hand. L.'s horse is slain; but he slays all who attack him, and reaches garden, where in tent, guarded by four knights, he finds Mordret chained. L. releases him, and they escape together. Belyas and Bryadas had wished to be knights of R. T. A. refused, not knowing them. They had sworn to keep fountain against all comers; L. has mortally wounded both. L. meets wounded knight, whom he heals at last, sending message to King B. that questers are found; also

---

[1] This does not fit in with indications of story, which would place Galahad's birth considerably earlier, L.'s visit to Corbenic being some two or three years previous.

APPENDIX 241

to those released at 'Verbodene berch,' bidding them meet him at court. Gawain is ready, but Ywein demurs, all are not found yet. G. says duration of quest should be year and day, they have been away three years. All agree to go. (This seems to indicate that 1533 was correct in not noting their departure earlier, as D. L. does, thus contradicting itself. Probably an earlier redaction did make them leave at once, while a later introduced more of L.'s adventures. This points to the later interpolation of 'tomb' adventures.) B. knights one of the squires, 'Axille die blonde,' and gives him the castle.

Line 27236. GAWAIN and comrades come to a castle by a deep water, where men are erecting lodges for a tourney. It is the castle of Galehoudijn, 'neve' of *Gawain* (obvious mistake for Gallehault), (1533, *son of Gallehault and la belle Géande*, but she was Gallehault's mother). Conceal their names, are well received and lodged outside castle. Hear a tumult, and see Agloval pursued by forty armed men. Go to his aid, and slay many. Their host is much distressed; they tell him they are of A.'s court. Galehoudijn arrives; is angry at first, but when Gawain reveals their names, is much rejoiced, does them great honour, and knights their host. (1533 *is very confused here, persistently calling Galehoudijn, Gallehault; correcting mistake, and then relapsing again.*)

Line 27735. LANCELOT[1] and MORDRET ride till nightfall. See white hart and leopards; decide to follow them. Two knights ride suddenly out of side road, unhorse them and take their steeds. Dwarf appears, will lead them to horses, if they will give him a gift. Promise; he leads them to two pavilions where they find their horses, and go off with them. Come to a hermitage, where they spend the night. L. asks H. of white hart; mystery may not be revealed till 'the good knight' come. Asks of king whom he slew, and who was mourned by maidens

---

[1] All this section of Lancelot's adventures, from his meeting with Sarras of Logres, differs very much from M. Paulin Paris's summary. Cf. *Romans de la Table Ronde*, v. p. 322 *seq*.

(cf. *supra*, p. 239), he was named Merlan, from 'die Marchen van Scollant,' a wicked man; L. did well to slay him. Next morning they ride away; are attacked by knights who stole their horses. M. overthrows them, and gives knights' horses to L. Spend this night with 'Vavasseur,' who tells them of Galehoudijn's tourney. They will go, host with four sons (*no number in* 1533) to attend them. Next morning they ride to hear Mass. Meet an old man who prophesies M. shall be ruin of kingdom and death of his father, 'who is a mightier king than K. Lot.' M., angry, smites off his head. L. finds letter on dead man saying who M. really is. Would slay him and avert mischief, but for love of Gawain, whose brother he is. Come to tourney. Kings of Norgales and of a hundred knights there. L. discomfits all comers. Then rides out of press followed by Bohort, who suspects his identity. Meet, and agree to ride to court together.

Line 28835. GAWAIN and his companions are much annoyed when they find they have missed L. again. Agree to return to court, each going his own way.

Line 29018. LANCELOT and BOHORT see a fire, hear cries for help. B. goes to see, and finds maiden and brother being ill-treated by eight knights; slays three, rest fly. B. returns to L. who has disappeared; spends night in forest. (1533, *goes with maid, who is daughter of king of a hundred knights, to lodging, then with brother to find L.; not doing so, returns and spends night with them. Departs next morning, and hears L. has been seen chasing a knight.*)

Line 29095. BOHORT, second visit to Grail castle. Tempts its adventures. Cf. *supra*, pp. 160, 233.

Line 29695. LANCELOT comes to two tents, light, and a maiden and dwarf in one, asks for lodging. Her lover will not allow her to give it. Knight and brother ride up, throw L.'s armour out of tent. Fight. L. slays one and wounds the other. Rides to a hermitage where he passes night. Next day meets two maidens sitting by spring, would eat with them. Maiden pursued by black knight runs up asking for aid, before

APPENDIX

L. can reach his sword she is slain. L. very angry smites off knight's head. Fourth night comes to forester's house in moon light.

Line 29952. LANCELOT and KAY. Cf. *supra*, p. 156.

Line 30380. LANCELOT after overthrowing knight of R. T. comes to two pavilions, in one of which is maiden who cured him of poison. Sees Bohort's son. Cf. *supra*, p. 157.

Line 30584. GAWAIN and his comrades return to court and hang up shield L. has thrown down in middle of hall; telling how they were overthrown. Queen much distressed that L. has not come, gives them rich garments in order of valour. Bohort is best, then Gawain, Hector, Gariëtte, Lionel, Bagdemagus (**1533** *omits Hector but gives others in same order*). Kay arrives in L.'s armour. Other knights overthrown by L. come and recognise shield. Next morning L. is seen coming, go out to meet him, joust, and Gawain overthrows him, L.'s horse being weary. Great Feast, A.D. 426 (**1533**, A.D. 225). A knight in white armour comes weeping, he is probably going to his death. Gives L. a letter—if he dies he is to read it aloud, if he survives return it. Sits in Perilous Seat, fire descends and consumes him. He was Brumal (**1533**, *Brumant*), nephew of King Claudas, who had vowed to prove himself a better knight than L. who dare not sit there. Queen and L. talk apart, and she tells him of Claudas's insult; he vows to avenge her, C. has taken Gannes, Benoyc and *Aquitaine*. (**1533**, *Gaule and Benoyc*—[but Gaule was not yet L.'s].) L. takes counsel with his friends and resolves on war. Brimol van Pleiche comes, was conquered by B. at bridge of Corbenyc (not recorded previously).

Line 31976. CLAUDAS prepares to resist A., gives all his nobles leave to go, richly rewards those who remain; is promised help from Rome.

Line 32394. Recital of knights' adventures, recorded above.

Line 32755. War with Claudas told at great length. Valiant deeds of Gawain, Hector, and Bohort. King and L. join army later. A.'s fight with Frollo and winning of Gaul is placed here. Claudas finally conquered, L. makes Hector king of Benoyc, Bohort of Gannes, Lionel of Gaule (cf. *supra*, p. 201).

Line 35465. Feast at Camalot. Arrival of Elaine, L.'s madness. Cf. chap. ix. pp. 161-163.

Line 35830. PERCEVAL. His arrival at court. Adventure with Patrides; fight with Hector. Grail is vessel out of which Our Lord ate Paschal lamb in house of Simon the Leper.

Line 36610. PERCEVAL and HECTOR come to house of a hermit who is priest to the fisher-folk, who provide him with fish, etc. After riding some time they come to house of a man, who had lodged L. six months before, knows H. for his brother by likeness, L. was mad then.

(This is not in 1533, which says, *Or dit le compte que grant piece chevaucherent P. et H. ensemble per mainte terre estrange pour scavoir se adventure les meneroit en lieu ou ilz peuffent trouver L. ains chevaucherent maint yver et maint este ensemble.*)

Line 36705. LANCELOT. Adventure at pavilion, imprisonment, and fight with boar (cf. p. 163). Breaks off short here, as if MS. came to an end and returns to

Line 36947. PERCEVAL returns to court. They do him great honour.

Damsel arrives (Grail messenger, but *Grail* is not mentioned). Castle Orguelous and Montesclaire ventures. (From this point source is analogous to Chrétien.) Gawain will go to Montesclaire, Ywein to Castle Orguelous, Kay and Griflet to 'Tere Dolorous' (not previously mentioned), Perceval will ride through land, jousting with all whom he may meet. Ginganbresil arrives, challenges Gawain. All ride forth, Gawain, Agravain, Gariëtte, Ywein, Perceval, Griflet, Kay and Mordret ride together for four miles, then separate.

Line 37105. GAWAIN adventure against Melias de Lis, and tournament as in *Conte del Graal*.

Line 37584. KAY and AGRAVAIN go to seek Dolorous Castle. Meet maiden, she will guide them thither if they dare

APPENDIX 245

to go there. Meet two knights who will joust, K. and A. overthrow them, are attacked by eight and finally taken prisoners, though A. defends himself stoutly. Will take them to Castle D., before they have gone half a mile P. rides out of side road. They attack him, but he puts them to flight, rescues K. and A., the three take castle and sent lord prisoner to A.'s court.

Line 37855. YWEIN and GARIËTTE meet a dwarf, who leads them to the Castle Orguelous. There they must joust against all comers. Ladies watch from battlements, and as each knight is overthrown his lady sends wreath of roses to victor. Thus they vanquish twenty. At last sixty at once attack and overpower them, and they are led to castle, where ladies insist on their being well treated.

Line 38000. MORDRET and GRIFLET are warned by hermit of danger they run in going to Montesclaire. Ride on and are taken prisoners by tyrant who will wed the lady of the castle.

Line 38133. PERCEVAL hears how Y. and G. have been vanquished at Castle Orguelous. Rides thither with Kay and Agravain. P. overthrows ten knights; K. and A. fifteen between them; when all attack them slay twenty, wound fifteen, and take castle, setting Y. and G. and the maidens free.

Line 38230. GAWAIN. Adventure with lady and chessmen in tower as in *Contê del Graal*. G. is sent to find the bleeding 'white' spear. Comes to hermitage, hermit tells him how Mordret and Griflet have been made prisoners at Montesclaire, and are to be hanged in the morning. G. will rescue them. Rises early, rides to hill where gallows already set up; frees M. and G. Tyrant appears, fight fiercely, G.'s strength increases at midday, overthrows tyrant, is fiercely attacked by his men.

Line 38990. PERCEVAL hears of M.'s danger; rides with Y., G., K., and A. to aid. Comes up in time to help Gawain against four hundred men. Slay tyrant and free maiden. Gawain wins sword ' metten vremden ringen,' which will break if an unworthy knight handles it. Next morning separate; G. goes to seek

Grail (which had not been mentioned before), others return to court.

Line 39140. GAWAIN. Adventure with wounded knight and Château Merveil. (Here we are told that *Merlin* made the *Lit Merveil*. Here too G. is warned he may not leave castle, but queen permits him to do so on condition he returns in evening.)

Line 40060. Adventure with Guiromelant. Lady is Orgeloise. The queens came into the land after the death of Uther, Pendragon, and *King Lot* (who in other romances is contemporary with Arthur), when there was civil war in Logres. G. is girded for the fight by Tristram (who has not previously appeared in the story). At prayer of Clareant a truce is declared, and A. says Guir. shall wed his niece. Kay bears tidings to G., who is so angry he vows he will not return to court. A. much distressed. Twenty-four knights vow to seek G. for a year and a day.

Line 40785. QUESTERS come third day into wood. Voice from thicket bids them stand; they may go no further unless they joust for it. Kay and Dodinel overthrown. Knight asks Tristram's name; he will not tell it unless knight tells his. He refuses; they fight fiercely till midday, when they rest. Knight sees others coming and fears to be known; flies into wood. Squire comes to seek T.; his wife is ill, must see him. T., K., and D. return. On way K. says he was overthrown unfairly. Knight is in wood, overhears, comes out and challenges K. and D.; puts them to the worse. T. and he fight again, lasts long, and T. is becoming exhausted, when maiden appears seeking knight; it is Lancelot. They go off together, and the three reach court safely.

Line 41013. PERCEVAL, who has separated from the others, comes to the Castle of Orgeloise, who is besieged by old lover whom she left when she rode off with Gawain. P. fights with and slays him. O. is hereafter known as '*die goede joncfrouwe.*'

Line 41160. AGLOVAL (who is seeking P.) meets knight, who will not reply to his greeting, but enters castle, arms himself, and attacks A. It is Gregorias, who stole Gawain's horse.

APPENDIX

A. slays him. Comes to castle, where old man receives him kindly. Greg. was his foe; his sons are out seeking him. All rejoiced to hear of his death.

Line 41420. GAWAIN. Visit to Grail Castle as in Montpelier MS. of *Conte del Graal*. Next day meets knight and maiden; former, hearing G.'s name, challenges him—he has slain his father. They fight, and desist, since it is no honour to fight with none to behold. Will fight it out before court. He is Dyandras. G. goes to Scavaleon to report ill-success of quest.

Line 41660. GARIËTTE and GRIFLET come to a tower where Hector is imprisoned; find two knights ill-treating maiden for advising H.'s release. Free her. H. appears to aid her (has escaped). Lord of castle pursues them with twenty men. Perceval and Agloval arrive; slay eleven, rest flee. All return to court.

Line 41845. GAWAIN goes to Scavaleon to fulfil compact with Ginganbresil. Dyandras comes and claims his fight. King consults counsellors; they judge that G. must fight *with both at once*. Squire goes to warn King A., who comes with court to witness fight. After a time would stop it, with king's consent, but Ginganbresil refuses. Gawain's strength doubles, and he conquers both. King and one hundred knights become A.'s men. Next day, rides homeward, stopping at castle of Tibaut of Tintavel, where G. is warmly welcomed. Then all go to Carlion.

Line 42540. Then follows *Morien*. Cf. *supra*, p. 150.

INDEX

ABEL, 180.
Ade, 12, 13.
Agloval, 36, 150, 162.
Agravain, 137, 149, 152, 157, 160, 186, 194, 195, 199.
Aguisel, 71.
Alexander, 81.
Arimathea (Joseph of), 121, 126, 127, 133, 134, 139, 209.
Armorica, 56, 57.
Arnoul, 181.
Arnout, *v.* Arnoul.
Arthur, 13, 15, 17, 21, 30, 32, 40, 41, 46, 47, 50, 51, 55, 56, 60, 62, 63, 65, 67, 71, 94, 103, 106, 107, 110, 113, 126, 135, 141, 154, 167, 184, 195, 196, 198, 199, 200, 201, 202, 203, 204.
Astolat (*v.* Escarloet), 194.
Avalon, 59, 60, 64, 65, 126, 153, 204, 205.

BAGAN, *v.* Vagan.
Balaan and Balaain, 73, 167.
Ban of Benoyc, 91, 92, 129, 143, 177, 185, 192, 200, 201, 210.
Barenton, 72.
Bath, 47, 48, 59, 60, 83.
Baudemagus, 41, 101, 137, 143, 154, 158, 170, 184, 185, 203, 204.
Beaurösch, 52.
Bedivere, 4.
Beforet, 12, 13, 14, 17.
Bel Inconnu, 97, 98.
Birch-Hirschfeld (Professor), 123.
Bleeding Tomb, 139.
Bohort, 21, 92, 121, 135, 136, 143, 144, 150, 153, 154, 156, 157, 160, 161, 163, 166, 168, 170, 178, 195, 197, 198, 199, 200, 201, 202, 205.
Boiling Fountain, 139.
Borron (Robert de), 122, 125, 126, 127, 128, 131, 133, 158, 163, 210.
—— pseudo *v.* above.
Bors, *v.* Bohort.
Briant des Illes, 129, 130.
Brimol van Pleiche, 160, 186.
Brisane, 142.
Broceliande, 72, 82.
Bromel le Plêche *v.* Brimol v. P.
Brunel du Plessis *v.* Brimol v. P.
Brut (*v.* also Layamon and Wace), 4, 6, 56, 71, 105, 106.
Brynhild, 47.

CÆRNANT, 82.
Cahere, 198.
Camalot, 83, 196, 197, 198.
Caradigan, 82.
Caradoc, 4, 91.
Carduel, 82.
Carlion, 83.
Cath Palug, 60.
Celidoine, 177.
Champagne (Marie de), 42, 48, 114.
Chapalu, *v.* Cath Palug.
Charrette (Chevalier de la), 5, 6, 7, 11, 19, 20, 21, 27, 30, 49, 50, 52, 53, 68, 81, 83, 101, 103, 112, 115, 116, 138, 143, 149, 185, 188, 194, 206, 212.
Charrette (summary of poem), chap. iv. 40-42.
Chastel du Trespas, 153, 154.

INDEX

Château Merveil, 121.
Chester, 82.
Chevalier au Lion (*v.* also Yvain), 6, 42, 50, 100.
Chevalier à la Manche, 18, 151.
Chrétien de Troyes, 5, 6, 7, 10, 19, 20, 24, 26, 27, 30, 31, 42, 43, 44, 45, 46, 48, 49, 50, 51, 52, 53, 95, 103, 115, 121, 131, 134, 140, 143, 149, 191, 210, 211, 212.
—— position in Arthurian cycle, chap. v. pp. 54-88.
Clarine, 11, 114.
Claudas (King), 4, 102, 129, 182, 183.
Claudins, 182, 183.
Cligés, 5, 6, 42, 68, 79, 81, 83, 115.
Conlaoch, 109.
Corbenic, 121, 138, 139, 159, 160, 161, 167, 168, 181, 182, 183, 186.
Cuchullain, 24, 58, 109.
Cybele, *v.* Sibile.

DIARMID, 109, 110.
Dinasdron, 82.
Dodine le Sauvage, 15.
Dodinel, 150.
Dover, 83.

ELAINE, 142, 160, 161.
Elayne, *v.* above.
Eleanor of Aquitaine, 48, 114.
Elidiâ, 16.
Eliezer, 139.
Erec, 5, 15, 16, 64, 71, 79, 82, 115.
—— (poem), 5, 6, 11, 27, 42, 53, 64, 69, 78, 80, 81, 83, 85, 115, 130.
Ernoulf, *v.* Arnoul.
Escalot, *v.* Escarloet.
Escarloet, 135, 187, 196, 197, 198.
Esealt der lange, 16.

FALERÎN, *v.* Valerin.
False Claimant (story of), 34, 35.
Fata Morgana, 19.
Fier Baiser, 18, 19, 98, 99.
Fisher King, 129, 138, 161, 168, 169, 192.

Foerster (Professor), 9, 10, 16, 17, 19, 20, 26, 44, 49, 50, 93, 188.
—— —— theory of Arthurian evolution examined, chap v. pp. 54-88.
Frazer (Professor J. G.), 72.
Frollo, 4, 102, 126.
Furnivall (Dr.), *v.* Queste.

GAHERET, *v.* below.
Gaheriet, 15, 143, 150, 154, 158, 159, 172, 195, 196, 198, 199.
Galagandreiz, 12, 26.
Galahad, 97, 120, 121, 123, 124, 125, 129, 132, 134, 135, 137, 138, 142, 145, 146, 161, 163, 164, 166, 167, 168, 169, 170, 171, 172, 174, 178, 182, 183, 184, 185, 189, 191, 208, 209, 210.
Galehault, 136, 138, 147, 149, 153, 205.
Galehodyn, 153.
Galobrus de la Vermeille lande, 130.
Gandîn, 51, 116.
Garel, 53.
Gareth, *v.* Gaheriet.
Gariëtte, *v.* Gaheriet.
Gawain, 2, 3, 4, 5, 6, 12, 14, 15, 16, 19, 21, 22, 24, 31, 32, 33, 35, 36, 37, 38, 41, 43, 51, 53, 57, 63, 67, 91, 93, 95, 99, 103, 108, 109, 110, 111, 112, 113, 114, 115, 117, 120, 121, 129, 136, 137, 139, 143, 149, 150, 151, 156, 157, 158, 161, 162, 166, 167, 169, 170, 173, 178, 183, 184, 185, 195, 196, 197, 198, 199, 200, 202, 203, 208.
Genewîs, 11, 17.
Geoffrey of Monmouth, 20, 55, 56, 102, 104.
Gildas, 46.
Ginganbrisil, 149, 150.
Giraldus Cambrensis, 64.
Girard de Viane, 71.
Glastonbury, 46, 48, 59.
Godefroy de Leigni, 42, 44.
Goothe, *v.* Goth.
Gorres, 43, 47.
Got, 174.

Goth, v. Got.
Graal, Conte del, 121, 189, 212.
Graalent, 64, 65, 77, 87.
Grail (Holy), 78, 80, 90, 97, 100, 120, 123, 129, 131, 133, 134, 137, 138, 139, 140, 141, 142, 145, 146, 161, 163, 168, 169, 173, 181, 191, 192, 208, 209, 210, 212.
Grail castle (v. also Corbenic), 121, 150, 183, 192.
Grail Quest, v. Queste.
Graislemier de Fine Posterne, 64, 65.
Grand S. Graal, 101, 121, 126, 127, 133, 137, 138, 139, 175, 179, 192, 209.
Griflette, 150.
Guendolen, 100.
Guerresches, 159, 198, 199.
Guinevere, 1, 2, 3, 14, 15, 16, 17, 19, 20, 21, 23, 32, 38, 40, 41, 43, 45, 46, 47, 50, 51, 52, 53, 59, 90, 96, 100, 103, 104, 106, 107, 108, 111, 112, 113, 116, 117, 129, 135, 138, 141, 142, 158, 182, 188, 197, 198, 199, 200, 202, 203, 207.
Guingamor, 64, 65, 77.
Guinglain, 19.
Gurnemanz, 13, 26, 28, 80.

Hagen (Herr P.), theory of Grail origin, 29, 52, 78.
Hartland (Mr. E. S.), 34, 62, 73, 84.
Hartmann von Aue, 5, 16, 26, 27, 49, 50, 51, 52, 53, 75, 80, 116.
Hector, 21, 136, 139, 143, 152, 153, 157, 161, 163, 178, 195, 198, 200, 201.
Heinzel (Professor), 129, 130, 213.
Hélie le Blank, 157, 170.
Henry II., 48.
Hertz (Professor), 26, 95.

Iblîs, 13, 14, 16, 17, 27.
Ider, 4.
Idylls of the King, 114.
Iseult, 1, 5, 37, 38, 45, 113, 116, 117, 197.
Isle of Women, 22.
Iwân de Nonel, 27.

Iwanet, 95.
Iwein (v. also Yvain), 4, 49, 50, 52, 53, 95.
—— (v. Hartmann von Aue).
Iweret, 12, 13, 27.

Johfrit de Liez, 12, 26.

Kailet, 27.
Kamalot, v. Camalot.
Karados, 203.
Karnachkarnanz, 27.
Kay, 4, 22, 30, 31, 40, 41, 44, 50, 51, 60, 151, 155, 156, 162, 200.
Kei, v. Kay.
Ker (Professor), 23, 24.
Kiot, 28, 29.
Krône (Diu), 15, 22, 58, 80, 121.

Lady of the Lake, 23, 36, 94, 99, 138, 152, 207.
Lady of the Fountain, 67.
Lamorak, 162.
Lancelot, not a character of early Arthurian tradition, chap. i. pp. 1-7.
—— origin of name, 8, 9, 10.
—— rescuer of Guinevere, 15, 16, 40, 43.
—— origin of legend, 21-25.
—— et le cerf au pied blanc, chap. iii., 30-39, 151, 206-207.
—— (prose), chaps. vi., vii., viii., 89-146.
—— (Dutch), 30, 31, 38, 130, 131.
—— comparison of text, chaps. ix., x., xi., 147-205.
Lanval, 64, 65.
Lanzelet, v. Zatzikhoven (Ulrich von).
Laudine, 70, 74, 75.
Laudunet, 10, 74, 75.
Layamon, 4, 27, 56, 93, 104, 105, 106, 111.
Limors, 12.
Lionel, 21, 92, 135, 136, 143, 152, 153, 156, 161, 166, 170, 178, 195, 200, 201.
Lohengrin, 210.
Lohot, 130,

INDEX

London, 83.
Lot (M. Ferdinand), 59, 62, 64, 74.
Lot (King), 13, 26, 93, 159.
Loth (M.), 60.
Louis VII., 48.
Lucan, 204.

MABÛZ, 13, 14.
Maelwas, 8, 10 (*v.* also Melwas).
Maheloas, 64.
Maimed King, 138, 161, 169, 192.
Malduc, 15, 16, 80.
Malduz, *v.* Malduc.
Malehault (Dame de), 101, 129.
Malmesbury (William of), 59.
Malory, 23, 45, 46, 49, 90, 101, 104, 108, 114, 131, 151, 165.
—— comparison of text, chaps. ix., x., xi., pp. 107-205.
Mantle (Lai), 14, 19.
Map (Walter), 122, 125, 131, 163, 184, 210.
—— (pseudo), as above.
Marie de France, 61, 65, 66.
Mathœus die felle, 154.
Mauduiz li Sages (cf. Malduc).
Maurîn, 27.
Meide-lant, 11, 14, 22, 94.
Meleagant, 40, 41, 42, 43, 47, 51, 52, 59, 60, 101, 118, 138, 143, 185.
Melians de Lile, 171.
Meliot de Logres, 158.
Melwas, 8, 46, 47, 59, 60, 118.
Méraugis de Portlesguez, 18, 73.
Merlin, 23, 34, 60, 91, 92, 103, 107, 117, 122, 126, 127, 138, 142.
—— (prophecies of), 100.
—— (Suite de), 23, 73, 92, 122, 137, 184, 185, 204, 209.
Modena (bas-relief at), 4, 56.
Mordred, 20, 93, 104, 105, 107, 108, 109, 111, 113, 115, 118, 126, 154, 156, 159, 162, 199, 202, 203.
Morgain la fee, 64, 99, 153, 156, 160, 199, 204, 207.
Morholt, 92.
Morien, 35, 37, 150, 174, 181, 207.
Mort Artur, 93, 104, 122, 126, 127, 135, 137, 138, 145, 148, 151, 159, 184.

Mort Artur, comparison of text, chaps. xi. 194-205.

NOHAN (Dame de), 97.
Norgales, 153, 196.
Nutt (Mr. Alfred, *Studies*), 120.

ORGUELLEUS DE LA LANDE, 80.
Orgeluse, 112, 149.
Orgeloise, *v.* Orgeluse.
Ossenefort, 79.
Oxford, 83.

PALLADA, 178.
Pant of Genewis, 11, 91.
Paris (M. Gaston), 8, 9, 16, 32, 35, 40, 44, 60, 110, 150, 151, 188.
—— (M. Paulin), 96, 101, 124, 127, 137, 149, 155, 190, 213.
Parzival (Wolfram von Eschenbach's), 26, 27, 28, 31, 94, 95, 96, 112, 118, 140, 181, 212, 213.
Patrides, 162.
Patryse, 195.
Pelles, King, 112, 138, 139, 160, 167, 168, 169, 183.
Perceval, 3, 5, 6, 24, 26, 33, 36, 42, 63, 69, 71, 78, 81, 83, 91, 95, 96, 98, 115, 118, 123, 124, 125, 126, 127, 129, 130, 131, 132, 133, 134, 135, 138, 139, 140, 142, 146, 149, 157, 158, 161, 162, 163, 167, 168, 170, 173, 174, 175, 178, 179, 181, 191, 192, 207, 208, 209, 210, 211, 212.
—— Didot, 93, 126, 128, 134, 140, 191, 192, 205, 212.
—— li Gallois, 107, 127, 129, 134, 140, 158, 181, 191, 212.
Peredur, 8, 9, 10.
Perilous Cemetery, 139, 158.
Perlesvaus (*v.* P. li Gallois), 130.
Perseus (Legend of), 34.
Philip of Flanders (Count), 78.
Pluris, 14, 15.

QUESTE, 34, 76, 101, 107, 120, 122, 123, 124, 125, 127, 128, 130, 131, 132, 133, 134, 135, 136, 137, 139, 140, 142, 144, 145, 148, 150, 153, 161, 208, 209, 210.

Queste, comparison of text, chap. x. 165-193.
—— Welsh, 148.

RAGUIDEL (vengeance de), 150.
Rajna (Professor), 6.
Rochedon (Duc de), 101, 153.
Rhys (Professor), 8, 10, 104, 108.
Rigomer, 18.

SCARLOET, v. Escarloet.
Schofield (Dr.), 87, 98, 99.
Schrienden Mose (den), 47.
Segramore, 5.
Shoreham, 83
Sibile (l'Enchanteresse), 153.
Siegfried, 19, 24, 47.
Sommer (Dr., *Sources of Malory*), 49, 90, 131, 151, 214.
—— Summary compared, chaps. ix., x., xi., pp. 147-205.
Soredamors, 81.
Sorelois, 153.
Sorestan, 152, 153.
Southampton, 83.

TANEBOR, 196, 197.
Tarquijn, v. Terriquen.
Terriquen, 152, 187, 200, 203.
Torec, 18, 151.
Tristan, 1, 3, 5, 6, 15, 16, 35, 37, 38, 51, 91, 92, 100, 103, 107, 109, 110, 111, 113, 116, 117, 125, 128, 137, 159, 162, 191, 197, 207.
Turquin, v. Terriquen.
Tyolet, 32, 33, 35, 63.

URRE OF HUNGARY, 187, 194.
Uther Pendragon, 142.

Uwayne, 172.

VAGAN, 170.
Valerin, 14, 15, 47, 48.
Villemarqué (M. de la), 8, 10, 101.
Vivienne, 99.

WACE, 20, 56, 72, 93, 104, 106.
Wallingford, 83.
Walter of Oxford, 105.
Wechssler (Dr.), 78, 101, 117, 121, 122, 123, 125, 127, 128, 132, 134, 137, 150, 159, 187, 191.
Widow of Ephesus, 69, 70, 76, 77.
Winchester, 83, 195, 196.
Windsor, 83.
Wolff (lais), 77.
Wolfram von Eschenbach, 52, 53, 94, 95, 121, 130, 134, 141, 149, 150, 191.
—— v. also Parzival.

YONET, 95.
Yvain, 45, 67, 69, 70, 71, 72, 73, 74, 75, 76, 77, 81, 82, 83, 85, 94, 95, 96, 129, 153, 154, 155, 156, 202.
—— v. also Iwein and Chevalier au Lion.

ZATZIKHOVEN (Ulrich von), 11, 17, 20, 29, 44, 46, 66, 80.
—— Lanzelet of U. v. chap. ii., 47, 66, 80, 91, 93, 94, 98, 99, 102, 206.
Zimmer (Professor), 9.

APPENDIX, pp. 215-247, not included in above INDEX.

LIBRARY OF DAVIDSON COLLEGE